JOURNAL OF LEGAL PLURALISM and Unofficial Law

NUMBER 65 / 2012.

Bibliographic information published by the Deutsche Nationalbibliothek
The Deutsche Nationalbibliothek lists this publication in the Deutsche Nationalbibliografie; detailed bibliographic data are available in the Internet at http://dnb.d-nb.de.

ISSN 0732-9113
ISBN 978-3-643-99865-1

A catalogue record for this book is available from the British Library

Zweigniederlassung Zürich 2012
Klosbachstr. 107
CH-8032 Zürich
Tel. +41 (0) 44-251 75 05
Fax +41 (0) 44-251 75 06
e-Mail: zuerich@lit-verlag.ch
http://www.lit-verlag.ch

LIT VERLAG Dr. W. Hopf
Berlin 2012
Fresnostr. 2
D-48159 Münster
Tel. +49 (0) 2 51-620 320
Fax +49 (0) 2 51-23 19 72
e-Mail: lit@lit-verlag.de
http://www.lit-verlag.de

Distribution:
In Germany: LIT Verlag Fresnostr. 2, D-48159 Münster
Tel. +49 (0) 2 51-620 32 22, Fax +49 (0) 2 51-922 60 99, e-mail: vertrieb@lit-verlag.de

In Austria: Medienlogistik Pichler-ÖBZ, e-mail: mlo@medien-logistik.at

In Switzerland: B + M Buch- und Medienvertrieb, e-mail: order@buch-medien.ch

In the UK: Global Book Marketing, e-mail: mo@centralbooks.com

In North America: International Specialized Book Services, e-mail: orders@isbs.com

JOURNAL OF LEGAL PLURALISM
and Unofficial Law

POLICY

The Journal of Legal Pluralism and Unofficial Law (JLP) is a refereed, independent, inter-disciplinary, international journal devoted to scholarly writing, documentation, information on current developments, and communications about all aspects of legal pluralism and unofficial law anywhere in the world and at any time. Issues 1-18 bear the name *African Law Studies*.

MANUSCRIPTS

Manuscripts for the Journal of Legal Pluralism should be submitted to the editor-in-chief:

Melanie G. Wiber
Department of Anthropology, University of New Brunswick
P.O. Box 4400, Fredericton, N.B.
Canada E3B 5A3
Fax: (+ 01) (506) 453-5071
Email: wiber@unb.ca

or to one of the associate editors. Unless the editors are otherwise informed, submission of a manuscript implies the undertaking that it is not currently being considered by another journal and that if accepted it will be available for publication.

Manuscripts must conform to the style and other instructions contained in the JLP 'style sheet' (to be found on the JLP web site under the title 'Author guidelines'), and should generally be submitted in electronic form.

SUBSCRIPTIONS

From nr. 49 (2004) the Journal of Legal Pluralism has been published by LIT Verlag, Münster-Hamburg-Berlin-Vienna-London, whose address for inquiries about subscriptions and for orders is Grevener St./Fresnostr.2, D-48159 Münster, Germany, Fax (+49) (0)251 23 19 72, vertrieb@lit-verlag.de.
Back numbers of African Law Studies and the Journal of Legal Pluralism to nr. 48 are available from William S. Hein & Co., Inc., 1285 Main Street, Buffalo, New York 14209-1987, USA..

INDEXES AND DATABASES

Articles appearing in the Journal of Legal Pluralism are indexed in the principal legal and social science indexes and online data-bases. It is planned to make available the full text of all articles published more than two years previously on the website of the Journal of Legal Pluralism at www.jlp.bham.ac.uk . Currently the site contains the full text of all articles in nrs. 15 to 57, and abstracts of articles in nrs. 43 to the current number.

CITATION

The Journal of Legal Pluralism and Unofficial Law should be cited as: *Journal of Legal Pluralism*.

CONTENTS

FROM THE EDITOR

This Number of the Journal of Legal Pluralism includes six contributions covering topics as diverse as legal philosophy on the nature of law, land grabbing through foreign direct investment, gender equality and maternal mortality, religious law, legal pluralism within state law, and law in colonial and post colonial settings. Geographical areas surveyed include Singapore and Australia, Nigeria, Israel, Tanzania, Nepal, and Kyrgyzstan, and Canada. The reader cannot fail to find something of interest in such a diverse and interesting range of topics.

I continue to owe a great debt to Gordon Woodman, who remains heavily involved in the editorial decisions and day-to-day work of producing the journal. Thank you Gordon, for your continued support.

And once again I remind readers that the next international meeting of the Commission on Legal Pluralism will be held in conjunction with the congress of the International Union of Anthropological and Ethnological Sciences. The IUAES congress theme is "Evolving Humanity, Emerging Worlds" (for more information see http://www.iuaes2013.org/index.html). It will take place in Manchester, UK from 5-10 August, 2013. See the Commission website (at www.commission-on-legal-pluralism.com) for information on panel organizers in legal pluralism and for the recent call for papers. I urge readers of the journal to consider submitting a paper abstract to one of the panel organizers and I look forward to meeting many of you in Manchester.

ABSTRACTS OF ARTICLES

JLP 65: 1-30

ALL LAW IS PLURAL. LEGAL PLURALISM AND THE DISTINCTIVENESS OF LAW

Mariano Croce

The present article pursues two basic aims. Firstly, it canvasses the idea that there is no normative difference between state law and other kinds of law, such as customary law or religious law, and that eventually there is not a clear dividing line between the various normative fields of social reality (from interactions of everyday life to legal activities). The author explores this 'panlegalistic' paradigm by integrating the analysis made by Gordon R. Woodman about the nature of customary law with a Wittgensteinian reading of the 'practice theory of norms' by Herbert L.A. Hart. After emphasising the conceptual advantages of this approach, the article puts forward an hypothesis meant to unravel a conceptual impasse which it incurs, that is, the impossibility of explaining what differentiates legal from social normativity. To this end, the author suggests that law should be seen as a trans-sectional and insulated venue, separate from everyday life, in which everyday reality can be renegotiated and rephrased by means of a special knowledge (usually mastered by a circle of experts) and a rigid set of conceptual categories.

JLP 65: 31-63

LAND GRABBING, INVESTMENT PRINCIPLES AND PLURAL LEGAL ORDERS OF LAND USE

Martina Locher, Bernd Steimann and Bishnu Raj Upreti

Recently, foreign direct investment in land, also termed 'land grabbing', has increased significantly in developing countries. In response to growing concerns about its detrimental impacts, the UN Food and Agriculture Organization (FAO), the World Bank and other multilateral organizations have come forward with two proposals, namely the *Voluntary Guidelines on the Responsible Governance of*

Tenure of Land, Fisheries and Forests in the Context of National Food Security (FAO 2012, FAO guidelines), to protect people's rights, and the *Principles for Responsible Agricultural Investment that Respects Rights, Livelihoods and Resources* (FAO et al. 2010, RAI principles), to make such investments more responsible. One of their central tenets is that investors and host governments respect local people's existing property rights over land by formalising them in a transparent and participatory manner.

The article challenges the two proposals – and thus much of the recent land grab debate – from a legal pluralism perspective, by showing that they do not adequately consider the existence of plural legal orders over land and the dynamics of power and everyday practices inherent in property relations. Referring to empirical evidence from Tanzania, Nepal, and Kyrgyzstan, we raise three fundamental concerns about the formalization of property rights. First, we demonstrate that the recognition of customary rights is a very complex and delicate endeavour, which risks neglecting existing property claims and rights. Neither of the proposals addresses this in a satisfactory way. Second, we understand that formalization by state intervention is sometimes necessary, but in those circumstances we cannot recommend the centralist approach of formalizing property rights, as proposed in the RAI principles. In many contexts, this approach has resulted in adverse effects for local communities rather than strengthening their rights. Third, a more rights-based vision as brought forward by the FAO guidelines still bears the risk of reinforcing unequal local power structures. Yet, this vision leaves it to local communities to decide whether their land should become a marketable good to outsiders or not. However, the introduction of such a property regime requires fundamental changes in governance. This cannot be addressed adequately within the framework of guidelines alone. Instead, more long-term strategies for the protection of customary rights are required. Thus, from an analytical perspective, a moratorium on 'land grabs' would be most appropriate. From a more pragmatic perspective though, we acknowledge the FAO guidelines and – to a much lesser extent – the RAI principles as more immediate efforts to reduce negative effects of 'land grabs'. However, investors and host governments should not mistake these guidelines as guarantors of ostensibly harmless land acquisitions. Finally, this article concludes that employing a legal pluralism perspective is very helpful in gaining a more holistic understanding of potential effects and proposed measures in the context of 'land grabs'.

JLP 65: 65-102

REPLICATING 'A MODEL OF MUTUAL RESPECT': COULD SINGAPORE'S LEGAL PLURALISM WORK IN AUSTRALIA?

Ann Black

Like other western nations with a Muslim minority, Australia too is debating the extent to which our government should recognize and make concessions to our small but growing Muslim population. In 2011, the Australian Federation of Islamic Councils made a submission to the government entitled 'Embracing Australian Values - Maintaining the Right to be Different', which advocated legal pluralism as the right of all Australians. It argued amongst other things that conflicts, especially ones involving family and inheritance matters, should be resolved according to the law and traditions of one's own religion. This was contentious in a nation where 'one law for all' has been the accepted approach for two centuries. It did however give rise to a debate on whether the nation can, or should, formally recognize certain aspects of Islamic law or support the establishment of a Syariah Court or tribunal. One of the models for legal pluralism often advocated is that of Singapore. Like Australia, Singapore has a minority Muslim population and also inherited the common law system during the era of British colonisation. This paper reflects on the pluralism debate in Australia and assesses the strengths and weaknesses of Singapore's plural model to determine whether it could, or should, be replicated 'down under'.

JLP 65: 103-132

SUBSTANTIVE EQUALITY AND MATERNAL MORTALITY IN NIGERIA

Ebenezer Durojaye

This article examines the relevance of substantive equality in addressing maternal deaths in Nigeria. The article argues that, aside from medical causes of deaths during pregnancy or childbirth, socio-cultural factors such as the low status of women and lack of respect for their fundamental rights often aggravate maternal deaths in Nigeria. While maternal death amounts to a violation of women's rights to health and life, it is contended that the application of the concept of substantive equality, as opposed to formal equality, can be helpful in addressing some of the root causes of maternal deaths in the country. This may require the government to take some practical steps such as awareness campaigns, law reforms and gender-sensitive budgeting towards improving the health of women. The article points out that the tension between international human rights law, statutory law and customary law in a pluralist state may have serious implications for women's fundamental rights, particularly the right to health. Therefore, the article argues that, in accordance with its obligations under international and regional human rights instruments, the Nigerian government needs to pay more attention to promoting and protecting women's rights, including meeting their health needs.

JLP 65: 133-163

LEGAL PLURALISM INCARNATE: AN INSTITUTIONAL PERSPECTIVE ON COURTS OF LAW IN COLONIAL AND POSTCOLONIAL SETTINGS

Ido Shahar

This article develops an institutional approach to the study of courts of law in colonial and post-colonial settings. Drawing on new institutional theory in organization studies, I argue that these courts often operate in an environment that is not only legally pluralistic but also institutionally pluralistic. Rather than inhabiting a single, coherent institutional field, many of them belong simultaneously to at least two institutional fields: a state-law institutional field and an indigenous one. Consequently, they are subject to contradictory pressures and demands, to which they respond by developing an especially dynamic and multi-faceted legal culture. In other words, these courts reflect and embody the pluralism of their environment. To illustrate this argument, I examine sharīʻa courts in contemporary Israel, which operate in a colonial-like setting characterized by both legal and institutional pluralism. I analyze two legal reforms that were promoted in these courts in the last few years, and attribute them to the courts' need to maneuver between contradictory pressures originating in two different institutional fields they belong to. Such institutional analysis, I contend, can help shed light on judicial policies that may initially seem irrational and incoherent.

JLP 65: 165-204

HALACHA, THE 'JEWISH STATE' AND THE CANADIAN *AGUNAH*: COMPARATIVE LAW AT THE INTERSECTION OF RELIGIOUS AND SECULAR ORDERS

Pascale Fournier

The *get* (Jewish divorce) can only be granted by the husband. Refusal by some Jewish husbands to grant the *get* has created the widespread problem of the *agunah* (chained wife) who, without a religious divorce, cannot remarry according to Jewish law nor have legitimate children in the eyes of her religious community. This article studies the measures put in place in Canada and Israel to address this social problem. It presents the results of two years of fieldwork among Canadian and Israeli Jewish women who went through divorce at the intersection of secular and religious legalities. In both polities, State responses are to varying degrees rendered less effective by social, religious and economic realities which lie beyond State law but have all sorts of crucial impacts on it. In the context of Jewish divorce, the Canadian civil State remedies are influenced by a web of alternative community responses and recourses available to women. Moreover, Israel's family law regime, while attractive to some Jewish women of the Diaspora, is also hopelessly ensnared in informal practices of rabbinical court judges, police, and rabbinical advocates, *most* of the time rendering Israeli policy responses unproductive. It seems clear that socio-legal research can no longer ignore the non-State legal ecosystem in which State law is grounded. This article thus seeks to further a new legal pluralist approach to research and legal practice, one which takes into account the relevance of *everyday* normativity and its potential usefulness to alleviate the plight of the *agunah*.

ABOUT THE CONTRIBUTORS

Mariano CROCE is a Pegasus Marie Curie Fellow at the Centre for Law and Cosmopolitan Values, University of Antwerp. He has held the post of Adjunct Professor of Legal Philosophy at Sapienza - University of Rome, and has worked for the Centre for Ethnic Minority Studies based at the School of Oriental and African Studies, University of London. His research includes legal theory, legal pluralism, political philosophy and socio-legal studies. Among his most recent publications are: *Self-Sufficiency of Law. A Critical-Institutional Theory of Social Order* (Springer, 2012); and, with Andrea Salvatore, *The Legal Theory of Carl Schmitt* (Routledge, 2012). Contact: mariano.croce@libero.it.

Dr Ann BLACK is a Senior Lecturer in Law at the TC Beirne School of Law, The University of Queensland, and is Deputy Director of its Centre for Public, International and Comparative Law. Her main area of research is the law of Asia with emphasis on the role of Islamic law, and how models of legal pluralism impact on gender, religion and political processes. While her recent book edited with Gary Bell, *Law and Legal Institutions of Asia: traditions, adaptations and innovations* (Cambridge University Press, 2011) reflects the Asia focus, another direction has been into the burgeoning area of legal and religious pluralism in Australia. It is an issue on which she has published widely with one paper, written with Kerrie Sadiq, 'Good and bad Sharia: Australia's mixed response to Islamic law.' *UNSW Law Journal* 17(1): 383-412, attracting considerable media and academic commentary. Contact: a.black@law.uq.edu.au.

Ebenezer DUROJAYE, LLB (Lagos), LLM, LLD (Free State), is the Coordinator/Senior Researcher for the Socio-economic Rights Project at the Community Law Centre, University of the Western Cape, Cape Town, South Africa. For more than a decade he has been involved in research and advocacy works on issues relating to socio-economic rights including the rights to housing and health in Africa. His areas of interest include focusing on human rights issues raised by access to HIV/AIDS treatment, intersection between gender inequality and HIV/AIDS response in Africa, women's health and adolescents sexual and reproductive rights in Africa. Contact: ebenezerdurojaye@gmail.com

Pascale FOURNIER holds the Research Chair in Legal Pluralism and Comparative Law at the University of Ottawa, Faculty of Law, where she is Associate Professor. She received her LL.B from Laval University (1997), her LL.M. from the University of Toronto (2000) and her S.J.D. from Harvard Law School (2007). Before arriving at the University of Ottawa, Pascale lectured at the State

University of Haiti, McGill University, the University for Peace in Costa Rica and the Institute for Women's Studies and Research in Iran. Her research touches upon law and religion, contemporary Islam and Judaism, children and women's rights in the context of legal pluralism, comparative law theory and the intersection of criminal law with family law and constitutional law. Her recent publications include: 'Calculating Claims: Jewish and Muslim Women Navigating Religion, Economics and Law in Canada' *International Journal of Law in Context* 8(1), 47-72 (2012); 'Honour Crimes and the Law - Public Policy in an Age of Globalization - Guest Editor's Introduction to the Special Issue' *Canadian Criminal Law Review* 16(2) 103-114 (2012); 'Borders and Crossroads: Comparative Perspectives on Minorities and Conflicts of Laws' *Emory International Law Review* 25()2, 987-1006 (2011); *Muslim Marriage in Western Courts: Lost in Transplantation.* Farnham, UK: Ashgate (2010). Currently in press are: (with Aida Setrakian & Pascal McDougall) 'No Fault Talaq: Islamic Divorce in Canadian Immigration and Family law', in Rubya Mehdi, Jørgen S. Nielsen & Werner Menski (eds.), *Anthology on Gender Equality and Muslim Law of Divorce*, DJØF Publishing: Copenhagen (2012); (with Aida Setrakian) 'False Jurisdictions? A Revisionist Take on Customary (Religious) Law in Germany' *Texas International Law Journal* 48(3) (2013); 'Quand 'l'Internationale', c'est aussi le national qui dérange: la théorie critique dans les coulisses du religieux', in Rémi Bachand (ed.), *Théories critiques et droit international*, Bruylant: Brussels (2013). Contact: Pascale.Fournier@uottawa.ca

Martina LOCHER, from Switzerland, is a PhD student and teaching associate at the Department of Geography, University of Zürich. She completed her Master of Geography in 2005 with a thesis on gender issues in an integrated nature conservation and development project in Nepal. From 2005 to 2009, she worked as a coordinator in an international research programme in Switzerland and in development projects with UNDP and GTZ in Bangladesh. Her current PhD research aims at contributing to a more detailed understanding of land acquisition procedures and the effects of transnational land deals for local livelihoods in Tanzania. Her publications include: '"We could show the men, that we are able to do it": Women's-development approach in the Kanchenjunga Conservation Area Project, East Nepal.' Pp. 267-284 in Smita Premchander and Christine Müller (eds.), *Gender and Sustainable Development: Case Studies from NCCR North-South.* Bern: Geographica Bernensia (2006); (with Ulrike Müller-Böker) '"But now men also listen to the women": Women's-development approach in the Kanchenjunga Conservation Area Project, East Nepal.' *Asiatische Studien / Etudes asiatique Suisse* LXI: 1113- 1139 (2007); '"How come others are selling our land?" Customary land rights, rural livelihoods and foreign land acquisition in the case of a UK-based forestry company in Tanzania'. Presented at *International Conference on Global Land Grabbing*, at the Institute of Development Studies, University of Sussex, Brighton (2011, draft conference paper). Contact: martina.locher@geo.uzh.ch.

Ido SHAHAR is a lecturer at the Department of Middle Eastern History at the University of Haifa, Israel. He has been a Post-Doctoral Research Fellow at the Hebrew University of Jerusalem, Tel Aviv University, University of Oxford, and Queen Mary University London. Shahar is a legal anthropologist specializing in Islamic law and its application, particularly in shari'a courts. His fields of research include the anthropology of law; the Palestinian minority in Israel; legal pluralism; and Muslim rural societies. He has published on these topics in *Islamic Law and Society, Theoretical Inquiries in Law, Political and Legal Anthropology Review*, and other journals. His book on the institutional and political dynamics of legal pluralism in Jerusalem is forthcoming from Ashgate. Contact: idoshah@gmail.com
Bernd STEIMANN received his PhD degree in geography at the University of Zürich, Switzerland in 2010. For his doctoral studies he based his field research in Kyrgyzstan, focussing on rural development and socio-economic disparities, the governance and management of alpine pastures, and processes of post-socialist transformation. From 2002 to 2005 he researched the often-strained relations between state and non-state actors in regard to forest management in Northern Pakistan. More recently he has worked as a research fellow at the University of Zürich and the Centre for Development and Environment (CDE) at the University of Berne, Switzerland. Today he works as a development policy coordinator with the Swiss NGO HELVETAS Swiss Intercooperation. Previous relevant publications include: *Making a Living in Uncertainty: Agro-pastoral Livelihoods and Institutional Transformations in Post-socialist Kyrgyzstan.* Bishkek and Zürich: Human Geography Series (26) (2010); (with Nadia Schoch and Susan Thieme); 'Migration and animal husbandry: Competing or complementary livelihood strategies. Evidence from Kyrgyzstan.' *Natural Resources Forum*, 34: 211-221 (2010); *Decentralization and Participation in the Forestry Sector of NWFP, Pakistan - The Role of the State.* NCCR N-S Dialogue Paper (7) (2004); and (with U. Geiser) 'State actors' livelihoods, acts of translation, and forest sector reforms in northwest Pakistan.' *Contemporary South Asia* 13(4): 437-448 (2004). Contact: bernd.steimann@helvetas.org

Bishnu Raj UPRETI, from Nepal, completed his PhD on conflict management from Wageningen University, the Netherlands in 2001. He specializes in conflict management and works as a senior researcher at NCCR North-South. He has written on the issues of resource conflict, peace, state-building and unconventional security. Some of his previous related publications include: 'Relationships between resource governance and resource conflict: Nepalese experience.' *Journal of Legal Pluralism* 50: 71-100 (2004); (with Ulrike Müller-Böker) *Nepal from War to Peace: Legacies of the Past and Hopes for Future.* New Delhi: Adroit Publishers (2009); (with Sagar Raj Sharma and Jagat Basnet) *Land Politics and Conflict in Nepal: Realities and Potentials for Agrarian Transformation.* Kathmandu: Community Self Reliance Centre, Human and Natural Resources Studies Centre, Kathmandu University and RCO NCCR North-South (2009); (with Sagar Raj Sharma, Kailash Nath Pyakuryal and Safal Ghimire) *The Remake of a State: Post Conflict Challenges and State Building in Nepal.* Kathmandu: HNRSC and South Asia Regional Coordination Office of NCCR North-South (2010); *Livelihood Insecurity and Social Conflict in Nepal.* Kathmandu: RCO NCCR North-South (2010); and (with Kailash Nath Pyakuryal) *Land, Agriculture and Agrarian Transformation.* Kathmandu: Consortium for Land Research and Policy Dialogue (COLARP) (2011). Besides conducting research, he also teaches at the School of Arts, Kathmandu University. He is actively engaged with policy makers, politicians and the national and international media on the issues of Nepal's armed conflict and peace process. Bishnu Upreti is currently the South Asia Regional Coordinator of NCCR North-South, a global research network active in addressing the challenges of sustainable development. Contact: bupreti@nccr.wlink.com.np.

ALL LAW IS PLURAL. LEGAL PLURALISM AND THE DISTINCTIVENESS OF LAW[1]

Mariano Croce

Introduction

The present article pursues two basic aims. Firstly, I shall canvass the idea that there is no normative difference between state law and other kinds of law, such as customary law or religious law, and that eventually there is not a clear dividing line between the various normative fields of social reality (from interactions of everyday life to legal activities). More precisely, I shall explain why some scholars (and above all some of those who belong to what today is known as 'legal pluralism') deem the traditional distinction between legal rules and other social rules either as an abstractive construal of monist state-centred theories, or else as a factual consequence of contingent socio-political arrangements. Such scholars forcefully argue that, at present, an increasing plurality of normative orders makes the distinction between the legal and the extra-legal outdated and urge legal theorists to dispose once and for all of the fictitious idea that law is something special. In reality, they conclude, the legal and the broader social are so intertwined that no distinctive line among good manners, religious precepts, and positive legal rules can be drawn. Subsequently, I shall argue that, while such a 'panlegalistic' approach represents a first decisive step towards a sound and open-minded understanding of legal phenomena, it is still possible to detect the traits that make law a special normative ordering. Indeed, in order to find a remedy to

[1] I am extremely grateful to Gordon Woodman for his meticulous and thoughtful reading of my article. His comments and suggestions have remarkably improved the original version of this writing.

the panlegalistic quagmire mentioned above, I shall contend that the distinguishing marks of law do not relate to its formal structure (in terms of rules and bodies of persons working therein), but to the role legal orderings perform in social reality.

To put it otherwise, this article has two sides that, I believe, belong to the same coin: in order to show that law is truly something special, we first need to follow the panlegalist (deconstructive) hypothesis that what separates legal from non-legal orderings does not concern their internal normative structure. Therefore, even though I believe that, as I shall argue in the last part of this article, the idea of a basic distinction between legal and non-legal practices can be successfully advocated, I shall previously show that those who support a panlegalistic approach convincingly prove that the investigation into the nature of law requires a novel theoretical approach and more adequate tools of analysis than those provided by monistic and state-centred paradigms. In arguing this, I shall demonstrate that this type of analysis finds support not only among legal pluralists. Indeed, I shall cast some light on the panlegalistic view by integrating the analysis of the nature of customary law offered by Gordon R. Woodman, a renowned legal pluralist, with a Wittgensteinian reading of the 'practice theory' of rules by Herbert L.A. Hart, one of the most respected exponents of legal positivism. Based on this analysis I shall highlight an impasse which the panlegalist hypothesis incurs: it is unable to clarify what it is that allows us to regard some orderings as legal and some others as simply social. At the end of this article I shall try to unravel this puzzle. If it is true that the investigation of the normative structure of law leads to the conclusion that there is no significant difference between law (whether it is state or non-state) and many social orderings of everyday life, I shall argue that the hallmark of law can be found elsewhere and that therefore the panlegalist hypothesis must be tempered. While doing this, I shall divert my attention from the formal structure of law to other relevant aspects of the legal practice and its typical way of functioning.

Preliminary considerations

1. The nature of Law

In an article devoted to analysing the risks and potentials inherent in the recognition of customary laws by state governments and their legal systems, Gordon R. Woodman provides some subtle conceptual indications that may slip the attention of a superficial reader. Though the title of the essay refers only to customary laws and rights, with a subtle argument the author comes to argue that every law is customary: "[A]ll law, including state law, is in the last resort customary law" (Woodman 2009a: 98). This conclusion will be reinforced by the results of my philosophical analysis; hence, I shall now assume it as unproblematic, and thus look at Woodman's considerations on customary law as referring to law in general.

Firstly, the author puts at the heart of law the controversial concept of 'acceptance', defined as a "relatively widespread observance of the norms of customary law in a particular group of humans" (Woodman 2009a: 92). Furthermore, here 'acceptance' figures as synonymous with 'observance'. This assumption has serious consequences for a vexed notion in the field of legal studies, namely the validity of legal norms. As I have suggested elsewhere (Croce 2009: 131-132; Croce 2012: Chap. 2), we may single out three basic kinds of legal validity, that some authors consider to be hierarchically ordered while some others consider them to be incompatible. These are: *practical validity*, i.e. the validity of a legal rule depends on adherence to some pre-legal natural or moral standard, such as natural human equality or some principle of justice (as many believers in natural law argue); *legal validity*, i.e. the validity of a legal rule depends on its belonging to a broader legal system (as many positivists argue); *effectual validity*, i.e. a legal rule is not valid unless it is felt as compulsory and then actually practised by those who actually practice the rule and in particular by officials (as many realists argue). It may seem that the 'acceptance as observance' perspective supports the third kind of validity, in that it maintains that a rule is valid insofar as it is effective. An important part of my analysis will be dedicated to showing that such an interpretation not only misinterprets Woodman's perspective, but would weaken it.

Secondly, in addressing the nature of law, Woodman mentions some well-known theoretical endeavours to capture the distinctive feature of legal rules and stresses that they all are to some extent reductive or misleading. Recalling the distinction advanced by Herbert L.A. Hart between 'primary' and 'secondary' rules, Woodman criticises those legal scholars who claim the law to be an ensemble of prescriptive norms. He shows that the law is composed of a full range of rules which have legal effects without all being commands or imperatives. As for instance Neil MacCormick (1998) puts it, such rules are *institutive* (that bring something into existence), *consequential* (that indicate what consequences the existence of that thing produces in the broader social context), and *terminative* (that determine when such a thing comes to an end). Not only, Woodman underscores, does the form of rules vary, but also the form of their observance does. In fact, most of these rules do not guide conduct by means of threats – as command-based positivist theories assert –, but require for the achievement of certain results specific types of behaviour (such as those needed for creating a company) or the performance of ritual acts (such as those needed for a marriage), often motivated by the requirements of the addressees themselves.

Thirdly, Woodman underscores a basic feature of legal rules, which has been largely discussed in the famed Hart-Dworkin debate. In arguing that the "major types of customary laws may be classified in terms of the types of populations by which they are observed" (Woodman 2009a: 94), he categorises religious law as a kind of customary law. But at the same time he invites us to bear in mind the basic distinction ("as far as it is possible to do so in practice") between religious injunctions that believers follow on the basis of their personal convictions and rules that they follow with regard to whether others follow them. As a consequence - and this is an important aspect of law - a legal rule serves as a *standard* for conduct within a population.

In sum, the conceptual background of Woodman's article is the following: the law is an ensemble of rules

(a) that are accepted and observed by the majority of a population;
(b) that have different forms requiring different types of observance;
(c) that are valid inasmuch as the members of a population consider them to be public standards.

Woodman's arguments are particularly instrumental in demystifying the monist state ideology that claimed that only state law was truly law while the other laws could only be defined as law-like. The author demonstrates that, inasmuch as every law is customary, the relation between state law and customary law is not to be seen as a relation between laws of different degree, value, or nature.

2. *The risk of objectifying and its opposite*

In a recent essay Woodman challenges the idea that law can be mapped (Bavinck and Woodman 2009). His negative conclusion is shared by many scholars in the ambit of legal pluralism, post-colonial studies and governmentality studies. Taken as the "anti-sovereign practice" *par excellence*, another scholar suggests that the "practice of travel" is able to unmask the "cartographic reason" of colonialism, which for a long time has enabled colonisers to impose their legal and political mentalities just by drawing a few lines on a piece of paper (Spanò 2009). The practice of travel discloses the imaginary and artificial nature of any material and symbolic border, which more often than not was a product of colonial exportation and served as an invasive means of violence and exclusion. This is why today – such theoreticians point out – western scholars are called upon to dispose of their instinctive inclination to map, so as to prevent themselves from exercising an objectifying symbolic violence that could be seen as an unintentional heir to the violence (both material and symbolic) of western colonisers.

These argumentations evoke the misgiving of Pierre Bourdieu over the fascination for logical models that according to many scholars (especially structuralists) allow the ethnologist to explain observed reality as no participant could. In *The Logic of Practice*, the French sociologist criticises the tendency to objectify shared by many philosophical and sociological schools. He expresses serious doubts about theories that look at social practices as if they were the application of some supra-subjective structures or schemes, of which the observed agents are supposedly unaware and which only an observer may come to outline. Bourdieu claims that when the observer superimposes a "logic" on the observed practices – that is, a "generative formula" as a set of independent and coherent axioms which the observer constructs in order to explain practices – she turns out to objectify and thus misread the practices, to such an extent that her observation is likely to reveal more about her (projective) relation to what she observes than about the nature of the latter. An objectifying approach to practices – which looks at their logical relations always in light of the model imagined by the observer – can hardly explain their true nature. To portray such a myopic tendency, Bourdieu uses the metaphor of the map:

> The logical relations he [the observer] constructs are to 'practical' relations – practical because continuously practised, kept up and cultivated – as the geometrical space of a map, a representation of all possible routes for all possible subjects, is to the network of pathways that are really maintained and used, 'beaten tracks' that are really practicable for a particular agent (Bourdieu 1990: 35).

Such "beaten tracks" are precisely what Woodman seems to have in mind when he focuses on the nature of norms and the possibility of mapping law: "[N]orms are considered to 'exist' only if they are socially observed, not merely if they are, according to doctrinal reasoning from an initial presupposition, 'valid'" (Bavinck and Woodman 2009: 199). However, a (justified) resistance to objectification should not induce us to take the opposite (wrong) direction, namely, to act on the assumption that there is nothing a scholar can take into account but factual behaviour. On this view, rules are just what people regard as rules and an observer may know about them just by looking at the concrete behaviours of rule-bearers. That is to say, rules are valid only when effective. By identifying the whole spectrum of validity with mere effectiveness one ends by reducing all kinds of rules to sheer facts and thus depriving them of their normative value. What such a conclusion leaves unexplained is why rules (whether legal or generally social) claim to govern the conduct of individuals and how they succeed in doing it. In fact, by interpreting validity in terms of effectiveness, rules are depicted as mere regularities of behaviour, which set standards by virtue of their being reiterated by the majority of a population and eventually turn out to be nothing but an articulation of a broader *ethos*. I shall take up this issue in more detail below.

But, as I understand him, Woodman does not take a stand for effectual validity. Customary law is not a simple reiterated custom. It is a normative device that governs and structures the interactions of rule-bearers and provides an orderly frame for their social life. Woodman seems to confirm my interpretation when, for instance, he says that the student of customary law should not attach "importance to the longevity of a social practice" (Woodman 2009a: 94-95). As Woodman describes it, customary law is a reflectively mediated instrument that human beings adopt so as to organise their social interactions and their common relation to the surrounding environment. An instrument which varies over time and is affected continuously by the continuous transformations of social reality: "A great deal of information attests to the increasing rate of change in customary laws as they adapt to modernisation in the societies in which they are observed" (Woodman 2009a: 95). But the soundest theoretical evidence for my interpretation is the distinction, underlined above, between rules followed by way of personal convictions (such as, for instance, "you must run thirty minutes a day in order to lose weight") and rules followed because of their public interactional value (such as, for instance, "you must stop when the traffic signal is red"). To corroborate my interpretation, I shall dwell on points (a) and (c) mentioned in the first section of the present article. I shall first concentrate on point (c), trying to elaborate on what Woodman may mean when he speaks of rules followed with "regard to whether others follow them," and then I shall turn to the point (a), analysing the notion of 'acceptance as observance'.

Back To Basics: Actions, Rules, Understanding

Legal rules cannot be said to guide conduct if they are followed without regard to whether others follow them. This assumption, that Woodman stresses *en passant*, is at the heart of the so-called "practice theory" of rules advanced by Hart in *The Concept of Law* (Hart 1994, first published 1961). The English scholar challenges many reductionist perspectives (such as positivism and realism) that claim to locate the core essence of rules in their being commands of a sovereign (J. Austin), or indications for officials (H. Kelsen), or means for predicting the future behaviour of officials (K. Llewellyn), or obligations psychologically interiorised by officials (A. Ross). In the *pars destruens* of his book, Hart shows why all such perspectives fail to account for the salient aspects of law, and in particular for the way law functions in social life. Hart is dissatisfied with these understandings of rules and law as they are more or less counter-intuitive. Not only do these accounts fall short of being convincing as to the way law really works in social life, but, according to Hart, they obscure how *ordinary people use rules*. I believe that the clarification of this Hartian point may help us understand both what Woodman means when he connects the law to observance within a population and why every type of normative order can be said to be inherently plural.

One of the renowned merits of Hart's practice theory is to show that it is not possible to give an adequate account of law from an "external point of view." An external observer – who merely focuses on the behaviour of observed individuals – would not be able to understand the way ordinary people use legal rules in social life and thus the relation between their conduct and the law. What is more, the programmatic twofold approach adopted by Hart[2] suggests that legal analysis alone can hardly explain any sort of normativity. Jurisprudence is not, *pace* Kelsen, an autonomous science, precisely because law is nothing but an articulation of social reality and legal rules are nothing but a special kind of social rules. Hence, the proper field in which we should carry out a dependable analysis on how legal rules work in social life is not the ambit of jurisprudence, but the general context of social interactions, so that "we must, for the moment, turn aside from the special case of legal rules" (Hart 1994: 55) and focus on the broader case of social rules.[3]

Whoever claims that an observer can account for rules by monitoring sheer behaviours turns out (whether consciously or not) to uphold the paradoxical

[2] In the preface to *The Concept of Law* Hart declares that his book can be regarded both as a work "designed for the student of jurisprudence" and "as an essay in descriptive sociology" (Hart 1994: vi).

[3] As Woodman shows in a recent review of a book on the nature of customary law, this is a process that must still be accomplished, as the attention of 'pure theorists' to empirical situations is scarce (Woodman 2009a).

conclusion that "the traffic signal in a busy street" is nothing but a "natural *sign that* people behave in certain ways, as clouds are a *sign that* rain will come" (Hart 1994: 90). Hart points out the difference between a *sign* which permits us to predict that something is likely to happen and a normative *signal* that an interactional practice establishes in a relevant context. This difference is rooted in the fact that, while certain phenomena happen independently of how people interpret them, a normative signal is intrinsically dependent upon the *meaning* that users give it. (Notice that this is not the same as the questionable distinction between 'brute' and 'institutional' facts, although this topic would merit further discussion). For instance, an external observer may not understand whether by shaking hands two persons are only greeting or are concluding an agreement; nor may the observer understand whether a person is nodding so as to indicate her assent or whether she is simply stretching her neck. The observer needs to *understand* (see Winch 1990; von Wright 1971) the shared meaning the agents give their actions. Rules are just like the actions in these examples: an observer must grasp their given meaning *in action*. But to convey the meaning of rules let me provide the further example (also used by Hart, Ross, Wittgenstein, and many others) of chess. An observer who intends to capture the rules of chess by recording the regularities in the behaviour of players may get into serious difficulty when she observes, say, every time the players move a piece they do so with their left hand, and every time they move the knight they do so in the typical 'L' move. By recording regularities the observer will hardly understand whether both of these actions are required by the rules or not. She will be helped by the fact that when a player happens to move a piece with her right hand her opponent gives no reaction, contrary to what happens when the player moves the knight as if it were a pawn.

By capitalising on reflections like these, Hart highlights the distinction between habits and rules. It may well happen that social agents feel habits to be essential, compulsory, or even oppressive, but, from a theoretical perspective, habits lack certain specific characteristics that rules have. Hart singles these out as follows:

1. As to habits, it is sufficient that behaviours converge, and "deviation from the regular course need not be a matter for any form of criticism." As to rules, on the contrary, "deviations are generally regarded as lapses or faults open to criticism" (Hart 1994: 55). In a word, rules are a basis for mutual *criticisms* between agents.

2. As to habits, no agent would feel it legitimate to criticise

someone who deviates from them.[4] As to rules, on the contrary, criticisms of deviations are regarded as legitimate or justified. In a word, rules are widespread standards whose infringement is considered as *a justified reason* for criticism.

3. As to habits, people behave in such a way that their behaviours converge unreflectively, i.e. without regard to whether each behaves as the others do: "[N]o members of the group need in any way think of the general behaviour, or even know that the behaviour in question is general." As to rules, on the contrary, it is vital that the agents follow them by considering whether the others do the same: "[I]f a social rule is to exist some at least must look upon the behaviour in question as a general standard to be followed by the group as a whole" (Hart 1994: 56). In a word, rules must have an "*internal aspect*" in the light of which people act reflectively, i.e. with regard to whether the rule really plays its role of a general standard.

Unfortunately, in the first edition of *The Concept of Law* Hart provides no solid justification for his analysis of social norms. On the one hand, his analysis simply amounts to quasi-sociological observations of certain crucial aspects of social reality that, on the contrary, require a robust philosophical investigation. On the other hand, Hart exempts himself from such a philosophical investigation by referring here and there to some authoritative thinkers such as J.L. Austin, L. Wittgenstein, and P. Winch. But this argumentative strategy turned out to be inadequate to counter copious criticisms. One of the sharpest is expressed by Joseph Raz in *Practical Reason and Norms* (1990). Here the author questions the idea that habits may be distinguished from rules by virtue of the fact that it is only the infringement of a rule that provokes criticism. One of the three "fatal defects" that Raz believes he has detected in the practice theory (Raz 1990: 53-58) is

[4] It may seem that a glaring contradiction arises between what I have just said and what I wrote some lines above, or rather, that "[i]t may well happen that social agents feel habits to be essential, compulsory, or even oppressive". In effect, as I shall say shortly, this contradiction seems to be also present in Hart's analysis, as some critics have pointed out. However I shall later say that, at the end of the day, Hart's second point is tenable and that there is an important difference between deviating from a habit and deviating from a rule and that it mainly relates to the reason for criticisms and their justification.

related to the fact that habits can well be regarded as bases for justified criticisms, and therefore this cannot be considered to be a distinguishing feature of rules. Raz claims that there can be a community "in which almost everybody believes that babies should be breast-fed or that children should be encouraged to learn to read when they are three years of age. This is generally done and people tend to reproach mothers who do not breast-feed or parents who do not teach their three-year-old children to read. Yet people in the community do not regard these as rules. They merely think that they are good things to do" (Raz 1990: 55). Under the pressure of this and other criticisms, this aspect of the practice theory has progressively changed over time. Eventually, many of Hart's epigones and to a degree Hart himself resorted to adopting a conventionalist approach, then interpreting the original version of the practice theory as a brilliant though approximate defence of legal conventionalism. In this way, Hart eventually dismisses the 'spiritual assistance' of the philosophers mentioned above for vindicating a tradition that among its leading figures lists David Lewis and Michael Bratman.

In my view, however, this solution brings out even more intensely the coherent *pluralist* outcome of Hart's practices theory. In his famous 'Postscript' (Hart 1994: 238-279), in which Hart tackles some of the various criticisms made by Ronald Dworkin, he declares that his initial programme was more ambitious than it later became, since when he wrote the first edition of *The Concept of Law* he believed that his analysis of social rules was a good interpretation of normativity in general, from morality to law. In the 'Postscript' Hart downgrades his powerful analysis of social normativity to a mere investigation of the convention lying behind the activities of legal officials: "I do not now regard it [the practice theory] as a sound explanation of morality, either individual or social" (Hart 1994: 256). Now Hart simply aims to show that the practice of law is based on the rule of recognition[5] as a *social* rule that sets a standard for officials and that must be accepted as a standard only by them. It is evident that this later perspective reinforces the conclusion at which Woodman hints when writing that "state laws are in reality further instances of customary laws, the populations which observe them being the officials and others who operate the various institutions of the state" (Woodman 2009a: 97). I believe that this conclusion can be even reinforced by an analysis of the original programme of the practice theory of rules. So, I first need to devote my attention to Hart's original portrayal of social normativity.

[5] That is to say, a standard specifying the features whose possession must be taken as a conclusive indication that it is a rule of the legal order. See Hart 1994: 114-117.

Social Practices as the Source of Normativity: the Criterion-Rules

As I stressed above, the assumptions that practices are the cradle of social rules and that they provide the foundation for every kind of normativity, whether moral or legal, are to be proven by means of solid philosophical arguments. In particular, we need to show how social practices produce binding criteria[6] that are inherently public and why therefore the adoption of their rules must be conditional on whether others adopt them. I shall now describe the way social practices yield such criteria and argue that they are indispensable if agents are to share common meanings and hence engage in functioning interactions.

We may describe social practices as *interactional contexts in which the conduct of the agents is governed by rules (or criterion-rules)*. There are three kinds of rule-governance: *intuitive*, *epistemic*, and *motivational*. The conduct of an agent is governed *intuitively* when she performs what the rule prescribes without them being aware of that and without them taking into account the advantages or disadvantages associated to rules (for instance, more often than not, one refrains from killing not because there is a rule forbidding murder, or one pays the bill not because there is an obligation not to breach contracts). The conduct is governed *epistemically* when the agent adopts the conduct *indicated* by the rule: the rule successfully governs the conduct of an agent, who complies with what the rule prescribes but is moved to action by other motives than the bare existence of the rule in question (for instance, one may act in accordance with the rule in order to achieve an aim that the rule makes achievable, or in order to do what they believe to be a good action). The conduct is governed *motivationally* when the agent is *motivated* by the fact that there is a rule claiming to govern their conduct: they follow the rule *because it is a rule*, i.e. because it is a standard that claims to guide conduct

As I said, rules are generally followed intuitively. But they are criteria that the agents are supposed to be capable – at least in principle – of bringing into a reflective, statable form. To put it differently, individuals must be capable of verbalising the criteria that provide a taken-for-granted basis for their interactions. I think it is crucial to prove this philosophically so as to show once and for all that every rule, *pace* Dworkin, is rooted in a social practice and thus that they are

[6] As I shall demonstrate later, the Hartian 'standards' owe much to the Wittgensteinian 'criteria'. This is why, for the reasons set out by Stanley Cavell (1979, chaps. I, II), I shall use the term 'criteria'.

really rules only if followed with regard to whether others follow them.[7]

A rule may be defined as a model of conduct meant to ensure the occurrence of the same behaviour on every occurrence of the relevant circumstances. To demonstrate that such a rule cannot be in any way a private affair, we have to show that - although a model may be produced by a subject in isolation - "the being a model" character of the model cannot stem from the activity of the very same subject who takes the model as binding.[8] I think that on this issue Wittgenstein provides some conclusive arguments. In many passages of *Philosophical Investigations*, he portrays rules as reiterated models of action from which ensues a *paradigmatic application*. Such a paradigmatic application institutes the criteria of correctness and incorrectness (of the action reiterated on the basis of the criteria) while the reiteration of the action (in the light of the paradigmatic application) confers on such criteria a general and public stability. The public dimension of the criteria secures their identity and constancy both in the different circumstances of private experience of single individuals and in the different experiences of the various individuals: the criteria, which embody their own paradigmatic application, represent for each and every subject stable guidelines for performing their own actions and understanding those of the others. On this reading, the paradigmatic application becomes the criterion of correctness for future applications. Any practice (that I may now describe as the *reiteration of an action under the guidance of the paradigmatic application*) establishes its own

[7] Famously, in order to controvert the idea that obligations come from social practices, Ronald Dworkin brings attention to the case of a vegetarian who says "that we have no right to kill animals for food because of the fundamental moral rule that it is always wrong to take life in any form or under any circumstance. Obviously no social rule exists to that effect" (Dworkin 1978: 52). As I shall show below, Dworkin misunderstands the essence of rules (or better, what I name "*the being rule*" *of a rule*), since the vegetarian, for example, needs a stable criterion to secure that in all circumstances in which she finds herself eating something, what she eats is not meat, and then may be corrected by others (whether vegetarians or non-vegetarians) when she erroneously bites into a pie containing meat. This aspect of rules will appear clearer after the introduction of the Wittgensteinian distinction between a necessarily and a contingently private language.

[8] In this regard I disagree with Jules L. Coleman who, in analysing the case of personal rules, maintains that the Hartian 'internal point of view' is the human *psychological* ability to transform a proposition into a rule (see Coleman 2001: 88).

paradigm of correctness and renders it into a normative criterion for assessing the actions that are performed in the light of the paradigm. In other words, the practice defines its own criteria for recognising the relevant circumstances (i.e. when the rule needs to be applied) and indicates the correct pathways for applying the rule. In such a framework, the *private* application of a rule is simply inconceivable. Let me explore this issue more in depth.

Wittgenstein argues that it is only if the rule is followed publicly - so that the criterion defined within the practice may be used by a *plurality* of agents - that we may assess whether a subject is following a rule *correctly*. To put it differently, the criterion we adopt for assessing the possible application of a rule is the *intersubjective interaction*, one of the primary and evident manifestations being the reaction of others to the infringement of the rule. Without this kind of intersubjectivity there would be no criterion of assessment: not only would the subject be unable to establish, in the restricted sphere of her individual experience, whether she is following the rule correctly (in fact, I shall indicate below, she may only *think* she is following it correctly), but in addition there would not be any rule at all. That is, there would not be any need for a stable and public criterion for assessing whether an application is correct or not, and conversely there would not be any application which might be taken as paradigmatic. This is evidence that the possibility of assessing the correctness of a single application represents the *condition of existence* of rules - that is, practices are conditions of existence of rules.

To prove this proposition, Wittgenstein needs to rule out the conceptual possibility of a private language, or rather, of a set of rules that a subject in isolation could follow by self-obligation. In doing so, he shows that the *publicity* of a rule is a distinctive feature of every rule.[9] A private language should be based on private rules, that the speaker may follow privately. To deny such a possibility, Wittgenstein vindicates the crucial distinction between *following* a rule and *thinking to follow* a rule: "That's why 'following a rule' is a practice. And to *think* one is following a rule is not to follow a rule. And that's why it's not possible to follow a rule 'privately'; otherwise, thinking one was following a rule would be the same thing as following it" (Wittgenstein 2009: §202). To substantiate his

[9] I would like to remark that these considerations do not apply only to the rules of language, as some legal philosophers assert (see Schiavello 2009: 56-60), since the so-called 'private language argument' refers to the human ability to institute, recognise, and follow rules in general and in particular social rules.

assertions, Wittgenstein - who is generally inclined to highlight the inconceivability of some possible counter-argumentations rather than to provide structured justifications - envisages a subject who gives a name to her sensations. Not only does the very same activity of naming presuppose that "much must be prepared in the language" (Wittgenstein 2009: §257). In addition, Wittgenstein claims, if the subject allots the letter 'S' to her sensation and keeps a diary about its recurrence so as to identify S precisely when it occurs, she is doing nothing but adopting a procedure that may help her to *remember* correctly the connection between her definition and the recurrence of S. It is as if she tried to express her sensation as a mental image so as to recognise it correctly when it occurs again. But the subject, Wittgenstein argues, just lacks a criterion of correctness that permits her to test whether S_1 is the same as S or whether she is associating them erroneously. In Wittgenstein's words: "Let us imagine a table, something like a dictionary, that exists only in our imagination. A dictionary can be used to justify the translation of a word X by a word Y. But are we also to call it a justification if such a table is to be looked up only in the imagination? - 'Well, yes; then it is a subjective justification'. - But justification consists in appealing to an independent authority - "But surely I can appeal from one memory to another. For example, I don't know if I have remembered the time of departure of a train correctly, and to check it I call to mind how a page of the timetable looked. Isn't this the same sort of case?" No; for this procedure must now actually call forth the *correct* memory. If the mental image of the timetable could not itself be *tested* for correctness, how could it confirm the correctness of the first memory? (As if someone were to buy several copies of today's morning paper to assure himself that what it said was true.) Looking up a table in the imagination is no more looking up a table than the image of the result of an imagined experiment is the result of an experiment." (Wittgenstein 2009: §265). In a word, if justification consists in appealing to something independent, the criteria must be public and must be managed publicly.

Let me conclude this Wittgensteinian detour by underlining that the private language argument does not concern the *pragmatic* difficulty that a subject may encounter in trying to remember correctly her sensations. Wittgenstein does not deny the pragmatic possibility that a single individual may establish certain procedures and follow them in isolation. Actually we may well imagine a particularly gifted subject capable of successfully recognising each of her sensations. The problem is primarily *conceptual* and concerns the normative structure of rules and their functions. The activity of the isolated subject who establishes and follows certain procedures is parasitic on public rule-following, in that the method she adopts in following the rule privately amounts to an attempt to institute a criterion for assessing her own actions in the relevant circumstances.

She determines and establishes some criteria that may help her recognise the recurrence of an identical situation and therein adopt identical conduct. This is arguably a clarification of the distinction between a *necessarily* and a *contingently* private language. Wittgenstein distinguishes between a private idiolect that in principle none can understand but its inventor, and a language that is private by accident, being based on rules that in principle others may understand (Wittgenstein 2009: § 243). He wishes to rule out the conceptual possibility only of the former, since the latter is a case where rules play the same role as they play in public contexts. C. Peacocke explains this clearly: "Wittgenstein thought that if only the rule-follower and not anyone else could know whether he is following a rule, we would not in such a case be able to say what is the difference between there really being a rule the agent is following and his being under the false impression that there is. This, Wittgenstein continues, is an unacceptable conclusion if following a rule is to place any restrictions on what the rule-follower does. Hence it is not possible that the subject alone can know whether he is following a rule: the conclusion is that there must be public criteria for whether someone is following a rule" (Peacocke 1981: 75).

In sum, by showing that the *"being a rule" of a rule* does not relate at all to any private experience of the rule-followers (a feature of rules that Hart often remarks against Scandinavian realists, but with no further philosophical justification), Wittgenstein shows *ipso facto* that the existence of a rule requires the presence of (at least) two individuals. That is, the correctness of rule-following can never be proven by private evidence, but it is (implicitly and most often tacitly) confirmed by reference to a coordinated interaction among agents. This understanding of rule-following clarifies the original Hartian account of social rules as public standards for justified criticism. On this reading, what Wittgenstein names 'criteria' in rule-following coincide with Hart's 'standards' in social rules, which I hereafter will name 'criterion-rules'.

Now that I have shown why criterion-rules must always be presupposed if subjects are to assess the application of a rule as correct or incorrect, I can turn to focus on practices. These are contexts where agents are expected to be able to *assess the correctness* of their actions and those of others in the light of the gap between them and the criterion-rules and thus to *criticise* actions that depart from criterion-rules. As Hart correctly emphasises, this is the key difference between habits and rules.[10]

[10] On this issue Hart is more convincing than Wittgenstein, as the latter is inclined to liken rules to institutions, customs, and usages (see Wittgenstein 2009: §199), and therefore to obscure the significant differences amongst these four elements of

It is essential to point out that rules, in this broad and basic sense, are neither commands nor external constraints for actions. The criterion-rule is an *epistemic indication* about what the agents do. Criterion-rules are primarily *epistemic devices*. In a previous article A. Salvatore and I characterised this feature of rules by saying that they

> are deemed to constitute a specific language which confers on social reality a complex of meanings: only by enjoying this language may we understand what happens around us (in terms of social actions) and distinguish, for example, the movement of the autumn leaves in the wind from that of two dancers (Croce and Salvatore 2007: 17).

Only by capturing this essential feature of rules may we understand why they are, as Hart partly explains, *reasons for action*. In the vast literature on this subject-matter we can often notice an underlying and somehow neglected confusion between *motives* and *reasons*. For instance, in discussing the way the rule of recognition can guide the conduct of officials, many conventionalist advocates struggle to demonstrate that such a rule *figures as a motive* in the practical reasoning of officials. Such a confusion is severely condemned by P. Winch, one of the acknowledged inspirers of Hart. In his *The Idea of a Social Science* (first published in 1958), Winch stresses that "the terms 'reason' and 'motive' are not synonymous" (Winch 1990: 82). If we are to look for the motives of behaviour we should carry out an analysis aimed at explaining the *causes* that brought about that behaviour. Reasons on the contrary are those *considerations appropriate* to the context that *makes the behaviour intelligible*. Thus reasons are *meanings* indicating what kind of things are the things people are doing. Hence, as far as I understand it here, let me clarify with an example what it means to say that *a rule is a reason for action*. If Tom is used to having breakfast in the same café every morning and every morning he meets Kate there, and then one morning Kate does not come, Tom will have no justified reason for criticising Kate. But if Tom and Kate have an appointment and Kate breaks it, Tom does have a justified reason for criticism. In the former case, it is a habit, a routine, in that the agents reiterate their behaviour - moved by the sheer motive of having breakfast - with no consequence that may provide grounds for criticism. In the latter case, on the contrary, beyond the sheer motive of having breakfast, Tom and Kate are involved in an activity which is an *autonomous source of obligations*: both are called upon to plan their

social life. See also Croce 2012: Chap. 3.5.

action so as to meet each other in the café. In this case their motives may be different (Kate may just desire to hold a pleasant conversation while having breakfast whilst Tom may hope to make Kate fall in love with him), but their common reason for action is the appointment. In other words, while the criterion-rule is the pivot of the practice (or, we may say, 'the appointment practice is based on a mutual agreement that gives rise to a mutual obligation to be at a specific time in a specific place'), the reason lies in the fact that such a criterion-rule represents what every agent knowingly and consciously takes into consideration for planning their actions (so that, say, if Tom knows that Kate generally considers appointments as approximate arrangements that do not give rise to any obligation, Tom will be less inclined to be absolutely punctual). This is also why it would not affect the inner nature of the general practice of fixing appointments if the real motive beneath this particular appointment was the intention of Tom to entice Kate in order to rob her. In fact, both of them regard the appointment as a reason for action apart from their personal motives for action. This reason is public, common, independent of what the agents actually do, and is used by the agents both in planning their actions and in criticizing the actions of the others if they disregard it.[11] In short, such a rule governs (at least intuitively) the conduct of Tom and Kate while planning their actions on the basis of the appointment.[12]

In sum, practices are contexts in which conduct is governed by rules that serve as public and intersubjective criteria for the mutual assessment and criticism of actions. Such criterion-rules are among the considerations that are at the basis of the actions of the subjects involved in the practice, i.e. in principle they can be pointed to as reasons for action (that is, they may be shown to govern or guide

[11] It is worth mentioning what D. Bloor writes as regards the practice of marriage:

> Suppose someone were to go through the ceremony with deliberate, inner [...] intention to deceive. Could such a person argue [...] that they were not really married because, as they were getting married, they were thinking of themselves as engaged in a deceit, rather than a real marriage? Would that invalidate the marriage? Certainly not. [...] The reason is that the oversubtle deceiver *was well aware that it was a marriage he was going through. His being aware of what he was doing was part of what made up the deception.* (Bloor 2001: 106, italics added.)

[12] In case Kate, forgetful of the appointment, went by chance to the café at the agreed time, her conduct may be said only to conform to the rule.

actions) regardless of whether they figure as motives for these actions.

By capitalising on the analyses of Wittgenstein and Hart, I may pinpoint more clearly the two essential features of criterion-rules that have been discussed in the previous pages.[13] The first is their *ideal-normative force*: notwithstanding their pragmatic derivation, criterion-rules must never be identified with practices. The second (converse) feature is their *pragmatic nature*: the existence of criterion-rules always depends upon there being concrete practices in which they serve as criteria. To put it differently, on the one hand, criterion-rules are *conditions of thinkability* for practices, in that practices are intelligible and describable only in light of the criterion-rules that regulate them. (This is what Coleman labels the "explanatory power" of criteria.) On the other hand, conversely, practices are *conditions of existence* for criterion-rules, in that the latter always emerge out of the former. In sum, criterion-rules could not exist without practices and also practices could not be thought without criterion-rules. Owing to their implicit and unreflective nature, criterion-rules are "the result of ongoing negotiations," and thus "there may well be disagreement about their content" (Coleman 2001: 99). To make criterion-rules explicit agents need often to engage in negotiations, i.e. reflective processes whose propositional results are always fallible and revisable. Suffice it to mention the general difficulty of formulating the fundamental rules or the recommended conduct of some widespread practices, such as friendship or love relationships, the implicit character of which is brought into question only when some conflict occurs.

This philosophical perspective may cast light on point (c) of Woodman's analysis, i.e. on the fact that rules can be distinguished from non-rules as the former are to be followed by a person with regard whether others do the same. Actually, criterion-rules are epistemic devices which enable people to interact, to understand each other's actions, and to criticise others when they contravene rules. Thus rules are common and shared insofar as they are indispensable criteria for understanding and assessing the behaviour of others and for planning our own actions, and thus engaging in those common activities that are at the basis of our social life. (Imagine what might happen if we were to follow the rules of a grammar, to fix appointments, to enter into marriages, to stop at red signals, with no regard to whether others give these activities the same meaning we give them).

[13] Here I follow Coleman (2001: Lect. VII), even though, as I have already remarked, his conventional approach ends up narrowing the original scope of Hart's practice theory.

A Conceptual Impasse: the Priority of Legal Standards

Based on what I have thus far argued I can say that Woodman and Hart come to the same conclusion as to what law is: law is a *social* practice in which some rules are accepted as public standards that are meant to guide (at least epistemically) the conduct of a specific population. Within this practice – whose existence and validity depend on the reflective attitude of its members – agents adopt a set of rules as reasons for action and standards for criticism. Hart then was right when placing emphasis on the broader case of *social* rules to explain what the *legal* rule of recognition is. This special rule is what makes the practice of law intelligible to those who are engaged in it. The rule of recognition (which should be better described as a multiple set of 'practices of recognition'[14]) guides – at least epistemically – those who regard themselves as members of a population which is actually determined by the existence of a common set of rules. As a consequence, Hart and Woodman can be said to agree on the fact that state law, like many other rule-governed contexts, is a set of rules which has its own relevant population (officials and more generally all those who belong to the state organisational machinery) while the members of this population regard legal rules – and in particular those which instruct them on how to recognise, amend and enforce the rules addressed to lay people – as standards to be followed because they provide some sort of guidance. Yet, if this conceptual definition of law is sound, law turns out to be a practice among many other practices, from more fluid (such as appointment-fixing) to more solid ones (such as football).

But Hart and Woodman endorse highly different positions as to this latter conclusion. Indeed, it is well known that Hart continues to advocate a positivist (although inclusive) and finally monist view, according to which the legal practice is a special one, which has a neat pre-eminence over the others. On the face of it, he has to tackle a tricky question: if, from a conceptual vantage point, law is a practice like many other social ones with their standards and their populations, why should it be so special? What entitles the practice of law to override the rules of other practices? It seems to me that Hart is able offer no conceptual solution to this issue. As a matter of fact, his theory provides the grounds for holding that, at least conceptually, law has no special pre-eminence over other similar practices. In

[14] As Frederick Schauer points out, this term comes "closer to capturing the amorphous and shifting nature of what is an acceptable legal source as well as the way in which much of the development over time takes place from the bottom up rather than from the top down" (Schauer 2004: 1934).

effect, as already pointed out by Ralf Sartorius some decades ago, the analysis of law as a social practice proves to be applicable to a broad series of rule-governed social practices. Sartorius (1971) notices that Hart's formal definition of law perfectly fits many other social organisations, in which both primary and secondary rules and different groups of law-appliers and law-abiders are clearly distinguishable. This is the case with political parties, trade unions, corporations, educational institutes, sporting clubs, and criminal organisations: in all of these contexts there are closely defined meta-rules that entitle specific groups to administer rules of conduct. If this is so, the only viable conclusion is that, as Schauer tellingly remarks, "once we see that this analysis applies as straightforwardly to football and religious duties as to legal duties, we have not made much progress in trying to understand the institution of law, other than it being just one more system of rules" (Schauer 2010: 16). In other words, this entails that - at least from the point of view of a conceptual analysis of the normative structure of law - nothing can really account for the pre-eminence of the legal practice over the others. On his part, Hart seems to be aware of this, and indeed in the 'Postscript' he admits that it is

> quite vain to seek any more specific purpose which law as such serves beyond providing guides to human conduct and standards of criticism of such conduct. This will not of course serve to distinguish law from other rules or principles with the same general aims; the distinctive features of law are the provision it makes by secondary rules for the identification, change, and enforcement of its standards and the general claim it makes to priority over other standards. (Hart 1994: 249.)

In sum, Hart fails to explain what justifies the "priority" over standards to which he refers when talking about law. If this is true, then Woodman's conclusion seems far more coherent with the Wittgensteinian interpretation I have provided in the previous section. He frankly argues that legal scholars need to recognise "that there is not a clear dividing line on the spectrum which runs from the state legal norms forbidding murder to the norms of etiquette and good manners" (Woodman 2009a: 100). This conclusion is conceptually sounder since the reference to the inborn sociality of the rule of recognition proves that state law in reality is nothing but a further instance of social practices governed by rules, whose population is "the officials and others who operate the various institutions of the state" (Woodman 2009a: 97).

However, this conceptual conclusion raises a recurring problem, which has dogged the entire debate over legal pluralism: Should we really accept, as Woodman explicitly suggests, that "all social norms must be included within the category of 'law'" and that therefore scholars should give up hope of finding a clear dividing line between the social and the legal? (Woodman 2009: 100.) Should we acknowledge that the distinctive line between the legal and the non-legal - when it is present - is nothing but a *historical* product that was able to transform *a* normative system in *the* legal order? Is law's being considered as a supreme ordering merely due to transient contingencies or even power differentials, on whose basis a societal party was able to transform into "law" its inner normative order? I think it is possible to provide a solution which is not necessarily at odds with the analysis provided thus far: state law (and every other kind of law) is not different from other normative orderings because of any inner properties of its rules or other aspects belonging to its formal structure. Rather, a rule-governed context's being a law entails a particular way of functioning of its rules and its inner knowledge. I shall briefly try to vindicate this solution in the following pages.[15]

Looking for the Distinctiveness of Law: a Semiotic Hypothesis

If so far I have been proceeding *with* Woodman, in the rest of the present article I shall go *beyond* Woodman (but, at least I think, not *against* Woodman). The hypothesis I shall put forward is that, although legal rule-governed contexts are structurally similar or even identical to many other non-legal rule-governed contexts, law is something special. In particular, even though there can well be many more types of law than state law, all those types share some basic traits that allow defining them as 'legal'. These traits do not inhere in the formal structure of legal orderings, but in the type of knowledge and categories that are at work within them: an ordering is legal if it is able to serve as "a symbolic grammar in terms of which reality is continually constructed and managed in the course of everyday interaction and confrontation" (Comaroff and Roberts 1981, 247). This way of conceiving law helps solve the conceptual impasse which the panlegalist approach incurs: the speciality of legal rules is not due to the role of standards they play within their relevant population, but to the special role they play as semiotic

[15] I would like to clarify that this kind of analysis would require much more space and a sounder justification than the rough and concise sketch I shall provide. Anyway, what I shall say will simply endeavour to synthesise what I argue in Croce 2012 and in particular in Part III.

tools for rephrasing social reality. To prove this hypothesis, I must temporarily withdraw from the field of legal theory to adopt a socio-anthropological approach that may bring out those elements which enable genuinely *legal* orderings to serve as venues of negotiation and management of social reality.

With an analysis which fits not only the modern juridico-political scenario (dominated by the pre-eminence of state law) but rather captures a relevant feature of the legal practice, Pierre Bourdieu proves that law always *tends to present itself as an autonomous field*, based on an *autonomous body of knowledge and rules*. He portrays law as an arena whose boundaries are safeguarded by a limited range of social agents who possess a "technical competence", or rather, the "socially recognized capacity to *interpret* a corpus of texts sanctifying a correct or legitimized vision of the social world" (Bourdieu 1987: 817).[16] In other words, among the basic constituents of law there seem to be not only rules and their serving as standards for the population who follow them, but also its *special stock of knowledge* and the *role of those who master such knowledge* by virtue of their exclusive technical competence. In this reading, law would be characterised by elements which go well beyond its formal structure, that is, the *way legal knowledge operates in social life*, its *claim to self-sufficiency* and its *separateness from everyday knowledge*. I shall now clarify these relevant characteristics and also spell out some of the ambiguities that may affect them.

Bourdieu appears to suggest that the mentioned characteristics are circularly connected to one another. Legal rules can successfully claim to override the rules of the other practices because the stock of legal knowledge is independent of both the knowledge of everyday life and the sectorial knowledge of other social fields. In short, law's normative claim of pre-eminence is legitimised with a circular recourse to its own self-sufficiency. At the same time, in order for law's knowledge to preserve its special position, it must be kept and managed by a limited circle of reliable people, who act as custodians of the legal borders. In this sense, law ends up being *independent because separate* and *separate because*

[16] Needless to say, he explicitly refers to contemporary Western legal systems, well institutionalised and highly proceduralised. Nonetheless, as I shall argue, I think that Bourdieu's analysis is applicable also to contexts in which such a technical competence is poorly institutionalised and left to flexible procedures. To prove this, in Croce 2012 I take into exam both a non-modern and a non-Western case: Roman law and the *mekgwa le melao* of Tswana people. In the following paragraphs I shall briefly mention the latter case.

independent.

Bourdieu's analysis shows how the different distribution of legal knowledge and its custody by a restricted range of experts make law appear as less and less dependent on extra-legal factors. Legal rules are seen as the pure outcome of an independent, autonomous and self-sufficient activity. Those who occupy an official role in the legal field are regarded as the 'authorised interpreters' of legal knowledge and as privileged players. Nevertheless, even if the role of experts turns out to be crucial, it does not represent a distinctive trait *in se* and *per se*. Rather the distinction between experts and lay people is primarily *instrumental in preserving the autonomy of the legal field and the self-sufficiency of its knowledge*. Indeed, legal knowledge grounds itself on an alleged self-sufficiency even when experts are not present or when they are not formally recognised as a well-established group (in fact, members of this group can be elders, savants, chiefs or priests who operate as 'legal' experts only in temporary and circumstantial conditions). Also in these latter cases, law acts as *a stock of knowledge* - distinct from, and independent of, every other kind of knowledge that is present in society[17] - whose decisions and settlements are seen as valid because they are founded on a common *trans-sectional* basis, which transcends the opposite interests that are at the origin of the conflict (be this basis a primeval tradition, an ancestral past, the wisdom of ancestors, the revelation of God or a democratic constitution). In other words, 'legal' decisions are based on what John Peristiany calls "a common *religio*" (Peristiany 1954: 48), as the law fulfils the need "to discover how sectional interests may be transcended" (Peristiany 1954: 39-40).

In my view, this is also what emerges out of John L. Comaroff and Simon Roberts's cutting-edge analysis of the *mekgwa le melao ya Setswana* in *Rules and Processes*. As far as I understand them, the two anthropologists prove that, even in circumstances that are far from our specialised legal systems, there is a special stock of knowledge that is used to produce particular effects on social reality. They claim that Twsana do not possess "a separate class of *legal* norms, functionally and conceptually distinguished from other types of precept" (Comaroff and Roberts 1981: 9). In fact, the stated rules found in Tswana communities is a vast and undifferentiated repertoire that extends from rules of etiquette to rules dealing

[17] I am by no means saying that legal knowledge is completely separate from the problems of daily life. I am rather saying that law sieves and parses everyday reality through its language and its categories without merging with everyday language and categories.

with major crimes. When Tswana find themselves speaking of *mekgwa le melao*, they mobilise a vast set of concepts, such as manners, etiquette, polite behaviour, custom, usage, habitual practice, taboo, duty, obligation (Comaroff and Roberts 1981: 71). This suggests that we can hardly consider it to be an ordered and differentiated set of legal rules. Yet, what counts here is the role that this repertoire plays in social life: the hybridity and flexibility of *mekgwa le melao* is instrumental in *legitimising competing constructions of reality* and *imposing an order on everyday events* (Comaroff and Roberts 1981: 78). Comaroff and Roberts depict *mekgwa le melao* as a *semiotic code*, based on a shared but separate stock of knowledge, which in given circumstances is employed so as to yield, renegotiate, and revise the Tswana view of social reality. They point out that, when discussing in reference to this repertoire, speakers adopt a *formal code*, marked by *stylistic formality, reliance on metaphors and impersonal and authoritative quality*. These marks make it clear that the speakers are appealing to "the transcendent legitimacy of shared values" (Comaroff and Roberts 1981: 86). In doing so, the authors emphasise that the parties treat the set of Tswana rules in a very particular manner: when Tswana enter the dispute and refer to *mekgwa le melao*, they come to adopt the *special language* that pertains to the legal field. More precisely, Comaroff and Roberts speak of an 'insulation', which is meant to separate the language typical of *mekgwa le melao* from the language of everyday life. In the legal field, there cannot be any reconstruction of facts and events that does not employ this insulated formulaic language.

The two anthropologists support this idea by discussing some concrete cases in which it is shown how Tswana processes favour a constant interplay between rules and facts. They explain how the rules of *mekgwa le melao* enable to describe facts in a certain manner, while in turn facts, described in a certain manner, enable potential conflicts between rules to be overcome. In other words, what is a stake in the cases that the authors consider is both *the way in which rules are used to elucidate facts* and *the way in which these facts*, elucidated in such and such a way, *retroact on the normative repertoire*.

This in my view helps solve the conceptual impasse of panlegalism: even though legal and non-legal orderings may exhibit the same formal structure, legal orderings claim they possess a stock of knowledge which allows a collectivity (or better, the vast arrays of practices, institutions, and organisations that comprise a given collectivity) to discuss and resolve their conflicts within an *extra-ordinary domain*, in which special categories are at work. Based on this, I would like to make the claim that we can call legal only those rule-governed practices that, in spite of the formal characteristic they share with many other practices, claim to be *trans-sectional and insulated venues, separate from everyday life, in which everyday reality can be renegotiated and rephrased by means of a special knowledge (usually mastered by a circle of experts) and a rigid set of conceptual categories*. Needless to say, this does not exclude the possibility that many *social* rule-governed practices regulate the everyday life of their members more closely and more effectively than *legal* practices;[18] nor does it exclude the possibility that, in addition to state law, many types of practices can be subsumed under the description of the legal practice provided above. Nonetheless, it is my contention that, on the basis of what I have argued, the number of rule-governed practices or contexts (whether institutionalised or not) which can be regarded as genuinely legal is significantly smaller than the overall number of rule-governed practices or contexts.[19]

The traits of law discussed so far – that is, the separateness of legal knowledge, the insulation of law's categories, the rigidity of legal language – are variable factors that, to a greater or lesser extent, pursue the same goal. They all aim to prevent the law, its stock of knowledge, and its categories from merging either with the unspecialised knowledge of everyday life or with the specialised knowledge of other rule-governed practices. These factors create a *protective*

[18] It is worth adding that legal orderings can share many of the rules of other non-legal rule-governed contexts residing in in their jurisdiction. In this regard, in Croce 2012: Chaps. 7, 9 and 10, I argue that the legal practice is above all a jurisdictional device, which does not (at least primarily) create new rules, but selects rules and models that are already at work in the social realm and translate them into its special and formulaic language. Social rules and models are thus typified and transformed, but never (or seldom) created *ex novo* by legal experts.

[19] It is also important to stress another remarkable difference connected to what I have thus far said: while rule-governed contexts in general are frameworks of meanings and rules, which are designed to mediate between those who operate within their borders and the external environment, the law *mediates among rule-governed practices and contexts*. This may help us solve the puzzle related to the role of those (lay people) who do not belong to the relevant population of the legal practice. Indeed the legal field primarily serves as a stable frame in which lay people can interact by following firm procedures, using a special language and adopting rigid categories. This suggests that *lay people are constantly involved in the production of legal outcomes*. What is produced in the legal field impacts on everyday life only as long as these productions can be effectively and intelligently employed in the various rule-governed contexts to which lay people belong.

membrane that surrounds law so as to subtract it from the sticky fluidity of social interaction. Only if it actually achieves this separateness can law play the role of conflict-neutraliser and provide a platform where social subjects can semiotically deconstruct and reframe their own conflicting views. Only in a condition of separateness and insulation can the parties interact in the legal domain in such a way for them to renegotiate social realty with recourse to a special set of categories. In most geo-historical contexts, a specialised body of experts, who are considered as independent from the parties in conflict, are called upon to organise *the public representation* of dispute in compliance with the formality of the legal language and with the firmness of its categories. Legal settlements are recognised as impartial precisely because they are made by a third party who has recurred to a trans-sectional body of knowledge and rules, which was previously agreed upon by the conflicting parties and which enables them to rephrase facts and events.[20]

The Space for Legal Pluralism

So far I have reached two conclusions. In the first sections I have argued that, under a structural-formal viewpoint, the official law of a given geo-historical context appears as a social practice among others. This analysis invites us to put into question the taken-for-granted pre-eminence accorded to state law, whose formal structure proves to be identical to many other social practices. Afterwards I

[20] It can be rightly argued that there are contexts in which there is no third party who acts as a judge. *Contra* this latter observation I would briefly mention these words by Adamson Hoebel:

> On an even more primitive level, if an aggrieved party or his kinsmen must institute and carry through the prosecution *without the intervention of a third party*, there will still be a 'court' *if the proceedings follow the lines of recognized and established order* – there will be then at least *the compulsion of recognized 'legal' procedure*, though the ultimate court may be no more than the '*bar of public opinion*'. When vigorous public opinion recognizes and accepts the procedure of the plaintiff as correct and the settlement or punishment meted out as sound, and the wrongdoer in consequence accedes to the settlement because he feels he must yield, then the plaintiff and his supporting public opinion constitute a *rudimentary sort of 'court'*, and *the procedure is inescapably 'legal'* (Hoebel 1954: 25, emphasis added).

have argued that the label 'law' cannot be stretched to cover all those entities that are governed by rules and in which a set of people look at rules as standards. To unravel such a panlegalistic impasse, I have shown that, in order for a practice to be defined as legal, it must possess certain specific qualities that distinguish it from other rule-governed practices. This analysis provides us with sounder criteria to establish whether a given ordering can be really called 'legal' and if it is able to serve as a venue for the renegotiation of social reality.

However, to conclude, I would like to underline that this view by no means reverts to legal monism. Not only because there can well be a geo-historical situation in which more than one practice claims to serve as a trans-sectional and special venue (as the European Middle Ages vividly shows), but also because it is important to cast due light on the perennial symbolic struggles around the legal practice and its boundaries. If the legal practice is what allows a collectivity to renegotiate and reframe social reality, the control over legal knowledge, the technical competence it involves and the categories it deploys grant the possibility of significantly impacting upon social signification and producing durable effects on social reality. To quote Berger and Luckmann: "He who has the bigger stick has the better chance of imposing his definitions of reality" (Berger and Luckmann 1966: 127). This is why all social entities that comprise a given geo-historical context are engaged in a struggle over the *stock of symbolic and material power* which is always related to the *custody of legal rule and knowledge*. Different normative rule-governed orderings (such as religious and ethnic groups, associations, businesses, civic organisations) compete with each other to affect both the special venue in which they enter when they need to solve disputes and the instruments they use to negotiate reality. This is a blatant situation of *legal* pluralism, in which a plethora of normative actors wage a symbolic war to affect the *definition of social meanings as filtered by law*. If this is so, then legal pluralism can be regarded as a permanent condition of social reality: a perennial struggle for determining the contours of lawfulness.

References

BAVINCK, Maarten and Gordon R. WOODMAN
2009 'Can There be Maps of Law?' Pp. 195-218 in Franz von Benda-Beckmann, Keebet von Benda-Beckmann and Anne Griffiths (eds.), *Spatializing Law: An Anthropological Geography of Law in Society*, Farnham: Ashgate.

BERGER, Peter L. and Thomas LUCKMANN
1966 *The Social Construction of Reality: A Treatise in the Sociology of Knowledge*. London: Penguin.
BLOOR, David
2001 'Wittgenstein and the Priority of Practice'. Pp. 103-14 in Theodore R. Schatzki, Karin Knorr-Cetina and Eike von Savigny (eds.), *The Practice Turn in Contemporary Theory*. London: Routledge.
BOURDIEU, Pierre
1987 'The force of law: Toward a sociology of the juridical field.' *Hastings Law Journal* 38: 814–813.
1990 *The Logic of Practice* (trans. Richard Nice). Stanford, Calif.: Stanford University Press [Original *Le sens pratique*. 1990, Paris: Les Éditions de Minuit.]
CAVELL, Stanley
1979 *The Claim of Reason. Wittgenstein, Skepticism, Morality, and Tragedy*. Oxford: Oxford University Press.
COLEMAN, Jules L.
2001 *The Practice of Principle. In Defence of a Pragmatic Approach to Legal Theory*. Oxford: Oxford University Press.
COMAROFF, John L. and ROBERTS, Simon
1981 *Rules and Processes. The Cultural Logic of Dispute in an African Context*. Chicago/London: The University of Chicago Press.
CROCE, Mariano
2009 *La conquista dello spazio giuridico. Potere statale e amministrazione della giustizia*. Napoli: Edizioni Scientifiche Italiane.
2012 *Self-Sufficiency of Law. A Critical-Institutional Theory of Social Order*. Dordrecht: Springer.
CROCE, Mariano and SALVATORE, Andrea
2007 'Ethical Substance and the Coexistence of Normative Orders. Carl Schmitt, Santi Romano, and Critical Institutionalism'. *Journal of Legal Pluralism and Unofficial Law* 56: 1-32.
DWORKIN, Ronald
1978 *Taking Rights Seriously*. Cambridge, Mass.: Harvard University Press.
HART, Herbert L.A.
1994 *The concept of Law*. 2nd ed. Oxford: Oxford University Press. (1st ed. 1961)
HOEBEL, E. Adamson
1954 *The law of primitive man. A study of comparative legal dynamics*. Cambridge: Harvard University Press.

MACCORMICK, Neil
1998 'Norms, Institutions, and Institutional Facts'. *Law and Philosophy* 17(3): 301-345.
PEACOCKE, Christopher
1981 'Reply: Rule-following: The Nature of Wittgenstein's Argument'. Pp. 72-95 in Steven H. Holtzman and Christopher M. Leich (eds.), *Wittgenstein: To Follow a Rule*. London: Routledge and Kegan Paul.
PERISTIANY, John G.
1954 'Law'. Pp. 39-49 in Edward E. Evans-Pritchard, Raymond Firth, Edmund R. Leach, John G, Peristiany, John Layard, Max Gluckman, Meyer Fortes and Godfrey Lienhardt, *The Institutions of Primitive Society: A Series of Broadcast Talks*. Oxford: Basil Blackwell.
RAZ, Joseph
1990 *Practical Reason and Norms*, 2nd edition (with new postscript). Oxford: Oxford University Press
SARTORIUS, Rolf
1971 'Hart's Concept of Law.' Pp. 131-161 in Robert S. Summers (ed.), *More Essays in Legal Philosopy: General Assessments of Legal Philosophies*. Berkeley and Los Angeles: University of California Press.
SCHAUER, Frederick
2004 'The limited domain of the law'. *Virginia Law Review* 90: 1909–1956.
2010 'Was Austin right after all? On the role of sanctions in a theory of law'. *Ratio Juris* 23(1): 1–21.
SCHIAVELLO, Aldo
2009 'Il diritto è una ragione per l'azione. La presunta svolta convenzionalista del positivismo giuridico contemporaneo'. *Politica & Società* 1: 47-70.
SPANÒ, Michele
2009 'Dislocare il governo. Post colonialismo e governamentalità'. *Politica & Società* 2: 65-90.
WINCH, Peter
1990 *The Idea of a Social Science and its Relation to Philosophy* 2nd ed. London: Routledge. (1st ed. 1958)
WITTGENSTEIN, Ludwig
2009 *Philosophical Investigations*, 4th ed. (translated and edited G.E.M. Anscombe, Peter M.S. Hacker and Joachim Shulte). Malden, MA: Blackwell Publishing.
WOODMAN, Gordon R.
2009a 'Diritto consuetudinario e diritti consuetudinari: una considerazione comparativa sulla loro natura e sulle relazioni tra tipi di diritto'. *Politica & Società* 2: 91-107.

2009b 'Book review'. *Journal of Legal Pluralism and Unofficial Law* 59: 161-167.

Von WRIGHT, Georg H.

1971 *Explanation and Understanding*. London: Routledge and Kegan Paul.

LAND GRABBING, INVESTMENT PRINCIPLES AND PLURAL LEGAL ORDERS OF LAND USE[1]

Martina Locher, Bernd Steimann and Bishnu Raj Upreti

Introduction

In recent years, foreign direct investment in land has increased significantly in developing countries. Land acquisition in a developing context by foreign investors is often referred to as 'land grabbing'. In response to the growing concerns about the effects of land grabbing, various multilateral organizations including the UN Food and Agriculture Organization (FAO) and the World Bank have recently come forward with guidelines and principles to make such investments more responsible and transparent. One of the central tenets in the *Voluntary Guidelines on the Responsible Governance of Tenure of Land, Fisheries and Forests in the Context of National Food Security* (FAO 2012, in short 'FAO guidelines') and the *Principles for Responsible Agricultural Investment that Respects Rights, Livelihoods and Resources* (FAO et al. 2010, in short 'RAI principles') is that investors and involved host governments recognize and respect local people's existing property rights over land and other natural resources. To this end, it is suggested that prior to any large-scale land deals, existing property rights should be formalized in a

[1] This article is partially based on work conducted within the framework of the 'Special Research Project: Transnational Pressure on Land' of the Swiss National Centre of Competence in Research North-South (NCCR North-South): Research Partnerships for Mitigating Syndromes of Global Change. We would like to thank Norman Backhaus, Thomas Breu, Boniface Kiteme, Peter Messerli and Oliver Schönweger from the 'Malindi team', Craig Hatcher and the anonymous reviewers for their contributions and constructive feedbacks on the paper.

transparent and participatory manner. Thus, the two proposals build on the assumptions that all kinds of property rights over land can be formalized, and that such formalization is required in order to support the interests of local stakeholders.

In this article we want to critically examine and challenge these assumptions from a legal pluralism perspective. Referring to the four layers of social organization brought forward by F. and K. von Benda-Beckmann (1999; see also F. von Benda-Beckmann et al. 2006), we first show that the proposed guidelines and principles - and thus much of the recent land grab debate - do not adequately account for the existence of plural legal orders over land and other natural resources, and that they largely ignore the dynamics of power and everyday practices inherent to property relations. Based on this, we raise three fundamental concerns about the idea of formalizing property rights in a legal pluralism context, and discuss them in the light of empirical evidence of competing claims over land resources from Tanzania, Nepal, and Kyrgyzstan.

The article demonstrates that the identification and recognition of customary group or individual rights is a very complex and delicate endeavour, which entails the risk of neglecting existing claims and rights of local people (this is our first concern). Neither of the proposals addresses this in a satisfactory way. Nevertheless, there are cases where formalization by state intervention is necessary, namely when local individuals and communities[2] are at risk of losing their rights against their will, or if it is their own wish to enter deals with outsiders. In such cases, from a legal pluralism perspective, a centralist approach to formalizing customary land rights as proposed in the RAI principles cannot be recommended. In many contexts, it has resulted in adverse effects for local

[2] We use the term 'local community' interchangeably with 'local people' or 'local stakeholders'. However, we are aware that local communities are by no means homogenous and do not necessarily experience the same consequences when 'land grabs' take place. In this article, we only distinguish between local elites and 'common' members of local communities. Other important characteristics in the context of 'land grabbing' include gender (see Behrman et al. 2011) and indigeneity (Sawyer and Gomez 2008). For critical thoughts on the notion of 'community' related to natural resource management and land reforms, see Sikor and Müller (2009: 1310f).

communities rather than strengthening their rights (our second concern). A more "security and rights-based vision" (Assies 2009: 586) as brought forward by the FAO guidelines still bears the risk of reinforcing unequal power structures within local communities (our third concern). Yet, we argue, this approach is more promising in terms of leaving it to local communities to decide whether their land and natural resources should become a marketable good to outsiders or not. However, the introduction of such a property regime requires broad changes in governance. This cannot be addressed satisfactorily within the framework of investment guidelines. Instead, more long-term strategies on how to protect customary rights are required.

Foreign direct investments in land and current proposals for a 'Code of Conduct'

In recent years, foreign direct investments in land have become a key factor of rural transformation in the Global South. Based on a new database it is estimated that between 2000 and April 2012, foreign land purchases and leases amounted to more than 80 million hectares (Anseeuw et al. 2012: 3). Deininger refers to 57.8 million hectares of intended or actual land deals in the year 2009 alone (Deininger 2011: 220). So far, most of these deals have taken place in Sub-Saharan Africa, yet large agricultural land reserves are also at stake in post-Soviet Eurasia, Latin America and Asia (Visser and Spoor 2011; Borras and Franco 2010; World Bank 2010; GRAIN 2008). Foreign investors often belong to either emerging and highly dynamic economies such as those of China or the Gulf states, or to developed economies from Europe and the US. The actual transaction of farmland usually happens in close collaboration with respective national governments in the host countries (Deininger 2011: 224; Borras and Franco 2010; GRAIN 2009). Some of the key drivers behind these investments are an increasing demand for food and non-food agro-products, such as biofuels, due to an ever-growing world population, changing nutrition patterns, and climate change and energy supply concerns. As a consequence, and in addition, land itself is also increasingly viewed as a central commodity and an object of speculation (Gonzalez 2010; Zoomers 2010; Cotula et al. 2009).

Along with the increasing pace and extent of these investments or 'land grabs', a growing number of observers started to raise concerns about their environmental, economic and socio-political consequences. The main points of critique pertain to the detrimental effects of large-scale plantations if compared to smallholder agriculture. These include impacts on natural resources such as water, soils, and biodiversity, but also on the livelihoods of the affected population, e.g. through reduced food security or income opportunities (de Schutter 2011; Cotula et al. 2009). Considerable attention has also been paid to the consequences of such investments for local people's property rights over land and other natural resources, and thus their capacity for self-determination (Borras and Franco 2010). In recent years, civil society organizations have documented numerous cases where local people's property rights were ignored and violated by investors and involved government agencies alike, sometimes even leading to forced displacements (see e.g. GRAIN 2009). Also the World Bank (2010) has reported such cases. In addition, recent analyses suggest that a weak general recognition of land rights at country level correlates with high levels of foreign demand for that land (Alden Wily 2011; Deininger 2011: 218; Visser and Spoor 2011: 319f; Mann and Smaller 2010).

While certain sectors such as the extractive industry have taken up these concerns by agreeing on (voluntary) principles for responsible investment, no global consensus has been reached yet in terms of land- and water-intensive agro-investments. However, at the international level, two prominent proposals for such a Code of Conduct have been released, which have been subject to a more or less broad consultation process among multilateral organizations, national governments, and civil society organizations.

A first initiative was taken by the FAO, which brought forward the "Voluntary Guidelines on the Responsible Governance of Tenure of Land, Fisheries and Forests in the Context of National Food Security" (FAO 2012). They build on the final declaration of the 2006 International Conference on Agrarian Reform and Rural Development, which emphasized the importance of secure and sustainable access to land, water and other natural resources, as well as of economic, social and cultural rights of marginalized and vulnerable groups in terms of land and natural resource issues (FAO 2006). To carry the dialogue further, the FAO initiated a broad, participatory process to develop practice-oriented, voluntary guidelines on the responsible governance of natural resource tenure. More than 90 FAO member countries, several UN agencies and other international organizations, farmer associations, representatives from the private sector as well as civil society organizations (CSOs) participated in the process, which consisted of three rounds of negotiations facilitated by a working group of the Committee on World Food Security (CFS). The active involvement of CSOs seems particularly noteworthy; not only did they participate in the official negotiations, but they additionally held a series of regional civil society consultations, which were facilitated by the International Planning Committee for Food Sovereignty (IPC). Thus, the FAO's consultation process developed into a highly contentious debate, but in return was positively acknowledged by a broad range of stakeholders. In their final version endorsed by the CFS on May 11, 2012, the guidelines mainly address potential host states rather than investors. Consequently, they refer explicitly to existing binding international law such as the universal declaration on human rights or international conventions on indigenous people or biodiversity. This is also why they gained the support of several important international agrarian movements such as La Via Campesina, the IPC, and others (Borras et al. 2011).

In a second initiative, the World Bank Group, the FAO, the International Fund for Agricultural Development (IFAD), and the United Nations Conference on Trade and Development (UNCTAD) joined to propose *Principles for Responsible Agricultural Investment that Respects Rights, Livelihoods and Resources* (FAO et al. 2010). Being the result of negotiations among officials of the involved organizations rather than of a broad consultation process, these so-called 'RAI principles' have been promoted since early 2010, most prominently in the World Bank's report on land-related investments (World Bank 2010). Their intention is to provide guidance for host countries and investors on how to prepare strong domestic legislation and carry out socially responsible investments respectively (FIAN 2010a). They consist of seven key principles addressing the issues of property rights, food security, transparency, participation, economic viability, as well as social and environmental sustainability. However, unlike the FAO guidelines, and despite a consultation process initiated in early 2010, some of the governments most directly concerned as well as civil society organizations have repeatedly denounced the RAI initiative for a striking lack of consultation in its early stages. In addition, it has been criticized for its reliance on the mainstream tools of 'good governance' and on corporate social responsibility frameworks rather than on binding human rights obligations. So far, it has also remained unclear as to how the RAI principles will be linked to the FAO guidelines (de Schutter 2011; Li 2011; FIAN 2010a).

The Notion of 'Property Rights' in the FAO Guidelines and the RAI Principles from a Legal Pluralism Perspective

Proponents of large-scale investments in land have often argued that they invest in 'unused land', 'reserve agricultural land' or 'idle land' only, i.e. land which was not used for any form of production and for which no local claims existed whatsoever (World Bank 2010; Woertz et al. 2008). Critics have remarked, however, that much of this seemingly 'unused land', which is usually in the formal ownership of the state, is subject to long-standing, often vague and informal tenure rights of the local population, be it individuals or groups, and that the neglect of such rights may trigger conflict and undermine effective land use and management (Cotula et al. 2009; Haralambous et al. 2009). Both the FAO guidelines and the RAI principles have taken up this concern. In principle, both proposals demand that governments and investors recognize and respect existing property rights to land and associated natural resources, namely by demarcating and formalizing these rights prior to any investment-related land transfer. For the detailed formulations in both proposals regarding the notion of property rights see Table 1.

Table 1: Selected main elements of the FAO guidelines and the RAI principles

	FAO guidelines: Voluntary Guidelines on the Responsible Governance of Tenure of Land, Fisheries and Forests in the Context of National Food Security (FAO 2012)	*RAI principles:* Principles for Responsible Agricultural Investment that Respects Rights, Livelihoods and Resources (FAO et al. 2010)
Main demands	"Where informal tenure to land, fisheries and forests exists, States should acknowledge it in a manner that respects existing formal rights under national law and in ways that recognize the reality of the situation..." (16).	"Existing use and ownership rights to land, whether statutory or customary, primary or secondary, formal or informal, group or individual, should be respected." (First of the seven RAI principles: 2)
Procedure	"States should allocate tenure rights and delegate tenure governance in transparent, participatory ways, using simple procedures that are clear, accessible and understandable to all, especially to indigenous peoples and other communities with customary tenure systems" (13).	Investors and government agencies must identify all right holders and legally recognize, demarcate and register their existing rights and uses. This is followed by "negotiation with land holders/users, based on informed and free choice" (2). Demarcation should be done "in a participatory and low-cost way that can be implemented quickly" (4).

Objective, expected outcome	States should "protect tenure right holders against the arbitrary loss of their tenure rights" and "[p]romote and facilitate the enjoyment of legitimate tenure rights" (3). Ultimately "These Voluntary Guidelines seek to improve governance of tenure of land [...] with the goals of food security [...], poverty eradication, sustainable livelihoods, social stability, housing security, rural development, environmental protection and sustainable social and economic development" (1).	Recognition of land rights "can greatly empower local communities and such recognition should be viewed as a precondition for direct negotiation with investors" (2). Ultimately, the objective is to avoid "[l]oss of land and other resource rights to an investment project without recognition of quite valid sensitivities and without full compensation" and "...the disruption of livelihoods and the dislocation of communities" (3). Further, another objective seems to be to prevent "public criticism of large-scale investment" due to such neglects (3).
Other Comments	"States should, in drafting tenure policies and laws, take into account the social, cultural, spiritual, economic and environmental values of land, fisheries and forests held under tenure systems of indigenous peoples and other communities with customary tenure systems" (15). Recognizing other than central state practices: "States should respect and promote customary approaches used by indigenous peoples and other communities with customary tenure systems to resolving tenure conflicts within communities..." (15).	Acknowledging that the formal recognition of group rights may be difficult and may foster individualisation of former common property (3).

Challenging the two proposals from a legal pluralism perspective

Since the consultation processes began in 2010, much criticism has been raised against the two proposals, not least regarding their approach to property rights. Many observers consider it naive to believe that legal recognition of land rights can guarantee their protection from 'unfriendly takeovers'. It has also been remarked that the simplistic focus on 'existing land rights' disregards the resource needs of future generations, thus underestimating new local claims that may arise in future (Borras and Franco 2012: 54, 2010: 517; de Schutter 2011; Li 2011; FIAN 2010a: 3; Scoones 2010).

In addition to these legitimate points of critique, a closer look at the two proposals from a legal pluralism perspective raises a number of further caveats and concerns. These mainly pertain to their somewhat simplistic notion of 'property rights' and the measures proposed to strengthen and protect them. We have chosen the legal pluralism perspective, because we consider it particularly useful for analysing the complexity of land tenure in contexts where different understandings of property converge.[3] First of all, legal pluralism accounts for the co-existence of parallel legal systems or institutions (F. and K. von Benda-Beckmann 1999). This is in contrast to a legal centralist perspective, where "law is and should be the law of the state, (...) exclusive of all other law, and administered by a single set of state institutions" (J. Griffiths 1986: 3). The debate on whether and how non-statutory legal systems should be formalized (e.g. Fitzpatrick 2005; Meinzen-Dick and Mwangi 2008; Assies 2009) will be taken up towards the end of this article. Second, from a legal pluralism perspective, engaging with property means to

[3] Borras and Franco claim that it would be more appropriate to focus on "rural poor people's effective control" - in Ribot's and Peluso's words 'access' - instead of property, and thus on the question of which people have "the ability to benefit from things" - in this case land - by drawing on different "bundles of powers" (Borras and Franco 2012: 55, following Ribot and Peluso 2003: 153, 154). While we agree with this view to some extent, we also see some challenges related to the use of this concept in this context (particularly in cases where people have rights to land, but too little power and thus no ability to use it). We have chosen the perspective of legal pluralism, as we consider this framework with its broad definition of property as useful for analytical purposes in relation to the FAO guidelines and particularly the RAI principles, which focus on land (tenure) rights (not land access).

acknowledge that it encompasses more than (private or common) ownership of a resource (Wiber 1992: 470). Instead, property rights are better understood as bundles of rights (or "web of interests", see Meinzen-Dick and Mwangi 2008), since different individuals or groups can have different rights over the same resource at the same time. The different types of rights can be broadly grouped into two categories, i.e. *use rights* (the rights to access and use or withdraw a resource) and *control rights* (the rights to manage a resource, to exclude others from using it, or to alienate it to others through sale, rental, or gift) (Benda-Beckmann et al. 2006; Meinzen-Dick and Pradhan 2001; J. Griffiths 1986; see Ostrom 2003 for a detailed categorization of different property rights). Third, legal pluralism means to acknowledge that property is not just a specific right or relation, but "concerns the ways in which the relations between society's members with respect to valuables are given form and significance" (Benda-Beckmann et al. 2006: 14; see also Sikor and Müller 2009: 1311; Meinzen-Dick and Mwangi 2008: 36). Consequently, property is always seen as embedded in a specific social and political context, encompassing a wide variety of different arrangements at different levels. These can include more formal aspects such as written rules, less formal ones such as people's beliefs and values, but also concrete practices related to property (Mehta et al. 2001; Wiber 1992; A. Griffiths 1998). The work of Benda-Beckmann et al. (2006), who distinguish four 'layers of social organization', helps to analytically grasp this plurality behind property relations. The first layer includes *ideologies and culture*, where neoliberal concepts of private property may collide with traditional or religious concepts of common property. The second layer focuses on *legal regulations*, which are usually directly related to ideologies and culture, but are more specific in the sense that they define concrete rules and procedures. This includes state law, but also customary or religious law. The third layer refers to people's actual *social relations related to property*. These are often multifunctional and reflect local power relations shaped by community and kin or by social, political or economic dependencies (e.g. patron-client relations), rather than abstract norms defined by state, customary or religious law. Thus, disputes over land tenure can only be understood within a wider socio-political context (Lund 1998). The fourth layer emphasizes that it is in people's concrete, everyday *property practices* (e.g. fencing or paying land rent) where ideologies, laws, and social relationships regarding property are reflected, negotiated, reproduced, and eventually transformed. In this context, we consider 'forum shopping' (Meinzen-Dick 2009: 3; Meinzen-Dick and Pradhan 2001: 11; cf. K. von Benda-Beckmann 1981) a useful concept[4]. It describes the practice of

[4] When introducing the concept termed 'forum shopping' in her work in 1981, K. von Benda-Beckmann described it as the practice of certain stakeholders appealing

certain stakeholders manoeuvring between different norms and regulations to secure their claims over resources. Consequently, property rights and the ways in which resources are used do not simply derive from statutes or formal rules, but "should be understood as negotiated outcomes" (Meinzen-Dick 2009: 3).

To some extent, the examined guidelines and principles account for these aspects of legal pluralism in property rights. The FAO guidelines state explicitly that resources have not only an economic and a political value, but that they can also have social, cultural, and spiritual values (see Table 1 above). In this way, they refer at least indirectly to the layer of ideas and ideologies related to resource property. The RAI principles distinguish not only between use and ownership rights, but refer explicitly also to statutory and customary, primary and secondary, formal and informal, as well as group and individual forms of property (see Table 1). They thus acknowledge that property rights over resources can take multiple forms and that there may be other layers of legal regulation besides statutory law. Nevertheless, both documents still build on a rather static understanding of property, since they largely ignore the dynamics of concrete social relationships and property practices. Neither the FAO guidelines nor the RAI principles acknowledge that property regimes may be contested, that they may be subject to ambiguous rules, and that especially powerful rights holders may draw on different legal systems to legitimize their property claims. In short, the social embeddedness of property and related aspects of power are largely absent from these documents. This is particularly problematic because both proposals seem to assume that property rights over land and other natural resources can and should be formalized, and that such formalization necessarily supports the interests of all local stakeholders.

In the following, we raise three fundamental concerns from a legal pluralism

to different institutions (i.e. forums) representing different legal systems in order to solve conflicts in their favour. In this article, we use the concept in a broader sense for the practice of using different norms and regulations to support claims over resources, without necessarily appealing to conflict resolution forums. While a cognate term such as 'shopping for normative orders' or 'shopping for legal systems' would be more precise for this broader concept, we use 'forum shopping' by referring to Meinzen-Dick who describes it as a process in which "individuals and groups make use of one or another of these legal frameworks as the basis for their claims on a resource" (Meinzen-Dick 2009: 3; see also Meinzen-Dick and Pradhan 2001: 11).

perspective, focusing on the identification of plural legal arrangements (our first concern) and the process as well as potential consequences of the proposed formalization (our second and third concerns). We will discuss our concerns in light of empirical evidence from three different regional contexts, i.e. Kyrgyzstan, Tanzania, and Nepal. Only part of this evidence (i.e. the evidence from Tanzania) stems from explicit empirical research on what is now called 'land grab'. We intentionally use material from other contexts in which existing patterns of land rights have changed and resource claims of various actors compete with each other. We are convinced that much can be learnt about the complexity of dealing with multiple socio-legal arrangements in land issues and the potentials and pitfalls of formalization procedures also from other (and earlier) cases, as has been argued and demonstrated also by Hall (2011) and Li (2011: 285f).

First Concern: Non-Statutory Legal Orders of Land Use are Difficult to Identify

Our first concern is that the formalization of property rights is a very delicate endeavour. Formalization as a first step requires the identification of claims (Meinzen-Dick and Mwangi 2008: 38). Claims are based on legal orders, and these are expressed in ideas and ideologies, concrete social relationships, and property practices, particularly where property rights are not (only) defined through statutory law. Elements in these layers of social organization are often difficult to identify and recognize, as we will show in the following two examples.

Tanzania: Challenges in identifying customary property rights

The example of a UK-based forestry company acquiring land in Tanzania illustrates challenges for outsiders to identify customary property rights during the land acquisition process (Locher 2011). In this case, a village assembly in the Southern Highlands had decided to hand over a certain area of reserve village land to the investor (Chachage and Baha 2010). The land is far from the core settlement and at present not used by the villagers. It is known under a specific name given by local people who had been living there before they were resettled by the socialist government during the 1970s. The decision was recorded in the meeting minutes accordingly, and a committee was formed to show the area to the district officials so that they would demarcate it for the land transfer. However, as Locher (2011) illustrates, the committee was headed by the village chairman who did not originate from that particular area. Since he did not know the exact boundaries of the respective area, he only showed it roughly to the district officials by pointing at it from afar. Hence, a considerably bigger area than what the village assembly had agreed upon was transferred, and several parcels, which according to customary law belonged to local households, were transferred, too. Further, some of those parcels were used by households from a neighbouring village, who had been provided use rights by the landholders. Unfortunately, the concerned households only realized that their land was transferred to the investor once the deal was made. They had to struggle for more than a year until their claims became formally accepted. They did not succeed, however, to revoke the transfer and finally felt forced to agree on the offered compensation. The example shows that detailed knowledge about complex customary property rights is not shared by everyone in a village, not even necessarily by elected village representatives. This lack of specific knowledge is likely to be more pronounced in respect of secondary property rights. In such cases, sometimes only those directly involved know their property arrangements and exact boundaries. Boundaries of individual property are not visibly marked, but are both conveyed verbally by referring to natural landmarks and reproduced through regular use such as planting crops. However, some land is not used intensively and there are also fallow periods. This makes it particularly difficult for outsiders to physically detect customary property rights in short visits.

Nepal: Dispute over ownership of a land pooling Joint Venture Project

In Nepal, particularly in the capital and big cities, real estate companies have emerged as key players in the housing sector market. They acquire fertile agricultural lands from farmers at cheap rates and sell high priced houses or house construction sites, thus earning huge profit margins (Shrestha 2011; Upreti et al. 2008; Upreti 2004b). In order to prevent such exploitation, the Bhaktapur Municipality together with the Kathmandu Valley Town Development Plan Executive Committee recently initiated a Joint Venture Project (JVP). In 2009, they accumulated approximately 30 ha of land from different landowners. The objective of this land pooling JVP was to improve the housing standards in the residential areas by providing basic requirements such as open spaces, food paths, drinking water, electricity, waste collection points, children's play areas. Once the land was endowed with all these facilities, the JVP intended to sell it for fixed prices, whereas the former landowners were provided right of pre-emption. However, the land soon became a major source of contestation among the involved stakeholders. While the JVP claimed full control rights (including access, withdrawal, management, exclusion and alienation rights; see Ostrom 2003;

Schlager and Ostrom 1992), the original land contributors argued that the JVP had no exclusive alienation rights, even if the project was exercising other control rights. In addition, many landowners, farmers, bureaucrats and politicians, who had not directly contributed their land to the JVP, have started to object to the JVP work by claiming different rights such as their freedom to use the surrounding open spaces for cultural, religious and social activities, which was altered after the land was taken by the JVP. The affected people cite their historical association, cultural and religious values, as well as their land use practices in order to oppose the provisions of the JVP.

Conclusions from the presented cases

The two cases from different contexts illustrate that 'existing property rights' over land resources can only be understood if conceptualized as overlapping 'bundles of rights'. Local claims and rights often coexist and overlap in terms of scale and time, and build on a broad variety of normative and cognitive frameworks as well as resource-related practices of access and use. Tanzanian smallholders convey their right to use certain land parcels from long-standing social relations and regular use practices, and Nepali land users interpret the rights to the JVP land according to their own customary and religious frameworks. Thus, local claims and rights not only build on different legal regulations but are also superimposed and further adapted by individual social relations, beliefs and practices.

Consequently, local people's perceptions of 'legitimate' and 'illegitimate' property rights often differ and even conflict with each other. The example from Tanzania shows that elected representatives (who are usually among the first ones to be involved in a participatory planning process) are not necessarily aware of all the flexible and often-changing tenure arrangements. In both cases, these coexisting and competing claims have become publicly contested in the course of an external intervention, such as the appearance of an investor seeking to acquire arable land in Tanzania and the municipality authorities acquiring land for a housing improvement project in Nepal. Apparently, both interventions have failed to sufficiently account for existing claims and rights, even when they tried to do so in a participatory manner (as in Tanzania) or sought to make access to land resources more equal (as in Nepal). This raises the question, whether and how locally existing claims and rights can be 'recognized' in the course of a large-scale investment in land. The complex endeavour is even more delicate for investors that usually deal with formal authorities who often themselves do not know or recognize the plural legal arrangements at the local level.

In any case, trying to identify existing rights by adopting a 'quick' and 'simple' procedure (as suggested in the two proposals) seems not only unrealistic but also irresponsible, given the conflicts and displacements that this may cause. We will take up this thought again towards the end of this article.

Second Concern: Centralist Approaches to Formalizing Property Rights Allow the State Administration to Expand its Influence at the Cost of Local Communities

Our second concern is that the formalization of hitherto non-formalized property rights allows superior levels of the state administration to expand their influence and increase their control over subordinate levels of the administration as well as over local communities and individual resource users. While this is not negative *per se*, under certain circumstances it can result in adverse political and financial pressure upon local communities and resource users. Thus, land titling may run counter to the declared intention of the FAO guidelines and the RAI principles to strengthen local communities and to ensure the effective use of scarce natural resources.

Nepal: Formalization and legalization of property rights as a means to expand state influence and control

Until 1950, land rights in Nepal were shaped by various cultural, social and normative practices and plural legal arrangements such as state, folk, customary, indigenous, and religious law (Upreti 2004a). In 1951, Nepal started a land reform to formalize and legalize property rights, which has been a major agenda for six decades. In the course of the reform the state changed all existing forms of land ownership into the *Raikar* ownership system. *Raikar* denotes an ultimate state ownership over all land, which is then cultivated by individuals as direct tenants of the state. The reform thus did away with six existing different forms of land control rights (Pyakuryal and Upreti 2011; Alden Wily et al. 2009; Caplan 2000; Thapa 2000; Regmi 1999). Studies show that at the operational level such expansion of state control and influence created numerous complications and led to many local conflicts (Upreti 2010; Upreti et al. 2008). The government argued though, that it was necessary to merge all land tenure systems in the country into one form of ownership in order to reach the declared objectives of improving land management, increasing agricultural production and productivity, and ensuring access to land for the landless (Kshetry 2011; Shrestha 2011). However, the reform provided a conducive (and to some extent manipulative) framework for a close nexus between the bureaucracy of government land administration and powerful elites to reap the benefits of the reform (Pyakuryal and Upreti 2011; Alden Wily et al. 2009). Basnet documents that when the land reform was implemented through the Lands Act 1964, the poorest 65 percent of the total population held 15 percent of land as opposed to 3.7 percent of the population, the rich peasants and feudal lords, who held 39.7 percent of land (Basnet 2011: 143). After the reform, according to the UNDP (2004), the 5 wealthiest percent of the people in Nepal own 37 percent of all arable land, whereas the poorest 47 percent own only 15 percent of all land. Though these figures show a gradual improvement over time they also demonstrate that the poor, marginalized and landless were not among the main beneficiaries of the most hyped land reform programme in Nepal. However, government officials not only gained control over land resources, but greatly expanded their influence over local communities. By using their authority, connection and influences, political and bureaucratic elites manipulated the provisions of the different land-related acts and regulations in order to exploit local people. This has also created problems in food production and security (Ghale 2011; Upreti et al. 2008), as it altered the existing agricultural practice, moving away from food production to non-agricultural commercial activities, and consequently food insecurity became more prevalent (Khatri and Upreti 2012).

Kyrgyzstan: Private arable land as a liability for the less wealthy

Agrarian reforms in Kyrgyzstan gained momentum in late 1993, when in view of the rapid impoverishment of the rural population, the central government declared the de-collectivization of former collective and state farms compulsory. Consequently, most of the hitherto state-owned arable land within these farms had to be equally distributed on an individual basis to all current and former farm employees and their family members. The land was first distributed in the form of land-use rights, which were converted into private ownership rights in 1998. However today, less wealthy households are often unable to cultivate all the land they received (Steimann 2011). They either lack the financial and technical means or the skills and knowledge required to do so. In addition, many irrigation schemes are in bad shape, and the allocation of water by local committees is often subject to arbitrariness and corruption (Lindberg 2007). At the same time, selling land is difficult because the concerned plots are usually far from the village and of bad quality; further, a nationwide moratorium on land sales was not lifted before

2001, this seriously slowed down the emergence of a functioning land market in rural Kyrgyzstan. Returning the land to the state is also not possible. As a consequence, a great deal of arable land has fallen out of production in recent years (Mamytova and Mambetalieva 2008). Nonetheless, irrespective of whether rural households use all their arable land or not, they are obliged to pay land taxes to the communal authorities. In addition, arable land serves as a basis for assessing a household's entitlement to state child allowances. This means that rural Kyrgyz households are taxed and assessed on the basis of land assets that many of them can neither use nor sell. In this way, private land ownership has turned into a liability for many among the less wealthy. At the same time, it has given the state an opportunity to exert pressure upon the local population. For instance, communal authorities use the threat of tax increases as an effective means to get their way in the course of local conflicts (Steimann 2011: 182).

Conclusions from the presented cases

The two examples may illustrate very different processes, yet they both show how legal centralist approaches, which define statutory law as the main or only normative framework (J. Griffiths 1986), inevitably lead to the expansion of power of the state administration. In many cases, this happens at the expense of local communities and resource users. Political elites in Nepal capitalize on the land reform by adjusting certain provisions of the new land acts and regulations to expand their influence and power at the local level. The Kyrgyz state endowed rural people with private property over land but not the means and structures required to effectively use it; since land is subject to taxes it has become a liability for many.

This raises considerable doubts as to whether a centralist approach can really do justice to legal plural orders over land property. It seems instead that the statutory recognition (or redefinition) of existing claims and rights strengthens the state administration rather than local communities. This confirms again that property is not just about questions of legal regulation and economic efficiency, but is always embedded in a concrete social and political context and is thus closely linked to issues of power and domination. In other words and with reference to the four layers of social organization of Benda-Beckmann et al. (2006), by enforcing statutory law as the dominant or only normative framework, the state gains authority over the layer of ideologies and culture and the layer of legal regulations. Hence, it automatically gains considerable control over the layers of social relations and people's property practices and thus over local patterns of power and domination.

Third Concern: Formalizing Property Rights Bears the Risk of Reinforcing Unequal Local Power Structures

Our third concern is that even if the central state introduces formalized property rights with the best intentions, it still runs the risk of reinforcing unequal local power structures. The implementation and maintenance of a respective regime and thus the expansion of state authority to the local level in a way that supports local people is complex and often beyond the state's capacity. The new legal provisions may be difficult to understand and become commingled with previous property regimes, thus providing ground for contestation. In such situations, local elites may benefit much more from formalization procedures than the poor. Since property regimes are always embedded in networks of dominance and dependence, local elites are usually in a better position than the less wealthy and less powerful to get their existing claims recognized, or to defend them towards external actors. To a large extent, this is to do with the practice of 'forum shopping' (see text and footnote on page 9), which allows especially wealthier and well informed people to manoeuvre between various normative and cognitive orders to defend their claims over resources.

Kyrgyzstan: Privatization of arable land and redefinition of pasture use rights

In rural Kyrgyzstan, the rapid privatization of state-owned farmland contributed to the reproduction of existing disparities between rural elites and ordinary workers (Steimann 2012). In most cases, the distribution of land and other farm assets was carried out by a local commission consisting of former farm leaders, agronomists, local elders, and other well-respected people. Building on two case studies from Central Kyrgyzstan, Steimann shows that the result was often a land distribution that was equal in a quantitative, but not in a qualitative sense (Steimann 2011). In fact, many among the local elite managed to secure undivided land parcels close to their own house, while less well informed people - mostly ordinary farm workers and their family members - often received their land share in the form of several divided parcels. Since these were usually far from the village and difficult to access and irrigate, this has seriously hampered people's ability to benefit from their land in the long run. The same study shows how new claims to farmland emerged once the official privatization procedure was over. In view of their ever-increasing flocks, wealthier local households were soon in need of additional arable land for the production of sufficient winter forage. To this end, many of them have begun to irrigate and cultivate land from a communal land fund. They claim rights to these areas based on arrangements during the Soviet times, yet they use the land without the consent of the communal authorities in charge of the fund and thus without paying any use fees. Such illicit appropriation has become possible because communal control over this land has always been very weak. However, in cases where the local authorities detected such practice, the concerned households usually formalize their claim *ex post* by concluding a lease contract. Wealthy rural households thus make use of their possibilities of 'forum shopping' - i.e. manoeuvring between non-formal appropriation (based on an earlier normative order) and formal recognition - to secure their private claims over land resources. Bichsel et al. emphasize that the new Kyrgyz land property regime thus continues to be conditioned by its preceding regime and by related social relations and local power disparities - irrespective of a seemingly clear allocation and legal recognition of private and common property rights over land and other natural resources (Bichsel et al. 2010: 264f).

Another example of the central state's incapacity to fully implement formalized land rights is the case of the Kyrgyz pastures. Unlike arable land or livestock, pastures were not privatized after the Soviet collapse, but remained in the ownership of the state. In the late 1990s, a legal framework for pasture use and management was put in place, which allowed individuals and groups to lease pastures from the state. However, the law left many loopholes, and the state authorities were neither able nor willing to enforce it. The result is that pastures have remained highly contested between different actors at various levels (Steimann 2011). At the local level, households have repeatedly secured their access to pastures either by abiding by state law (i.e. conclusion of a formal lease contract), or by negating it. In the latter case, this mainly happened with reference to individual customary use rights (usually based on pasture use practices from Soviet times), or by insistence on often-vague notions of pastures as a common pool resource. This coexistence of norms and claims has repeatedly led to conflicts when leaseholders tried to bar non-leaseholders from using 'their' pastures. Again, in the course of these conflicts, the wealthier leaseholders are usually in a better position than their less wealthy competitors due to their ability to practice 'forum shopping'.

Tanzania: Knowledge and power differences in defending and registering customary land rights

The Tanzanian land law (URT 1999a, 1999b) is praised for respecting customary rights and providing management responsibility over rural areas to village bodies (Knight 2010; Alden Wily 2003). Evidence from two case studies, based on qualitative interviews conducted by Locher shows, however, that the law is complex and difficult to understand for many among the local population and even for government officials. It is thus a challenging task for district officials to teach the often-illiterate local population the necessary knowledge on defending and registering non-formal rights. Village leaders - who are usually more educated and have more regular contacts with district officials and better access to the relevant legal documents - often have a lead over other villagers in terms of relevant knowledge and may be able to take advantage of that situation. The formalization of land property also requires registration at village and district level and includes certain costs for landholders. Thus, it might be less accessible for poor people (personal communication by Locher 2011; see also Knight 2010; Pedersen 2010; Odgaard 2006). Also when it comes to defending customary rights, local elites are often in a better position than other villagers, as one example related to the above mentioned case in the Tanzanian Southern Highlands (see first concern) shows: When district officials by mistake were in the process of demarcating an area which was used by several villagers under customary law, a well situated businessman, who has considerable knowledge about the statutory land law, stopped the officials from surveying his plot. Realising that the village council was the proper authority to impede the demarcation process, he managed to get support from council members (personal communication by Locher 2011). At the same time, other villagers failed to defend their customary rights and lost them to the investor against their will (Locher 2011).

Conclusions from the presented cases

The cases from Kyrgyzstan and Tanzania show that the redefinition of land ownership or use rights by the state may create situations in which legal provisions are unclear or not implemented strictly (for Tanzania see also Pedersen 2010, 2011). The presented examples show that in such situations, even under very different circumstances, local elites often benefit disproportionately from land titling processes. They either build on good connections with state representatives, use their economic potential to practice 'forum shopping', or benefit from the fact that they are more knowledgeable in terms of rules and procedures than other people. That way, former Soviet elites directed the Kyrgyz land privatization according to their own needs, wealthier Kyrgyz households refer to either statutory or customary law to claim access to communal land and pastures, and Tanzanian village leaders can register their land rights easier than poor or vulnerable groups. Also during the land reform in Nepal (see our second concern), a similar process was observed. Local elites who had access to the state power centres and privileges managed to leverage the land-related state structures, institutions, acts and regulations. Thus, despite the declared objective of a more equitable land distribution, mostly large landowners (who frequently control more land than the legal maximum) have benefited from the land reform, while the poor, marginalized and lower sections of society were often badly affected (Kshetry 2011; Pyakuryal and Upreti 2011; Alden Wily et al. 2009; Upreti et al. 2008). All this again illustrates how strongly social power relations determine property regimes. As Meinzen-Dick and Pradhan point out, property rights "are only as strong as the institutions or collectivity that stands behind them" (Meinzen-Dick and Pradhan 2001: 11). Consequently, socioeconomic disparities and the resulting power relations have a considerable influence on what people can or cannot do to claim and secure property rights over resources. This becomes particularly problematic in the case of secondary use rights of landless people, who are often unable to secure their already weak claims in the course of a land titling process (see also FIAN 2010b: 3). The evidence presented here also suggests that even well intended participatory processes can hardly avoid being strongly influenced or captured by local elites.

Discussion

Already before the recent rise of foreign direct investments in land, there has been much debate on the use of formalizing poor people's property rights over land and other resources as a means to reduce poverty. In reaction to the wave of neoliberal (land) reforms in the wake of the Washington Consensus, land titling was promoted as the 'silver bullet' for the poor (de Soto 2003). Yet, critics have repeatedly remarked that formalized property rights are no guarantee that poor people can actually access and cultivate land, or can derive any other benefit from it, e.g. through land markets (Borras and Franco 2010; Sikor and Müller 2009: 1309; Cotula et al. 2006; Fitzpatrick 2005). Assies shows for instance that the expectation that formal land titles facilitate access to credit often does not hold true in practice, either because banks are not interested in the provision of small loans to poor people, or because smallholders fear using their land as mortgage security (Assies 2009: 582).

Besides the debate on the use of land titling, there is also some debate on different ways of formalizing customary rights and the related overall objectives. Focusing on the formalization of existing property rights over land and other resources as suggested by the FAO guidelines and the RAI principles we have raised three concerns by arguing from a legal pluralism perspective and building on evidence from Kyrgyzstan, Nepal and Tanzania. In the following, we discuss our concerns in light of the existing debate.

Centralist approaches to formalization of existing tenure rights

Assies shows that in principle, the whole formalization debate has evolved around two contrasting objectives or visions (Assies 2009: 574f, referring to Payne 2000), he names them legal centralist, "marketability-based vision" (where formalization mainly serves to turn land into a marketable good), and "security and rights-based vision" (which aims at strengthening local people's rights and self-determination). According to John Griffiths, notions such as 'recognition' or 'formalization' of existing rights are typical reflections of a legal centralist approach, because they imply that customary laws must ultimately be recognized by a single validating source, i.e. statutory law (J. Griffiths 1986: 8). Such an approach is suggested by the RAI principles. However, a centralist or 'state-led' land reform does not only have important limitations in achieving its targets (Sikor and Müller 2009) but – as we argue in our second concern – it also inevitably strengthens the state administration at the expense of local communities and individuals. While this is not negative *per se*, our examples have shown how involved state representatives can leverage their position in a formalization procedure to lead reforms astray. Whereas the RAI principles largely ignore this apparent problem, the FAO guidelines propose a series of measures that states can take to recognize property rights in a fair and transparent manner. They thus rather suggest an orientation towards a security and rights-based vision.

Approaches that recognize pluralism and their implementation challenge

The FAO guidelines propose that: "States should consider adapting their policy, legal and organizational frameworks to recognize tenure systems of indigenous peoples and other communities with customary tenure systems" (FAO 2012:14). They are thus in line with what Assies suggests for the implementation of a security and rights-based vision (Assies 2009: 586). Assies proposes to 're-institutionalize' existing property regimes wherever possible, i.e. to allow for an overall legal recognition of plural customary tenure regimes, rather than to forcefully subject them to a single, national property system under statutory law (Assies 2009: 586, referring to Bruce 1998). This approach "does not prescribe a specific approach to land reform" but is based on pluralism (Toulmin and Quan 2000: 5, cited in Ubink 2009: 9). An approach that "accommodate[s] the complexity of rights and practices at multiple levels, including especially the local level" (Meinzen-Dick and Mwangi 2008: 43) may also allow recognizing overlapping bundles of rights or protecting existing common property rights from the risk of being privatized in the course of a formalization procedure.[5] We conclude that formalization of land tenure needs to be anchored at the local level. The example of Tanzania, whose Village Land Act of 2001 provides customary rights - be they registered or not - the same legal status as statutory rights under the Land Act 2001, is an attempt in that direction. However, the implementation of such types of land reforms faces its own challenges (Sikor and Müller 2009; for Tanzania see Pedersen 2010, 2011). First, there is often a lack of commitment on different state levels to fully implement respective laws and allocate the necessary means to the local level (Knight 2010: 258). After all, letting others participate in the formalization of property rights means sharing power over resources.[6] Knight thus concludes that if a reform is not to "face a kind of subtle bureaucratic mutiny" (Knight 2010: 259), it requires broad changes in governance: "state officials need new powers, roles and responsibilities if a new law strips them of their previously-held authority" (Knight 2010: 258).

Second, as we have demonstrated in our examples related to the third concern, and as Wiber states: "The consequences of the introduction of state law into minority regions are not, however, always those planned by state bureaucrats" (Wiber 1992: 487). Formalization processes can be very complex endeavours, which may kindle latent conflicts (Assies 2009: 584; see also Cotula et al. 2006: 20). Hence, they require, besides political will, considerable capacities on the part of the involved state authorities - capacities lacking in many of the countries affected by large-scale foreign investments in land (see also Li 2011; Pedersen 2011). As a consequence, local elites outside the state institutions or certain skilful groups often benefit disproportionately from land titling processes, while claims and rights

[5] On the complexity of formal recognition of group rights in general see Alden Wily 2006 and Fitzpatrick 2005, and for Nepal see Alden Wily et al. 2009 and Upreti et al. 2008.

[6] For a conceptual analysis of the reciprocal constitution of property and authority see Sikor and Lund 2009.

of the less wealthy and powerful are infringed upon (see also Ubink 2009; Meinzen-Dick and Mwangi 2008; Sawyer and Gomez 2008; Cotula et al. 2006). Since wealth and power disparities are essential constituents of property regimes, even participatory approaches cannot always avoid 'elite capture' or other types of struggles within local communities. Thus, even a clear political will for 're-institutionalization' cannot ensure that all people get treated in a fair manner.

Avoid legal intervention whenever possible

Due to the outlined challenges, Fitzpatrick suggests that the extent of external legal intervention in customary land systems "should be determined by reference to the nature and causes of any tenure insecurity" and intervention should be avoided whenever possible (Fitzpatrick 2005: 449). This means that in those cases where customary property regimes have worked considerably well so far and where local individuals and communities show no interest in selling their rights to outsiders, the state's role should be limited to recognising existing customary rights as a whole and protecting them against external threats. Thus, existing claims and rights would remain embedded in a given social context and not be incorporated into the mainstream market system. Land would thus remain out of reach for investors. This is much in line with the demands of global farmer organizations such as La Via Campesina who have been fighting for an overall recognition of customary property regimes beyond statutory law since the 1990s (La Via Campesina 2011). It is certainly not in line, however, with the intentions of the RAI principles, which - even more than the FAO guidelines - emphasize the ostensible advantages of land as a marketable good.

The complexities of participatory land titling

Nevertheless, there may be justified needs for state interventions at the local level. Customary property regimes may fail to de-escalate local resource conflicts, or - more essential in the context of foreign investments - communities may explicitly wish to create marketability for their land resources. In these situations, Fitzpatrick recommends certain forms of state regulation. However, he also warns of "quick-fix attempts to impose formalized titles on fluid customary interests" (Fitzpatrick 2005: 472). In such cases, participatory approaches are a must. Yet, as we argue in our first concern and unlike suggestions by the FAO guidelines and the RAI principles, these can neither be 'simple' nor 'quick'. Identifying customary property rights is a delicate endeavour, because it usually concerns overlapping bundles of rights, which are embedded in a social and political context and constantly reproduced through people's relations and everyday practices. Our example from Tanzania shows that even elected village leaders are not always aware of all existing claims and (secondary) rights. Yet if common knowledge regarding detailed property rights is absent within a community, it can take a lot of time and money to identify different groups of stakeholders, to understand local patterns of domination and dependency, and to carefully select adequate representatives. In cases where certain land rights are held by external actors (e.g. in the form of patron-client relations), participation may even need to be scaled up beyond the local level.

Concluding Remarks

When analyzing potential economic and socio-political effects and proposed measures in the context of 'land grabs' it is crucial to gain a holistic understanding of land tenure systems. This article concludes that employing a legal pluralism perspective is very helpful in this regard. Adapting this perspective and using also empirical cases beside the classical examples of 'land grabbing', we have demonstrated that the identification and recognition of customary property rights over land is a very complex and delicate endeavour, which risks neglecting locally existing property claims and rights. Unfortunately, neither the RAI principles nor the FAO guidelines address this challenge in a satisfactory way. First, both initiatives propose to identify existing rights in a participatory manner, an approach that is certainly indispensable yet anything but 'quick' and 'simple'. Second, the centralist approach to land tenure in the RAI principles does not allow acknowledging legal plural orders and the social embeddedness of local property regimes. Third, even a more security and rights-based vision as brought forward by the FAO guidelines entails the risk of elite capture and of reinforcing unequal power structures within local communities. To some extent, however, it allows for the incorporation of land-related cultural, social and normative practices and of plural legal arrangements and thus for the protection of locally existing tenure rights. It further leaves it to local communities to decide whether their land and natural resources should become a marketable good to outsiders or not. However, in many countries the realization of this vision would require the adaptation of whole legal regimes and national regulations which takes, besides political will, a lot of time for implementation and involves fundamental changes in governance. Further, careful participatory land use planning at the local level could prove to be an additional tool to reduce negative effects of foreign land acquisitions. Completed before any external interests arise, it serves as a basis for local communities to take decisions regarding the availability of land for potential investors. However, the introduction of meaningful nationwide land use planning is a major endeavour. All of these challenges cannot be addressed adequately and convincingly within the framework of such guidelines alone. Instead, more long-term strategies for the protection of customary rights are required. Thus, from an analytical perspective, a moratorium on 'land grabs' as postulated by some civil society organizations (IPC 2011) would be most appropriate. From a more pragmatic perspective though, we acknowledge the FAO guidelines and - to a much lesser extent - the RAI principles as more immediate efforts to reduce negative effects of 'land grabs'. However, investors and host governments should by no means mistake these guidelines as guarantors of ostensibly harmless land acquisitions, as the complexity of plural land orders cannot be underestimated. Even when following the guidelines the risk of infringing upon local people's land rights continues to be very high.

References

ALDEN WILY, Liz

2003 *Community-based Land Tenure Management: Questions and Answers about Tanzania's New Village Land Act, 1999.* IIED Issue paper no. 120, London: International Institute for Environment and Development.

2011 '"The law is to blame": the vulnerable status of common property rights in Sub-Saharan Africa.' *Development and Change* 42: 733-757.

2006 'The commons and customary law in modern times: rethinking the orthodoxies.' Pp. 17-20 in Esther Mwangi (ed.), *Land Rights for African Development: From Knowledge to Action.* CAPRi Policy Briefs, Washington: International Food Policy Research Institute (IFPRI).

ALDEN WILY, Liz, Devendra CHAPAGAIN, and Shiva SHARMA

2009 *Land Reform in Nepal - Where is it Coming from and Where is it Going?* Kathmandu: DFID.

ANSEEUW, Ward, Mathieu BOCHE, Thomas BREU, Markus GIGER, Jann LAY, Peter MESSERLI, and Kerstin NOLTE

2012 *Transnational Land Deals for Agriculture in the Global South. Analytical Report based on the Land Matrix Database.* Bern, Montpellier, Hamburg: CDE, CIRAD, GIGA.

ASSIES, Willem

2009 'Land tenure, land law and development: some thoughts on recent debates.' *The Journal of Peasant Studies* 36: 573-589.

BASNET, Jagat

2011 'Land rights movement and agrarian change (Chapter 7).' Pp. 141-160 in Kailash Nath Pyakuryal and Bishnu Raj Upreti (eds.), *Land, Agriculture and Agrarian Transformation*. Kathmandu: Consortium for Land Research and Policy Dialogue (COLARP).

BEHRMAN, Julia, Ruth MEINZEN-DICK, and Agnes QUISUMBING

2011 *The Gender Implications of Large-Scale Land Deals*. IFPRI Discussion Paper 01056, Washington: International Food Policy Research Institute.

BENDA-BECKMANN, Keebet von

1981 'Forum shopping and shopping forums: dispute processing in a Minangkabau village.' *Journal of Legal Pluralism* 19: 117-159.

BENDA-BECKMANN, Franz von, and Keebet von BENDA BECKMANN

1999 'A functional analysis of property rights, with special reference to Indonesia.' Pp. 15-56 in Toon van Meijl and Franz von Benda-Beckmann (eds.), *Property Rights and Economic Development*. London: Kegan Paul International.

BENDA-BECKMANN, Franz von, Keebet von BENDA-BECKMANN, and Melanie WIBER

2006 'The properties of property.' Pp. 1-39 in Franz von Benda-Beckmann, Keebet von Benda-Beckmann, and Melanie Wiber (eds.), *Changing Properties of Property*. New York: Berghahn Books.

BICHSEL, Christine, Gilbert FOKOU, Asel IBRAIMOVA, Ulan KASYMOV, Bernd STEIMANN, and Susan THIEME

2010 'Natural resource institutions in transformation: The tragedy and glory of the private.' Pp. 255-269 in Hans Hurni and Urs Wiesmann (eds.) with an international group of co-editors, *Global Change and Sustainable Development: A Synthesis of Regional Experiences from Research Partnerships*. Perspectives of the Swiss National Centre of Competence in Research (NCCR) North-South, University of Bern, Vol. 5. Bern: Geographica Bernensia.

BORRAS, Saturnino Jr. and Jennifer FRANCO

2010 'From threat to opportunity? Problems with the idea of a "Code of Conduct" for land-grabbing.' *Yale Human Rights & Development Law Journal* 13: 507-523.

2012 'Global land grabbing and trajectories of agrarian change: a preliminary analysis.' *Journal of Agrarian Change* 12: 34-59.

BORRAS, Saturnino, Ruth HALL, Ian SCOONES, Ben WHITE, and Wendy WOLFORD

2011 'Towards a better understanding of global land grabbing: an editorial introduction.' *Journal of Peasant Studies* 38: 209-216.

BRUCE, John (ed.)
1998 *Country Profiles of Land Tenure*. Madison: University of Wisconsin, Land Tenure Center.

CAPLAN, Lionel
2000 *Land and Social Change in East Nepal: A Study of Hindu-tribal Relations* 2nd ed. Kathmandu: Himal Books.

CHACHAGE, Chambi and Bernhard BAHA
2010 *Accumulation by Land Dispossession and Labour Devaluation in Tanzania: The Case of Biofuel and Forestry Investments in Kilwa and Kilolo*. Dar es Salaam: Land Rights Research and Resources Institute (LARRRI/HAKIARDHI) and Oxfam.

COTULA, Lorenzo, Camilla TOULMIN, and Julian QUAN
2006 *Better Land Access for the Rural Poor. Lessons from Experience and Challenges Ahead*. London, Rome: IIED, FAO.

COTULA, Lorenzo, Sonja VERMEULEN, Rebeca LEONARD, and James KEELEY
2009 *Land Grab or Development Opportunity? Agricultural Investment and International Land Deals in Africa*. London, Rome: IIED/FAO/IFAD.

DEININGER, Klaus
2011 'Challenges posed by the new wave of farmland investment.' *Journal of Peasant Studies* 38: 217-247.

FAO (FOOD AND AGRICULTURE ORGANIZATION OF THE UNITED NATIONS)
2006 *Report of the International Conference on Agrarian Reform and Rural Development (ICARRD)*. Porto Alegre, Brazil, 7-10 March 2006.
2012 *Voluntary Guidelines on the Responsible Governance of Tenure of Land, Fisheries and Forests in the Context of National Food Security (11 May 2012)*. http://www.fao.org/nr/tenure/voluntary-guidelines/en, last accessed 18.06.2012.

FAO (FOOD AND AGRICULTURE ORGANIZATION OF THE UNITED NATIONS), IFAD (INTERNATIONAL FUND FOR AGRICULTURAL DEVELOPMENT), UNCTAD (UNITED NATIONS CONFERENCE ON TRADE AND DEVELOPMENT.) and WORLD BANK
2010 *Principles for Responsible Agricultural Investment that Respects Rights, Livelihoods and Resources: Extended version, January 25, 2010*. http://www.responsibleagroinvestment.org/rai/node/256, last accessed 18.06.2012.

FIAN (FOOD FIRST INFORMATION AND ACTION NETWORK)
2010a *Comparative Chart: FAO Voluntary Guidelines on Land and Natural Resources versus the Principles for Responsible Agricultural Investment.*

The Global Campaign for Agrarian Reform, October 2010. http://www.fian.org/resources/documents/others/fao-voluntary-guidelines-on-land-and-natural-resources-vs-principles-for-responsible-agricultural-investment, last accessed 18.06.2012.

2010b *Why We Oppose the Principles for Responsible Agricultural Investment (RAI)*. The Global Campaign for Agrarian Reform, Land Research Action Network. October 2010.

FITZPATRICK, Daniel

2005 '"Best Practice" Options for the Legal Recognition of Customary Tenure.' *Development and Change* 36: 449-475.

GHALE, Yamuna

2011 'Right to food and food security in the changing context (Chapter 2).' Pp. 27-56 in Kailash Nath Pyakuryal and Bishnu Raj Upreti (eds.), *Land, Agriculture and Agrarian Transformation*. Kathmandu: Consortium for Land Research and Policy Dialogue (COLARP).

GONZALEZ, Carmen G.

2010 'The global food crisis: Law, policy, and the elusive quest for justice.' *Yale Human Rights and Development Law Journal* 13: 462-479.

GRAIN

2008 *SEIZED! The 2008 Land Grab for Food and Financial Security*. GRAIN briefing, October 2008.

2009 *The New Farm Owners. Corporate Investors Lead the Rush for Control over Overseas Farmland*. GRAIN report, October 2009.

GRIFFITHS, Anne

1998 'Reconfiguring law: an ethnographic perspective from Botswana.' *Law & Social Inquiry* 23: 587-620.

GRIFFITHS, John

1986 What is legal pluralism? *Journal of Legal Pluralism* 24: 1-55.

HALL, Derek

2011 'Land grabs, land control, and Southeast Asian crop booms.' *Journal of Peasant Studies* 38: 837-857.

HARALAMBOUS Sappho, Harold LIVERSAGE, and Monica ROMANO

2009 *The Growing Demand for Land Risks and Opportunities for Smallholder Farmers*. Discussion Paper prepared for the Round Table organized during the thirty-second session of IFAD's Governing Council, 18 February 2009. Rome.

IPC (INTERNATIONAL PLANNING COMMITTEE FOR FOOD SOVEREIGNTY)

2011 *Landmark Conference on Land Grabbing: Large-scale Agricultural Investments Do Undermine Food Security*. IPC press release (April 2011).

http://www.foodsovereignty.org, last accessed 18.06.2012.

KHATRI, Shridhar and Bishnu Raj UPRETI
2012 *Nontraditional security challenges in Nepal.* NBR Special Report No 36, January 2012. Seattle and Washington: The National Bureau of Asian Research.

KNIGHT, Rachael S.
2010 *Statutory Recognition of Customary Land Rights in Africa: An Investigation into Best Practices for Lawmaking and Implementation.* FAO Legislative Study 105. Rome: Food and Agriculture Organization of the United Nations.

KSHETRY, Deependra Bahadur
2011 'Land reform and agrarian transformation (Chapter 5). 'Pp. 101-124 in Kailash Nath Pyakuryal and Bishnu Raj Upreti (eds.), *Land, Agriculture and Agrarian Transformation.* Kathmandu: Consortium for Land Research and Policy Dialogue (COLARP).

LA VIA CAMPESINA
2011 *It's Time to Outlaw Land Grabbing, not to Make it "Responsible"!* http://viacampesina.org/en/index.php?option=com content&view=article&id=1076:its-time-to-outlaw-land-grabbing-not-to-make-it-qresponsibleq&catid=23:agrarian-reform&Itemid=36, last accessed 18.06.2012.

LI, Tania Murray
2011 'Centering labour in the land grab debate.' *Journal of Peasant Studies* 38: 281-298.

LINDBERG, Emma
2007 *Access to Water in Irrigation Agriculture of Sokuluk River Basin, Kyrgyzstan.* Master thesis, Zurich: University of Zurich.

LOCHER, Martina
2011 '"How come others are selling our land?" - Customary Land Rights, Rural Livelihoods and Foreign Land Acquisition in the Case of a UK-based Forestry Company in Tanzania.' Presented on 7 April 2011 at the *International Conference on Global Land Grabbing*, organized by the Land Deals Politics Initiative (LDPI) in collaboration with the Journal of Peasant Studies and hosted by the Future Agricultures Consortium at the Institute of Development Studies, University of Sussex (draft conference paper).

LUND, Christian
1998 'Struggles for land and political power: On the politicization of land tenure and disputes in Niger.' *Journal of Legal Pluralism* 40: 1-22.

MAMYTOVA, Jyldyz and Gulnara MAMBETALIEVA
2008 'Kyrygzstan unveils food security plan.' *IWPR's Reporting Central Asia*, 526.

MANN, Howard and Carin SMALLER
2010 *Foreign Land Purchases for Agriculture: What Impact on Sustainable Development?* United Nations Sustainable Development Innovation Briefs (8), January 2010, New York: United Nations Department of Economic and Social Affairs.

MEHTA, Lyla, Melissa LEACH, and Ian SCOONES
2001 'Editorial: Environmental governance in an uncertain world.' *IDS Bulletin* 32(4): 1-9.

MEINZEN-DICK, Ruth
2009 *Property Rights for Poverty Reduction?* DESA Working Paper (91), December 2009. New York: United Nations.

MEINZEN-DICK, Ruth S. and Rajendra PRADHAN
2001 'Implications of legal pluralism for natural resource management.' *IDS Bulletin* 32(4): 10-17.

MEINZEN-DICK, Ruth and Esther MWANGI
2008 'Cutting the web of interests: pitfalls of formalizing property rights.' *Land Use Policy* 26: 36-43.

ODGAARD, Rie
2006 *Land Rights and Land Conflicts in Africa: the Tanzania Case.* Country policy study. Copenhagen: Danish Institute for International Studies.

OSTROM, Elinor
2003 'How types of goods and property rights jointly affect collective action.' *Journal of Theoretical Politics* 15: 239-270.

PAYNE, Geoffrey
2000 *'Urban land tenure options: titles or rights?'* Paper presented at the World Bank Urban Forum, Virginia, USA, 3-5 April.

PEDERSEN, Rasmus H.
2010 *Tanzania's Land Law Reform; the Implementation Challenge.* DIIS Working Paper 37, Copenhagen: Danish Institute for International Studies.
2011 *The Forgotten Villages - Land Reform in Tanzania.* DIIS Policy Brief, Copenhagen: Danish Institute for International Studies.

PYAKURYAL, Kailash Nath and Bishnu Raj UPRETI (eds.)
2011 *Land, Agriculture and Agrarian Transformation.* Kathmandu: Consortium for Land Research and Policy Dialogue (COLARP).

REGMI, Mahesh Chandra
1999 *Landownership in Nepal.* New Delhi: Adroit publishers.

RIBOT, Jesse C. and Nancy Lee PELUSO
2003 'A theory of access.' *Rural Sociology* 68:153-181.
SAWYER, Suzana and Edmund Terence GOMEZ
2008 *Transnational Governmentality and Resource Extraction. Indigenous Peoples, Multinational Corporations, Multilateral Institutions and the State*. Identities, Conflict and Cohesion Programme Paper Number 13, Geneva: United Nations Research Institute for Social Development.
SCHUTTER, Olivier de
2011 'How not to think of land-grabbing: three critiques of large-scale investments in farmland.' *Journal of Peasant Studies* 38: 249-279.
SCOONES, Ian
2010 *Investing in Land: a Commentary on the World Bank Report*. Brighton: Future Agricultures Consortium, 16 Sept 2010. http://www.future-agricultures.org/index.php?option=com content&view=article&id=7365:investing-in-land-a-commentary-on-the-world-bank-report&catid=81:fac-news&Itemid=472, last accessed 18.06.2012.
SCHLAGER, Edella and Elinor OSTROM
1992 'Property rights regimes and natural resources: A conceptual analysis.' *Land Economics* 68: 249-262.
SHRESTHA, Bharat
2011 *The Land Development Boom in Kathmandu Valley*. Kathmandu: College of Development Studies and the International Land Coalition.
SIKOR, Thomas and Christian LUND
2009 'Access and property: a question of power and authority.' *Development and Change* 40: 1-22.
SIKOR, Thomas and Daniel MÜLLER
2009 'The limits of state-led land reform: an introduction.' *World Development* 37: 1307-1316.
SOTO, Hernando de
2003 *The Mystery of Capital: Why Capitalism Triumphs in the West and Fails Everywhere Else*. New York: Basic Books.
STEIMANN, Bernd
2011 *Making a Living in Uncertainty: Agro-pastoral Livelihoods and Institutional Transformations in Post-socialist Kyrgyzstan*. Human Geography Series 26, Bishkek and Zurich.
2012 'Conflicting strategies for contested resources. Pastoralists' responses to uncertainty in postsocialist rural Kyrgyzstan.' Pp. 145-160 in Hermann Kreutzmann (ed.), *Pastoral Practices in High Asia. Dordrecht, New York:* Springer.

THAPA, Shankar
2000 *Historical Study of Agrarian Relation in Nepal (1846-1951).* New Delhi: Adroit Publishers.

TOULMIN, Camilla and Julian QUAN (eds.)
2000 *Evolving Land Rights, Policy and Tenure in Africa.* London: DFID, IIED, NRI.

UBINK, Janine M.
2009 'Legalising land rights in Africa, Asia and Latin America: An introduction.' Pp. 7-32 in Janine M. Ubink, André J. Hoekema, and Willem J. Assies (eds.), *Legalising Land Rights. Local Practices, State Responses and Tenure Security in Africa, Asia and Latin America.* Leiden: Leiden University Press.

UBINK, Janine M., André J. HOEKEMA, and Willem J. ASSIES (eds.)
2009 *Legalising Land Rights. Local Practices, State Responses and Tenure Security in Africa, Asia and Latin America.* Leiden: Leiden University Press.

UNDP (UNITED NATIONS DEVELOPMENT PROGRAMME)
2004 *Nepal Human Development Report 2004. Empowerment and Poverty Reduction.* Kathmandu: UNDP.

UPRETI, Bishnu Raj
2004a 'Land conflict in Nepal: Peasant's struggle to change unequal agrarian social relations.' *Community, Work & Family* 7: 371-393.
2004b 'Relationships between resource governance and resource conflict: Nepalese experience.' *Journal of Legal Pluralism* 50: 71-100.
2010 *Management of Natural Resource Conflict in Nepal: Conflicts over Land, Water and Forest Resources and their Resolution Systems.* Saarbrücken: Lambert Academic Publishers.

UPRETI, Bishnu Raj, Sagar Raj SHARMA, and Jagat BASNET (eds.)
2008 *Land Politics and Conflict in Nepal: Realities and Potentials for Agrarian Transformation.* Kathmandu: Community Self Reliance Centre, Human and Natural Resources Studies Centre, Kathmandu University and South Asia Regional Coordination Office of NCCR North-South.

URT (UNITED REPUBLIC OF TANZANIA)
1999a *Land Act (No. 4 of 1999).* Dar es Salaam: United Republic of Tanzania. http://faolex.fao.org/docs/pdf/tan23795.pdf, last accessed 18.06.2012.
1999b *Village Land Act (No. 5 of 1999).* Dar es Salaam: United Republic of Tanzania.

VISSER, Oane and Max SPOOR
2011 Land grabbing in post-Soviet Eurasia: the world's largest agricultural land reserves at stake. *Journal of Peasant Studies* 38: 299-323.

WIBER, Melanie G.

1992 'Levels of property rights, levels of law: A case study from the Northern Philippines.' *Man* (New Series) 26: 469-492.

WOERTZ, Eckart, Samir PRADHAN, Nermina BIBEROVIC, and Chan JINGZHONG

2008 *Potential for GCC Agro-investments in Africa and Central Asia.* GRC Report, September 2008.

WORLD BANK

2010 *Rising Global Interest in Farmland. Can it Yield Sustainable and Equitable Benefits?* September 2010, Washington DC: World Bank.

ZOOMERS, Annelies

2010 'Globalisation and the foreignisation of space: seven processes driving the current global land grab.' *Journal of Peasant Studies* 37: 429-447.

REPLICATING 'A MODEL OF MUTUAL RESPECT': COULD SINGAPORE'S LEGAL PLURALISM WORK IN AUSTRALIA?[1]

Ann Black

1. Introduction

For two centuries, the Muslim presence in Australia has always been a quiet one – Muslims found freedom to practice religion and be good Muslims and good citizens of Australia. Although Christianity was the dominant faith at the time of federation when the six British colonies came together to form the Commonwealth of Australia in 1901, a state religion was never imposed. Many free settlers had fled religious persecution in the sectarian struggles in Europe and Britain and so from its inception Australia was a secular nation[2] but along with a de-establishment clause the Australian *Constitution* provided for freedom of religion and of worship for all.[3] In this land of immigrants, the common law system was, rightly or

[1] The research for this paper was undertaken during my time of Fellowship in 2011 at the Asian Law Institute, National University of Singapore. I thank the members of ASLI, and also Noor Aisha Bte Abdul Rahman and Ahmad Nizam bin Abbas for their guidance.

[2] On the secular character of Australia, see Bouma et al. 2010: 4-6.

[3] *Australian Constitution* s116: The Commonwealth shall not make any law for establishing any religion, or for imposing any religious observance, or for

wrongly, seen as a uniting and equalising force for all Australians. It has remained an unashamedly 'one law for all' nation with both sides of politics in support of that stance. However, recently that 'one law for all' model has been challenged. One challenge has come from voices within the Australian Muslim community, or more accurately, communities,[4] who argue that a system of legal pluralism should replace the 'one law for all' approach. Singapore is given as a model for consideration as it has a respected common law system coexisting with a Syariah[5] court system with special laws enacted exclusively for Muslims. Singapore's model of legal pluralism is accepted by Muslims and by non-Muslims in Singapore and is promoted as a workable, on-going and respectful system of legal pluralism. This paper explores the viability for Australia of the 'Singapore model' which its advocates believe functions effectively because of "the mutual respect the Muslims and the non-Muslim community have for each other" (bin Abbas 2012: 163). It is beyond the scope of this article to assess other models, such as the English network of Arbitration Councils, which is an informal, non-government regulated scheme, whose decisions as arbitral awards may be enforced by the civil courts.[6] As Australia already has an ad hoc, unofficial system in which Muslims obtain

prohibiting the free exercise of any religion, and no religious test shall be required as a qualification for any office or public trust under the Commonwealth.

[4] Legal academic Jamila Hussain writes that it is "probably more correct to speak of Muslim 'communities' in Australia rather than 'the' Muslim community" (Hussain 2004: 202).

[5] *Shari'a, shariah, syariah, shariat* are transliterations from the Arabic script. The transliteration used in Southeast Asia is usually syariah, whilst in Australia *Sharia* is more commonly adopted. Both mean the same thing. In this paper Syariah is used when referring to Singapore and Sharia for Australia. Whilst there are debates about whether Sharia precisely equates with the 'Islamic law' the terms are often used interchangeably when English is used. Sharia refers to the divinely ordained law embodied in the *Qur'an* (actual word of God as revealed to the Prophet Mohammad), *Sunnah* (practices and traditions of the Prophet) and *fiqh* (jurisprudence). The *fiqh* is the means by which jurists can extend principles contained in the *Qur'an* and *Sunnah* to deal with new situations. There is a range of approved juristic techniques including *ijma* (consensus of scholars) and *qiyas* (analogical deduction and application) with *maslaha* (in the public interest) playing an increasing role. For an overview of Sharia from different perspectives see: Glenn 2004: 170 -221; and Hallaq 2009.

[6] See Bano 2007.

guidance and legal rulings on personal status matters and other issues meaningful in their lives, the possible transition from an informal 'shadow' system to a formal parallel court system - identified as the Singapore model - is the focus of the analysis that follows.

2. The Australian Context

Muslims have been in Australia for two centuries. Even from the early days of first European settlement when Australia was mainly a convict colony, there were some Muslims amongst the convicts, sailors and free settlers (Centre for Muslim Minorities and Islam Policy Studies 2009). Malay pearl divers came to the northwest and cameleers from Pakistan and Afghanistan opened up the desert interior and built the first mosques (Saeed and Akbarzadeh 2001). Today, Australia has approximately 500,000 Muslims.[7] They came with each wave of migration to Australia[8] from over 80 nations and comprise a substantial component of current migrant and refugee intake. Mosques, *masqids*, Islamic schools, organizations and community centres, *halal* stores, Islamic attire, prayer rooms[9] in public places are part of the fabric of Australian cities and some rural areas. In this nation of immigrants, 44 per cent of the 22 million Australians were born overseas or have a parent who was; four million speak a language other than English, 260 languages in fact; and identify with 270 ancestries (Department of Immigration and

---

[7] The precise numbers of Muslims is not known because many do not declare their religious status for census purposes. At the last census in 2006 the Australian Bureau of Statistics stated the number as 340,000 making Muslims the third largest religious group in Australia, after Christians and Buddhists. However it is believed this is an under-representation and that there has been considerable growth in the Muslim demographic over the last five years. See http://www.dfat.gov.au/facts/muslims_in_Australia.html.

[8] These waves include Afghani and Pakistani settlement in outback and rural communities from the 1860s; Albanian and Lebanese migration during the 1920s; significant Turkish and Lebanese migration from the 1960's onward, and from 1990s immigration from the Middle East, South Asia, Bosnia, and the Horn of Africa, also being a significant portion of our refugee intake. As well, there has been migration from South East Asia, South Africa and Fiji.

[9] Airports, universities, theme parks, shopping centres, government offices and other public places.

Citizenship 2011). The results from the 2011 census are not yet published, but in the previous census in 2006, 64% of the population was Christian (Bouma et al. 2010: 6-7), a decrease from the previous census, with Buddhism (2.1%), Islam (1.5%) and Hinduism (0.7%) increasing numerically. Every religion of the world has a base in Australia: Sikhism, Baha'i, Aboriginal spiritualism, Exclusive Brethren, Druid, Scientology, Paganism, Wicca and Satanism (Bouma et al. 2010: 6).

The challenge to 'one law for all'

The first challenge to 'one law for all' came from Aboriginal and Torres Strait Islanders. As the first peoples of Australia (also known as indigenous Australians), a case was put forward for differential treatment in criminal matters, which was designed to address concerns of significant over-represented in the prison population.[10] This resulted in the setting up of Murri (Hennessy 2007) or Koori Courts,[11] which are sentencing courts. These courts do not apply customary law and have no operation in family, inheritance or other matters although some recommendations for this have been made (Australian Law Reform Commission 1986).[12] The only jurisdiction they have is when an Aboriginal or Torres Strait Islander is accused of a minor criminal offence and pleads guilty. As sentencing courts, a magistrate sits with an Indigenous elder or elders to jointly determine a culturally appropriate sentence. The aim is to avoid incarceration or fines, and so give community based orders in the hope of rehabilitating offenders within the community. The establishment of these courts was not contentious and had overwhelming community support.

In contrast, it was highly contentious when some Muslim groups[13] and their representatives, made arguments for Islamic family, inheritance and possibly

[10] In Queensland in 2006, indigenous and Torres Strait Islanders were 3.5% of the population but comprises 27% of the adult prison population and 60% of juvenile detainees (Parker and Pathe 2006: 4).

[11] Koori Court is the name used in Victoria, and in New South Wales these are Circle Sentencing Courts.

[12] A report in Western Australia advised against the recognition of indigenous customary law (Law Reform Commission of Western Australia 2006).

[13] Australian Muslim Mission and Islamic Friendship Association of Australia.

contract law to be determined by Muslims, for Muslims. Such dispute resolution would be in accordance with Islamic law and would require separate Islamic legal institutions, referred to as Sharia courts, tribunals or councils, whose decisions should have formal recognition from the common law courts. Essentially a case was made for formal legal pluralism.

The desire for accommodation of Islamic law into Australia's legal system may have been bubbling along within Muslim communities and mosques for some time but the notion first entered the public arena in Ontario, Canada in 2005-6 (Boyd 2004). Ontario's foray into Islamic arbitration for family disputes ultimately failed, but it did give impetus to some Imams in Australia[14] to signal that similar options would now open up in Australia. It also raised the expectations of many Muslims. The issue picked up more momentum in 2008 with the famous speech of the Archbishop of Canterbury to the Royal Courts of Justice in England. Analysis of his speech and reaction to it from all quarters saturated our local media for some time. The views of Muslim spokespersons were sought, and these views were mixed, but within days of the Archbishop's speech, the government through our Attorney-General, Robert McClelland clarified Australia's 'one law for all' stance, stating "the Rudd government is not considering and will not consider the introduction of any parts of Sharia law into the Australian legal system" (Zwartz 2008).

These debates and reform agendas taking place in other parts of the world served to both inspire and conversely to quell local sentiments. There were other factors that also informed the desire amongst some Australians to formalize the place for Sharia. One is that Islamic law acts as a marker for identity, which is important for all religious and cultural minorities especially in democratic multicultural nations. This is true in Australia, just as it is in Singapore where Muslim Malays are an ethnic and religious minority. Professor Maznah binte Mohammad argues that Islamic law as administered through Singapore's *Administration of Muslim Law Act* Cap 3 (AMLA) has become integral to Malay identity in Singapore. If you remove it, you remove part of your identity. This, she sees as a shared identity that binds Muslims together to form a religious boundary – a 'ring fence'- within the territorial boundary of the nation state.[15]

[14] In 2005 Imam Abdul Jalil Ahmad, of the Islamic Council of Western Australia proposed setting up a Court in Western Australia comprised of ten Islamic leaders to deal with divorce and separation (Weber 2005).

[15] Personal communication with research scholar at Asia Research Institute, the

Furthermore, the world is now global and its people mobile. The Muslim population is not embedded nor settled in any one place and individuals and families can have multiple allegiances. Many who come to Australia intend to make it their home forever and do; for others their stay is to attain a qualification or career opportunity; for some it may not work out and they return to their country of origin or to 'greener' pastures in other places. If they marry in compliance with Islamic law or their Islamic marriage terminates in Australia, how will they give their changed status legal effect without a formal Sharia court/tribunal? Will the informal options using Imams and local entities now open in Australia have any legal standing in a Muslim country that applies Islamic law? The answers vary. Would an Iranian Sharia Court recognize an Islamic divorce decree given by an Imam or some informal body in Australia? The answer is no. Would the Syariah Court in Singapore accept such a decision as a legal divorce? The answer is maybe, as the court would look at the circumstances and make a decision on the substantive evidence presented. Even in England the Sharia Courts, which operate under a system of Islamic arbitration will not recognize a decision from Australia as the legal ruling is not valid under Australian law and no entity is recognized by Australian courts (Arshad, *Islamic Family Law* (2010: 36).

Another reason is that by not providing a regulated formal Sharia court system, unfairness and inequity, especially for Muslim women can result. The main example for this 'unfairness' is divorce. Whilst a Muslim husband can extra-judicially pronounce divorce, a wife usually cannot.[16] In the unofficial ad hoc system in Australia, there is no formal court for her to go to so a Muslim wife who wants to end an unhappy marriage has to find 'someone' or some 'organisation' she believes can affect such a religious divorce, usually an Imam or Sheik whose religious authority is informally recognised by the others. This has led to inconsistency and unaccountability, as individuals or groups can simply put themselves forward as sufficiently scholarly, pious or authoritative to make family law determinations, especially for the ethnic community with which they are aligned. These men may look to modernist interpretations or adhere to patriarchal and conservative ones. When conservative interpretation prevails, women can find it difficult to obtain a religious divorce, as for example a *khula* divorce may be

National University of Singapore. September 2011. See also previous note. On law as a marker of Muslim identity in Singapore see Abdul Rahman 2009: 112.

[16] It is possible for a marriage contract to specify that the husband delegates to his wife his authority to pronounce divorce, known as *talaq-i-tafwid*. This option however is not widely employed in marriage contracts.

refused unless the husband consents to it[17] or his statement of facts may be accepted in preference to a wife's. The result is some Muslim women are disadvantaged, even vulnerable, especially recent migrants who may have little knowledge of the local language or of avenues available outside their immediate family or mosque. It gives rise to phenomenon known as 'limping' marriages, where a wife can or has obtained a secular divorce, but a religious one is denied. This is well documented in Australia (Family Law Council of Australia 2001; Black 2010) and also in the United Kingdom (Law Commission 1972; Yilmaz 2003b; Muslim Arbitration Tribunal 2008) and in secular Muslim Turkey (Yilmaz 2003a).

Perspectives on the legal pluralism debate

Against a background of multiple rationales for a Sharia court-like institution, the Gillard government in 2011 set up a Parliamentary Enquiry into Multiculturalism.

The Minister for Immigration, Hon Chris Bowen, set out policy outlining Australia's model of multiculturalism (Department of Immigration and Citizenship 2011) which he argued differed from those in Europe, particularly Germany and the United Kingdom[18] because the first loyalty must be given to Australia - to the Constitutional, rule of law, democracy, freedom of speech and religion, English as the primary language and to sexual equality and tolerance. Other cultures and traditions can be celebrated, and each individual is free to keep his or her own linguistic, religious and ethnic heritage, but if there is conflict between these and

[17] In *khula* the wife requests divorce and in return provides her husband with compensation, which is usually the return of part or all of her *mahr* (marriage portion), or if deferred, to forego her rights to it, along with rights to maintenance during her *iddah* (divorcee or widow's waiting period before remarriage is permissible). There is debate on the matter of whether the husband must agree to this and whether his lack of consent negates *khula.* Jurisprudence developed over many centuries in which the dominant position was that a grant of *khula* was contingent upon the husband's consent. However, this traditional conservative position has been revisited and the consent fetter removed, especially in cases where arbitration failed to bring about agreement. Egypt, Bangladesh and Pakistan, for example, allow a woman to unilaterally apply to a registrar or a court who can grant *khul*a without the husband's consent.

[18] See generally Payrow Shabani 2007.

Australian values derived from the articulated sources of loyalty then "traditional Australian values win out. They must" (Bowen 2011). The other two defining features that the Minister identified were that it is citizenship-based multiculturalism,[19] which makes each and every Australian an equal partner in citizenship; and that it has received political bipartisanship. The Minister announced there would be a parliamentary enquiry into multiculturalism to which individuals and organisations could make submissions: 490 submissions were made.

Australia's national Muslim umbrella body, the Australian Federation of Islamic Councils (AFIC) made a submission via its President, Ikebal Patel, in April 2011 entitled 'Embracing Australian Values and Maintaining the Rights to be Different' (AFIC 2011). The submission advocated that "multiculturalism should lead to legal pluralism" arguing that conflicts should be resolved according to the law and traditions of one's own religion. In support it drew on the history of the Ottoman Empire with the millet system based on religious affiliation and a division of governance based on Muslim and *dhimmi* classification.[20] The AFIC submission challenged Australia's policy of multiculturalism on the ground that by limiting it to culture, religion and language and not extending it to encompass law, Australia was treating Muslims as 'second class citizens' by requiring them to live 'under one law: Western law'. On this point, it drew support from Gary Bell from the National University of Singapore who was cited in the submission as supporting multi-legal regimes:

> Multiculturalism applied to the law should lead to an acceptance and celebration of legal pluralism – Islamic law is part of a Muslim's culture and completely denying any recognition of this

[19] New citizens were to pledge "loyalty to Australia and its people ... whose democratic beliefs I share ... whose rights and liberties I respect ... and whose laws I will uphold and obey".

[20] Dhimmis were a protected minority, which meant adherents of Christianity and Judaism were allowed to follow their own family and religious laws with the community heads given jurisdiction over such matters. In the Ottoman Empire this was formalised as the millet system. The practice of allowing minorities to retain and administer different family, inheritance and religious laws from the Muslim majority has continued in most Muslim countries. Colonial rule further cemented pluralism, officially through parallel court systems and through laws applicable to specific religious or ethnic sectors.

> law goes directly against any profession of multiculturalism.[21]

The AFIC submission reasoned that Sharia was not immutable but adaptable and it was possible to have a moderate form of Sharia that could co-exist with the Australian legal system through a concept of 'twin tolerations' in which "Muslims in Australia should accept the Australian values", and Australia should provide a "public sphere for Muslims to practice their belief." The paper referred to the existing legal regulation of *halal* products and the pending changes to Australian taxation laws to give parity to Islamic financial products, as examples that demonstrated the workability of a plural legal system in Australia.

The reaction to the AFIC submission was swift. The media reported on the "call for Sharia law in Australia" (ABC News Online 2011; Hole 2011; Devine 2011; Kervalas 2011a) and featured the topic in subsequent news cycles. The government quickly quelled concerns. Attorney General McCelland stated there was no place for Sharia in Australian society, and the government strongly rejected any proposal for its introduction. He endorsed the Minister Bowen's stance by saying that: "Australia's brand of multiculturalism promotes integration. If there is any inconsistency between cultural values and the rule of law, then Australian law wins out" (Karvelas 2011b). Also retiring Chief Justice of the New South Wales Supreme Court, Jim Spigelman posited there was no basis for intrusion of Sharia or any body of religious law' into Australian law and legal system (Merritt 2011b). Instructive, however, was the reaction from some sectors of the Australian Muslim community, in particular from AFIC itself - the very body that had made the submission. Two days later a second submission was made to the Parliamentary Enquiry with a different focus, one that kept well away from law, and did not mention either 'legal' issues or 'pluralism' (Ibrahim 2011). Several state Islamic Councils also distanced themselves from the AFIC submission saying they were not consulted on it[22] and were more concerned with other issues, such as the carbon tax.[23] Some state Islamic Councils made their own separate submissions.[24] Muslim academics also entered the public debate, including Halim Rane of the Islamic Research Centre at Griffith University, who opined that Sharia law was not

[21] Whilst this quote from Assoc Prof Gary Bell was in the AFIC submission, no citation was actually provided.

[22] Islamic Councils in Queensland, New South Wales and Victoria said they had not been consulted and disagreed with parts of the submission (Merritt 2011d).

[23] Sherene Hassan of the Islamic Council of Victoria.

[24] For example see Islamic Council of Victoria 2011.

needed and not wanted by Muslims in Australia.[25] Ultimately, AFIC President, Ikebal Patel, retreated from his own submission. In an interview he said that, "it had been a mistake to even mention Sharia law and legal pluralism" and he remained "a supporter of secular law" (Merritt 2011a).

Yet, despite the responses and an apparent retraction from the call for legal pluralism, the issue remains a live one. AFIC's original submission to government remains. Moreover, there is support and continuing articulation by other prominent Muslim lobby groups[26] and individuals[27] that formal recognition for some parts of Islamic law is necessary. How many of Australia's 500,000 or so Muslims support this is not known. What is advocated seems to range from 'everything',[28] to certain discreet aspects notably family and inheritance, banking, finance and commerce, (Saeed 2010: 231; Hussain 2010) to 'nothing' (Halim Rane quoted in Merritt 2011c).[29] Views are diverse and sometimes divisive amongst Muslims, just as amongst non-Muslims. The desire in the wider Australian society to be inclusive and to counter, or at least reduce, disaffection amongst some sectors of the Muslim community is widely accepted. Whether formal accommodation of some aspects of Sharia would achieve this is unclear; however, the issue of whether we can, or should, established Sharia Courts or Islamic arbitration tribunals remains in the public arena. It warrants consideration and attention by Muslim and non-Muslim Australians. A shift to a plural system based on religious affiliation would be a very significant change to Australia's existing system of law.

---

[25] He added that Australian law meets the higher objectives of Islamic law. See Merritt 2011c.

[26] Islamic Friendship Association, Australian Islamic Mission, Islamic Council of Western Australia, Sharia4Australia.

[27] Individuals include Kaysar Trad, Zachariah Matthews, Abdul Jalil Ahmad, Ibrahim Siddiq-Conlon, and Sheik Mohamadu Nawas Saleem. Also there are individual members of the Australian National Council of Imams and the imam of the mosque at Hoppers Crossing in the Melbourne. See Karvelas 2011b. Also for divorce, see Essof 2011.

[28] Sharia4Australia organization.

[29] See also El Matrah 2009 in which a women's perspective is given on a Sharia tribunal.

3. The Singapore Model of Mutual Respect.

Is Singapore's model of legal pluralism one that Australia could adopt and implement? Unlike neighbouring Brunei Darussalam and Malaysia, where Muslims are in the majority, both Singapore and Australia are democracies with a multi-ethnic population in which Muslims are a recognizable minority group, 3% in Australia, and 15% in Singapore. Both were former colonies of Great Britain and share the institutions and processes inherent in the common law tradition. Whilst the Singapore model has many positive attributes that will be outlined, it must be borne in mind that it is a product of different historical forces and operates within a distinctive cultural context; neither of which is replicated in Australia.

A proven track record

The significance of the Singapore model is that it is not experimental. It demonstrates that legal pluralism can have long-term viability for Muslim minorities within a common law setting. Singapore's current conjoint system of Syariah and common law courts has been in operation since 1958 when the Syariah Court was first established under the *Muslims' Ordinance 1957* (subsequently amended)[30] and which post- independence was replaced by the *Administration of Muslim Law Act 1966* (AMLA).[31] On becoming an independent, democratic Republic, Singapore recognized that its Muslim citizens should have their personal law administered separately from non-Muslims. This was a smooth continuation of the legally pluralistic colonial model employed by the English from the 1820s, which allowed separate legal orders for personal law (Leong 2007: 885-887)[32] for Singaporeans. Sir Stanford Raffles negotiated with Sultan Hussein Muhammad Shah[33] that for all cases involving Malays in ceremonies of religion, marriages and inheritance "the law and custom of the Malays will be respected" unless "contrary to reason, justice or humanity" (Abdul Rahman 2009: 109). This was formalized

[30] *Muslims (Amendment) Ordinance 1960*

[31] Act 27 of 1966, 2009 Rev. Ed. Laws of Singapore.

[32] The *Mohammedan Marriage Ordinance* of 1880 allowed for the establishment of Kathi Courts.

[33] Singapore was under the control of the Sultan of Johore, and Sultan Hussein was supported in that position by Raffles. On the founding of Singapore, see Tan 2011: 331.

in three ways. First, by legislation, notably the *Mohammadan Marriage Ordinance* of 1880, which in 1957 became the *Muslims' Ordinance*. Second, by establishing Islamic courts with jurisdiction over Muslims, which under the 1880 *Ordinance* were the Kathi/Kadi Courts and but were designated in 1955 as Syariah, courts of law. Third, in keeping with colonial bureaucratisation, separate administrative bodies were formed, notably the Mohammadan Advisory Board in 1915, which became the Muslim Advisory Board in 1946. It has been rightly put that by the time of independence in 1965, so entrenched was the right and practice for Muslims to adhere to Islamic law that AMLA was facilitating "rather than creating a new jurisprudence of law" (bin Abbas n.d.).

Religious affiliation continues to determine the applicable law and court system for Muslims and for non-Muslims in a range of family law, succession and others matters. The High Court of Singapore has no jurisdiction to hear matters that fall within the exclusive jurisdiction of the Syariah Court.[34] In family law matters, Singaporeans, other than Muslims, have been under the jurisdiction of the *Women's Charter.*[35] Article 3 of the *Charter* sets out that it is to regulate "all persons in Singapore" and "domiciled in Singapore" but excludes Muslims from its application for certain matters, namely, the "solemnization of marriage, the regulation of spouses, the unnatural termination of marriage and ancilliary powers of the court".[36] AMLA sets out areas of exclusive jurisdiction, which for family law matters are set out in s. 35(3). However, the details and substantive aspects of what is "Muslim law as varied where applicable by Malay custom" in each of these areas is frequently left to the discretion of the court and the Legal Committee of *Majlis Ugama Islam, Singapura* (MUIS). Section 35 directs the *Majlis* or the Legal Committee to consider the tenets of the Shafi'i school and for determining the Muslim law for issues of inheritance s. 114 AMLA sets out seven texts recommended to the court.[37]

---

[34] *Supreme Court of Judicature Act* Cap 322, 2009 Rev. Ed. Laws of Singapore, s. 17A(1).

[35] Cap 353, 2009 Rev. Ed. Laws of Singapore.

[36] Under s. 3(2); Parts II to VI and Part X and ss. 181-182.

[37] AMLA s. 114 (1):

> In deciding questions of succession and inheritance in the Muslim law, the court shall be at liberty to accept as proof of the Muslim law any definite statement on the Muslim law made in all or any of the following books: (*a*) The English translation of the

There is also a dual system for registering marriages. The Registry of Muslim Marriages (ROMM) has exclusive jurisdiction to register marriages where both parties are Muslim, and the Registry of Marriages (ROM) registers all other marriages for Singaporeans including marriage between a Muslim and a non-Muslim. The result is that marriages between a Muslim and *kitabiyah* woman fall under the jurisdiction of the civil ROM registry. In some schools of Islam, Hanafi for example, a marriage between a Muslim man and woman who is a *kitabiyah* (person of the Book)[38], which includes Christians and Jews is lawful, though it is generally regarded as undesirable.[39] However, the Shafi'i school, which is the dominant legal tradition in Singapore and Southeast Asia, has traditionally held a narrow interpretation of *kitabiyah* requiring the woman to be a descendant from a lineage that was Christian before the time of the Prophet Mohammad, or Jewish before the time of the Prophet Isa; a condition that is almost impossible to fulfill, so in practical terms amounts to a de facto not de jure prohibition.

Who is a Muslim for the purposes of the *Womens' Charter* and for the application of AMLA? Section 2 of the AMLA gives little guidance as it provides simply that a Muslim is "a person who professes the religion of Islam" and states the court's jurisdiction is for actions and proceedings in which "all the parties are Muslim or where the parties were married under the provisions of Muslim law".[40] There is acceptance that a child born to a Muslim parent is by birth Muslim, as is a person who formally converts to Islam. Although this does not frequently arise, jurisdiction can be relevant in cases of mixed religious marriages or in situations of conversion, whether into, or out of, Islam especially for marriage validity[41] and for

Quaran, by A. Yusuf Ali or Marmaduke Pickthall; (*b*)*Mohammedan Law*, by Syed Ameer Ali; (*c*) *Minhaj et Talibin* by Nawawi, translated by E. C. Howard from the French translation of Van den Berg; (*d*) *Digest of Moohummudan Law*, by Neil B. E. Baillie; (*e*) *Anglo-Muhammadan Law*, by Sir Roland Knyvet Wilson, 6th Edition Revised by A. Yusuf Ali; (*f*) *Outlines of Muhammadan Law*, by A. A. Fyzee; (*g*) *Muhammadan Law*, by F. B. Tyabji.

[38] The 'Book' refers to lawgivers in the Abrahamic tradition. See generally Mohamad 2008: 8.

[39] The Prophet married a Christian and also a Jewish woman.

[40] AMLA s. 35(2)

[41] *Noor Azizan bte Colony (alias Noor Azizan bte Mohammad Noor) v Tan Lip*

inheritance distribution[42] as the estate of a Muslim must be distributed in accordance with Islamic inheritance laws.[43] There are difference views as to whether it would be the Syariah Court or the Civil Court that would make such a determination and possibly it falls with the jurisdiction of either court. In a plural system where legal consequences and legal status flow from the Muslim designation it can be crucial. Apostasy, whilst a sensitive issue in Singapore, is lawful and does not have the legal ramifications as are found in Malaysia where an apostate can face not only legal difficulty converting out of Islam, but criminal sanctions and/or detention in Rehabilitation Centers.[44] Singapore does not require religious affiliation on its Registration Identity cards, just race, and as 'Malay' is not defined in the *Constitution* as a person of the Islamic religion, it is possible in Singapore to be racially and ethnically Malay but not be a Muslim.[45] For determinations on religious adherence, a person could take an oath[46] in the Syariah Court declaring before Almighty God that he or she was, or was not, a Muslim or a fatwa of the Legal Committee of MUIS obtained. Alternatively, in the civil law tradition a statutory declaration could be made before a Commissioner of Oaths. Essentially, in Singapore it is for the parties to decide who is a Muslim for the purposes of the *Womens' Charter* and for the application of AMLA.

Although Singaporeans have greater autonomy over religious affiliation than in neighbouring countries of Malaysia and Brunei, where apostasy is unlawful, the Singapore model does not allow a Muslim to opt out of the jurisdiction of the Syariah Court in matters where it has been exclusively given to the Syariah Court. This legal requirement is seen differently by Singaporeans. Non-Muslims tend to call it a 'concession' (Leong 2007: 891). Some Muslims describe it as an 'honour' or 'privilege' given only to Muslims, (bin Abbas 2012: 163) others as their 'obligation or duty', and some have the view that it is a restriction on their rights as Singaporeans, as it "restricts the freedom of the individual to decide the forum

Chin (alias Izak Tan) [2006] 3 *Singapore Law Reports,* 707.

[42] *Re Mohammad Said Nabi, decd* (1965) 31 *Malayan Law Journal,* 121.

[43] AMLA ss. 111 and 112.

[44] See generally, Dawson and Thiru 2007.

[45] Contrast with Malaysia where s. 160 of the *Constitution* of Malaysia defines a 'Malay' as a person who 'professes to be a Muslim, habitually speaks the Malay language, adheres to Malay customs, and is domiciled in Malaysia or Singapore'.

[46] An oath in Islam is a religious as well as legal procedure.

to hear" his or her dispute. This is because Muslims are prevented from having those exclusive personal status issues determined by the civil court even where a Muslim wishes it or perceives that he or she may have a more advantageous outcome or have it resolved more quickly. (Abdul Rahman 2006: 429).

The longevity of the two separate legal regimes shows that co-existence cannot only work but can stand the test of time. Jurisdictional conflict does occur and depending on your view is either minimal or "notoriously difficult to resolve" (Leong 2007: 918) but legal uncertainties are worked through. On the whole,[47] the model seems to have a high level of acceptance amongst Muslims and Singaporeans in general with AMLA and the Syariah system "cherished by the (Muslim) community" (Abdul Rahman 2009: 109). If its existence and accepted operation has been an avenue for social inclusion and harmonious relations between the Singapore's different religious and ethnic groups, it warrants consideration in Australia. Western nations in general, Australia included, are concerned about disaffection and alienation of some Muslim citizens, especially amongst young people, many of whom are second and third generation. As well, in particular suburbs of large cities where there is a high concentration of Muslims from the same ethnic group, alienation from the wider non-Muslim society and a distrust of Australian institutions is evident (Human Rights and Equal Opportunity Commission 2004: 83). If Singapore's form of legal pluralism sends a message of respect for Sharia that is inclusive and affirming, and allows minority values and aspirations to be recognized in a way that may help counter ethnic and religious tensions, then there is much to commend it. Similarly, if the constitutionally sanctioned operation of Syariah Courts demystifies Sharia and provides a face of Islam that is rational, adaptable, moderate and demonstrably able to co-exist with other value systems and legal processes, then it could go a long way in reducing distrust, misconceptions and the alarm which some sectors of Australia view both Islam as a religion, (Dunn 2005: 8) and Muslims as citizens (Poynting et al. 2004; Centre for Muslim Minorities and Islamic Policy Studies 2009: 6; Human Rights and Equal Opportunity Commission 2004: 45). Whilst it would be simplistic to conclude that the presence of the Syariah Court and MUIS alone has resulted in a 'harmonious' Singapore, the end result is one that appears to be based on 'mutual respect', a phrase used by a Singapore lawyer (bin Abbas n.d.) to describe Singapore's system of legal pluralism.

[47] Cf Bahrawi 2007. See also Ahmed 2010.

Relationship with the civil courts

The longevity of legal pluralism in Singapore has meant that the Syariah and civil courts have had to establish a working relationship. The jurisdiction of each is delineated with regular interaction between the two. For example, the Syariah Court lacks powers of enforcement, so its orders for maintenance, *mutaah*,[48] marriage expenses, custody, and property division are enforceable (s. 53) but not reviewable by the civil court. They are enforced as if they were orders of the District Court. There are also cases in which each court will play a distinct role. In distributing a Muslim's estate, the Islamic laws of inheritance are applied by the Syariah Court in order to issue an inheritance certificate (AMLA s. 115), but all grants for probate and letters of administration are issued by the civil courts.[49] Also disputes over the validity of wills are heard in the civil courts but where the deceased was a Muslim a fatwa from the MUIS can be obtained on its compliance with Islamic inheritance laws (AMLA s. 114). A shared arrangement also operates within family law matters. Whilst the Syariah Court has exclusive power to hear and make an order on divorce it does not have power to determine matters of spousal maintenance or whether a protection order should be issued. These must be remitted to the civil court. In some matters the courts have concurrent jurisdiction. Whilst a Muslim couple must have their divorce heard in the Syariah Court, applications for child custody, access and distribution of matrimonial property can be made to 'any court', which enables a Muslim party during or after divorce proceedings in the Syariah Court to make an ancillary application to the civil Family Court where the civil law will be applied.[50] AMLA requires this to be with the consent of the parties and with the leave of the Syariah Court (AMLA s. 35A).[51] Although adoptions fall under the jurisdiction of the civil family court[52] the Court takes into account Islamic principles on adoption, for example, to allow the child to keep the name of her birth parents and not that of the adoptive family (Abdul Rahman 2006: 416). It appears that the Syariah Court applies the civil law of evidence. Section 42 AMLA states that the court will follow "the law of

[48] Payment of compensation to a woman divorced without fault.

[49] *Probate and Administration Act*, Cap 215, 2009 Rev. Ed. Laws of Singapore.

[50] *Supreme Court of Judicature Act* , Cap 322, 2009 Rev. Ed. Laws of Singapore s. 17A(2)

[51] Also *Supreme Court of Judicature Act,* s. 17.

[52] *Adoption of Children Act*, Cap 4, and generally see bin Abbas 2012: 174.

evidence for the time being in force in Singapore, and shall be guided by the principles thereof, but shall not be obliged to apply the same strictly." Also, the Syariah Court can apply legal principles from the civil law system when the issue is one not covered in by Islamic law (bin Abbas 2012: 174). Conversely, the civil courts will take legal advice on matters of Islamic law from the Majlis (MUIS). Lastly, the criminal offences contained in AMLA Part IX which include religious offences such as failure to pay *zakat* (a tithe), cohabitation outside of marriage, enticing an unmarried woman away from her *wali* (male guardian, usually her father), and teaching false doctrines about Islam[53] are heard, determined and sentenced in the civil courts.

The effectiveness of the relationship between the two legal systems is generally assumed, with lawyers in Singapore reluctant to be critical in any way although the phrase "this is very sensitive" was frequently used when questions regarding effectiveness were broached. Ahmad Nizam Abbas reflects the common sentiment that the plural system is working for the benefit of Muslim Singaporeans and is evolving into a professional one that ensures fairness and justice for all concerned (bin Abbas 2012). Conversely, Leong Wai Kum sees the dual court system as "potentially problematic" in resolving family law disputes and that "apparent and real conflicts do crop up" which cannot be resolved by "reference to a simple separation" of jurisdiction of the two court systems. He feels that as such conflicts are "notoriously difficult" to resolve, he awaits "the eventual integration of the entire family law in Singapore to regulate all Singaporeans" (Leong 2007). Abdul Rahman also sees "significant problems" in the current system but does not favour cessation of the dual system for family law but rather advocates for jurisprudential and legislative reform of the Syariah system. The problems she outlines arise because the "substantive law on marriage, divorce and ancillary issues is not comprehensively codified" in AMLA, so the interpretation of Syariah resides with the judges of the court and with MUIS. She feels the initial spirit of the framers of AMLA, which was attuned to the contemporary needs of women has been eroded by traditionalism,[54] which is important when Muslims are restricted from accessing the civil forum (Abdul Rahman 2006: 416).

[53] AMLA ss. 137, 134, 135 and 139.

[54] Defined by Mannheim as a "dogmatic attitude that clings firmly to old ways, resisting innovations or accepting them only unwillingly", and by Towler as a "style of religious belief whose essence is to cherish the entire tradition received as sacred such that if any part is threatened or called into question, it is the whole pattern which is put at risk" (Abdul Rahman 2006: 416).

Constitutionally sanctioned

Singapore's *Constitution* was drafted to entrench a form of legal pluralism. It creates a special legal status for Muslims in recognition of the fact that the Malays are "the indigenous people of Singapore".[55] The *Constitution* also guarantees its citizens "equality before the law" and "equal protection", but s. 12(3) makes it clear these guarantees do not extend to the regulation personal law, which is under AMLA. Similarly the protection from discrimination on grounds of "religion, race, descent or place of birth in any law or in the appointment to any office" given in s. 12(2) does not extend to "provisions of an institution managed by a group professing any religion" or "to persons professing that religion", or to provisions "restricting office or employments connected with any affair of any religion." The operation of s. 12(3) is to allow judges, registrars, counselors and all personnel in the Syariah Courts system and in the *Majlis Ugama Islam, Singapura* (MUIS), to be appointed and funded by the government on exclusive religious lines. By contrast, the Australian *Constitution* makes it unconstitutional for any religious test to be required as a qualification for any office or public trust under the Commonwealth. That may prohibit any Australian government establishing and funding a *Syariah* Court or Arbitral Tribunal where a qualification for judicial or arbitral appointment to office, is a religious one. Whilst s. 116 does not bind the states, family law is now a matter under Commonwealth not state jurisdiction.

Professional and transparent

The ad hoc system in Australia where informal tribunals and certain Imams hold themselves out as possessing authority and knowledge to make legal decisions for Muslims based on their understanding of Islamic law is neither transparent nor professional. These legal determinations are done 'behind closed doors', just as occurs with the arbitral bodies in the English scheme. In contrast, Singapore's model is quite professional and is open to scrutiny. Trials and hearings are in open court[56] with the power given in s. 46(2) AMLA for the court, if it thinks fit, to hold part or all of the proceeding in camera. This power is frequently exercised.

---

[55] Art. 152 *Constitution of Singapore.*

[56] *Administration of Muslim Law Act* Cap. 3 2009 Rev. Ed. Laws of Singapore ss. 32(1), 46, with the power given in s. 46(2) for the court, if it thinks fit, to hold part or all of the proceeding in camera. This power is frequently exercised.

Although decisions are not formally reported and published, as they are in the common law courts, the Syariah Court does have an internal system of records, which are made available to the legal representatives of the parties. This has allowed an informal system of precedence to develop that facilitates consistency and predictability. Appeals are also possible. Decisions of both the Court and the Registrars can be taken on appeal to the Syariah Appeal Board.[57] This degree of transparency and an appellate review are two important safeguards lacking in Australia's informal system.[58] In an unofficial system, if a group of Islamic scholars or an individual claims to have knowledge and authority to make determination on marriage, inheritance, divorce, financial matters how can this be checked? When hearings take place in private, without lawyers, without transcripts, and when there is no avenue of appeal to a higher authority it is almost impossible to know if the reasoning and application of Syariah law is fair and accurate. As well, there can be different outcomes on the same issue. The Singapore model provides oversight of legal decision-making with the safeguard of an appeal process.

Whilst AMLA does not lay down specific qualifications for judicial appointment whether as President, Deputy President, ad hoc Presidents or for Kadis, nor for its Registrars,[59] in practice the individuals appointed to these positions have knowledge and experience in both Syariah law and the common law. There were discussions in 1997 at a Parliamentary Select Hearing on specifying qualifications for the Syariah Court appointments. I It was decided not to proscribe these, but rather to leave it to the government, through the Ministry of Community Development, Youth and Sport to make appointments based on jurisprudential credentials, an upright and pious character, leadership qualities and familiarity with the civil law processes in Singapore.[60] The later was seen as important because the Syariah Court interacts with the civil courts and should not be in a

[57] AMLA s. 55. The minimum number for the Appeal Board is seven. Currently there are 16 members: seven religious teachers, five district judges and four lawyers. Four of the members are women (bin Abbas 2012: 185).

[58] See Black 2008: 217.

[59] The Registrar is a relatively new position, which was deemed necessary to reduce the increasing administrative load of the Presidents and to provide a filtering mechanism to determine the complexities of cases and the allocation of resources.

[60] Personal communication.

religious bubble removed from other legal and social processes.[61] Appointments do not come with security of tenure but are akin to ones made by the Singapore Legal Service. This is different from High Court judges in the common law system, who do have security of tenure. Parties are entitled to legal representation "by advocate or solicitor or by an agent, generally or specially authorized to so by the Court."[62] This does not exclude non-Muslim lawyers. Ahmad Nizam Abbas notes that as there are no mandatory requirements or qualifications specified for legal counsel, the "motivation to equip oneself adequately" in Syariah law and procedure, lies with the individual lawyer to engage in self-study, attend courses and seek guidance from experienced practitioners (bin Abbas 2012: 181).

Jurisprudential Consistency

Consistency in interpretation of Syariah provides a measure of certainty and predictability in the application of Islamic law in Singapore. Again this is absent in the ad hoc unofficial system in Australia. Jurisprudential consistency comes not only from the courts and the supervisory role of the *Majlis Ugama Islam, Singapura* (MUIS) Appeal Board but also from the MUIS Legal Committee, which can issue fatwas (legal opinions on matters of Islamic law). Section 31 AMLA sets out the composition of the legal committee, namely "(a) the Mufti; (b) two other fit and proper members of the *Majlis*; and (c) not more than two other fit and proper Muslims who are not members of the *Majlis*." The Mufti of Singapore is the Chairman of the Committee and the Mufti and Committee members are appointed by the President of Singapore, with the advice of the *Majlis* for the other members.[63] In keeping with the tradition of *ifta* (the issuing of fatwas) in Islamic law, a question requiring a fatwa on any point of Islamic law can be asked by "any person",[64] or by a court of law, including the Syariah Court.[65] The Committee can

61 President Alfian Kuchit studied *Syariah* at the International Islamic University, Malaysia and has an LLM from Columbia University.

62 *Administration of Muslim Law Act* Cap 3 2009 Rev. Ed. Laws of Singapore ss.32(1), 39.

63 *Administration of Muslim Law Act* s. 30.

64 *Administration of Muslim Law Act* s. 32(1).

65 *Administration of Muslim Law Act* s. 32(8).

also "of its own motion" make and publish any ruling or determination.[66] The process involves making a draft ruling which if it is unanimously approved by the Legal Committee[67] will be issued by the *Majlis,* and if not unanimous, will be referred to the *Majlis* who will issue the fatwas in "accordance with the opinion of the majority of its members".[68] The goal of consistency is further promoted by s33 AMLA which requires both the *Majlis* and the Legal Committee to "ordinarily follow the tenets of the Shafi'i school of law, unless it is not in the public interest to do so."[69]

The role of the Legal Committee provides not only the Syariah Court with an authoritative source for interpretations of Sharia law but fulfills that role also for the civil courts. Unlike the Syariah Courts, the civil courts are not bound by any ruling of the Legal Committee, though the cases show consideration and general respect for the Committee's rulings.[70] That the civil courts have one entity to which they can turn for an Islamic law opinion is a valuable attribute of the Singaporean model. In Australia, who can qualify as an expert in matters of Islamic law can be problematic and has to be established each time to the satisfaction of the court.

On the MUIS website some of the important fatwas are published in either Malay, English, or both languages, and include legal rulings on finance and estate matters; zakat; family matters including family planning; the permissibility of certain medical advances including the stem cell research; organ donation and transplantation; bone marrow transplantation; abortion; advanced medical

[66] *Administration of Muslim Law Act* s. 32(6).

[67] *Administration of Muslim Law Act* s. 32(4) includes those members present and entitled to vote.

[68] *Administration of Muslim Law Act* s. 32(7).

[69] *Administration of Muslim Law Act* s. 33(1) with s. 33(2) stating that 'the tenets of any of the other accepted schools of Muslim law as may be considered appropriate' can be used in such rulings, but that 'the provisions and principles to be followed shall be set out in full detail and with all necessary explanations'. Rulings can also be made when specifically requested 'in accordance with the tenets of [another] particular school of Muslim law', see AMLA s. 33(3).

[70] *Saniah Binte Ali & Anors v Abdullah Bin Ali* [1990] 1 *Singapore Law Reports*, 555.

directives; the permissibility of using ethanol as a food additive; and whether a particular group engages in deviant teachings (on Islam). These questions would resonate with many Muslim Australians who also seek guidance in similar matters. The role fatwas fulfill in the Islamic system is not limited to Muslim countries or to ones like Singapore that apply Syariah law. Fatwas are equally, if not, more important in countries like Australia with a preponderance of immigrants, rather than a long settled Muslim population. In order to accommodate Islamic religious requirements within a secular framework, fatwas are of particular significance for Australian Muslims (Black and Hosen 2009a; Black and Hosen 2009b). They facilitate social and cultural transformations, at a personal, individual and private level. Alexandre Caeiro's (2010) research in Europe found the demand for fatwas in the West appears greater than in Islamic countries. He argues this is because there is a discontinuation in the transmission of Islamic knowledge, which increases the need to find ways to adapt Islamic law for western context and allows women to find "elaborate strategies of survival" for the different normative orders (Caeiro 2010).

Without an equivalent of Singapore's MUIS Legal Committee or a government appointed Mufti, there can be confusion and inconsistency in the legal opinions provided, or alternatively, a plethora of views, which reflects the voluntary nature of *ifta* as a tradition and the diversity within the Australian Islamic community. Muslims in Australia turn to a range of sources for fatwas: to national organizations such as the Australian Federation of Islamic Council (AFIC), the Darulfatwa Islamic High Council, or the National Council of Imams (ANIC); to state organizations including state Islamic Councils and local *majlis ulama*; to local Sheikhs or an Imam at their mosque; or to a scholar or organization in their country of origin; and last, but importantly to the Internet's many online fatwa sites (Black and Hosen 2009a). The process of searching Islamic websites for religious rulings has been called 'fatwa shopping', or surfing the 'inter-madhab net' (Yilmaz 2005: 39). Potentially, it opens all sorts of new, alternative and diverse interpretations of Islam alongside the more traditional versions. Australian Muslims are big users of such services with the au (Australia) domain for just one site *Islam Q&A* well over a million and seventh out of 128 nations (after Saudi Arabia, the United Kingdom, France, the Netherlands and the United States).Whilst this might seem democratic there is also the concern that providing wide divergent views on what is *halal* (permitted) and what is *haram* (forbidden) could lead to information anarchy (Black and Hosen 2009a: 421). In the context of on-line use almost anyone can set themselves up as an authority and issue legal opinions. The practice of asking foreign Islamic websites[71] (not Australian ones) can also be problematic, as foreign Muslim scholars who answer the questions may not understand life in Australia. If the question closely relates to life and social interaction in Australia, the answer might not be contextually suitable.[72] Of course, Singapore's Muslims can also go on-line to surf the 'inter-madhab' net, but the presence of a national *ifta* body is a stabilising and unifying force.

Australia does have a Grand Mufti but *ifta* has not been undertaken in any public or open sense. Traditionally, and as occurs in Singapore, the Mufti is a religious authority to provide guidance and religious leadership where the majority of Muslims are of the same *madhab*, ethnicity and cultural background. Australia's diversity makes this very difficult. The Grand Mufti of Australia is not appointed by the government, but is elected by just one of Australia's several national organizations, once AFIC, but now, ANIC. The Grand Mufti therefore cannot speak on behalf of all Muslims, just the one representative body (Kilani 2011). In practice the position has been quite divisive. The first Mufti (1989-2006) was Egyptian born Sheikh Taj Din al-Hilali who proved to be a controversial figure in part because of inappropriate statements and actions.[73] The third[74] and current

---

[71] *Islam on-line*, based in Doha, Qatar with fatwas issued by a committee of scholars headed by Dr. Yusuf Qardawi.
<http://www.islamonline.net/livefatwa/english/select.asp>; *islamtoday*, based in Saudi Arabia with fatwas issued by committee of scholars supervised by Sheikh Salman bin Fahd al-Oadah.
<http://www.islamtoday.com/fatwa archive main.cfm>; *Ask the Imam,* South African site with fatwas issued by Mufti Ebrahim Desai, <http://islam.tc/ask-imam/index.php>; *Islam Q&A*, based in Saudi Arabia with fatwas issued under supervision of Shaykh Muhammad Saalih al-Munajjid ,
<http://63.175.194.25/index.php?ln=eng>; *Fatwa on-line*, Saudi Arabian site designed to give English speaking Muslims access to translations of officially published Arabic fatwas, <http://www.fatwa-online.com/>.

[72] An example given is the issue of saying 'Merry Christmas'. In Australia this is a cultural practice to mark the season not a religious observation or one identifying a theological battle between Islam and Christian. Overseas online websites routinely forbid it, for example, the Indonesian website, Syariah Online,
<http://www.syariahonline.com/new index.php/id/1/cn/24458> strongly forbids it as does, Islam Q&A, http://www.islam-qa.com/en/ref/947/Christmas.>

[73] For example, his sermons claiming women invite rape by the way they dress (with the uncovered meat for cats analogy); that women were Satan's messages

Grand Mufti, Dr Ibrahim Abu Muhammad, elected in 2011 by ANIC, is another Egyptian born scholar who has lived in Australia for two decades. However, like al-Hilali he does not speak English and relies on a translator for interviews and interaction with the wider community, Muslim and non-Muslim. Over one third of Australian Muslims are born in Australia and there is a growing number who only speak English. Although a highly respected scholar, his publications are in Arabic not in English. Such concerns over communication, authority and consistency in jurisprudence do not arise in the Singapore model.

4. Importing the Singapore Model to Australia

The legal pluralism model that operates in Singapore is an accepted part of the island's legal landscape - one that links back to the Raffles' era and the nation's founding. The resistance to enacting a similar scheme into Australia is essentially for the same reason that the Singapore model is accepted and works well in Singapore. Australia's 'one law for all' model is well entrenched and has garnished considerable respect, trust and allegiance. Although it is not without strong critics,[75] it has broad acceptance as an inclusive system in which no one is refused access on grounds of race or religion. The concept that adherents of one faith tradition could be required to go to a separate system of religious courts, Sharia courts, for personal status matters as happens in Singapore, runs counter to the established ethos of Australia and also counter to a cultural preference for secularism over religiosity,[76] and a long standing distrust of sectarianism. Whilst the plural system does embody the tradition and character of Singapore it does not reflect Australia's tradition and culture. There are philosophical, legal and

sent to deceive men; endorsement of the September 11 terrorist attacks; and calls for a jihad against Israel, a meeting with Hezbollah, a prescribed organization under Australian law; claims on Egyptian television that there was no freedom or democracy for Muslims in Australia and that English people are the most unjust and dishonest in the world especially Australians who came to Australia 'in chains'. See The Age 2006; Zwartz 2007.

[74] Imam Fehmi Naji El-lmam was in poor health for some time and stood down for that reason.

[75] As noted earlier in Part II – 'The Australian Context'.

[76] The pervasiveness and quality of secularism in Australia is explored by Bouma et al. 2010: 4-14.

practical arguments that mitigate against a formal Singapore–style model of legal pluralism.

Philosophical objections

A plural system with two streams of courts with concurrent jurisdiction based on religious affiliation, undermines something quite culturally entrenched in Australia. At Federation in 1900 when the colonies of Britain united to form the Commonwealth of Australia, and Christians made up over 95% of the population, the *Constitution* did not establish a state religion, opting instead for a de-establishment provision. At that time many people who came to start their lives afresh in a new nation did so because of religious and sectarian strife particularly in Europe and Great Britain. Unlike the 'pilgrim fathers' in America, the free settlers did not come to Australia to ensure their religion thrived, but rather to avoid the consequences that they had seen and experienced in the distrust and hatred arising from different beliefs in God. Anti-sectarianism informed Australia's secularism, in which there was always a space for the practice of religion.[77] This sentiment continues as many recent Muslim immigrants to Australia left their homeland, some as refugees, others voluntarily, because of similar kinds of religious intolerance arising from state preference for one sect over another, which manifests in disadvantage, even brutality and civil war along sectarian lines. Any assumption that the majority of Muslim Australians would want to go down a sectarian preference route or a form of differentiation by which they were treated differently from other Australians by being required to go to Syariah Courts to have a religious system of personal status law applied, rather than the family law of Australia, is likely to be false. The lesson from Ontario Canada's failed experiment of legislating for faith-based arbitration which would have allowed Muslims access to Sharia arbitration for family law matters (Black 2008: 215)[78] cautions against any assumption that most Muslims, particularly Muslim women, want this. The Director of the Islamic Women's Council of Victoria, Joumanah El Matrah, echoed similar sentiments. She argued:

> As Muslims, it is entirely bewildering that our concept, our cultural or religious recognition is now measured by the extent to

[77] These views are expanded by Voyce and Possamai 2011: 339, 343.

[78] Canadian Muslim women effectively argued that they wanted the same rights under the *Charter* as applied to every other Canadian.

> which the government is prepared to set us apart from the rest of Australian society. The legal ghettoization of Muslims does not recognize their difference: it would simply allow a government to delegate its responsibility for ensuring the rights and protection of people who are different. Essentially, it would be a government prepared to outsource and privatize justice and the protection of women. Establishing parallel system for Muslims does not ensure a culturally appropriate response to justice: it fundamentally locks out Muslims from services they as citizens have a right to access. (El Matrah 2009.)

However, it is equally clear as noted earlier, that there are Muslim spokespersons and representatives who believe that the 'one law for all' model is unfair and exclusionary. Formalisation of Sharia is advocated as a right that should come with citizenship in a liberal democracy (Ali 2011: 367). AFIC, for example, argued in its submission to government that in not recognizing Sharia law and in not allowing for Sharia Courts to be established, the Australian government is treating Muslims as 'second class' citizens.[79] This argument of exclusion is difficult to sustain because no religion has its body of law accorded legal recognition or is given preferential treatment. Islam receives preference in Singapore on the basis that Muslim Malays are the indigenous peoples of Singapore, but the spiritual traditions of Aboriginal and Torres Strait Islanders, the indigenous peoples of Australia, do not receive similar priority, nor does Christianity as the religion of the majority. El Matrah rejects the frequently made comparison equating the rights of indigenous Australians with those of Muslim Australians as 'unethical.' She writes that Muslims were "part of the process that dispossessed indigenous Australians" so indigenous entitlements are beyond "anything a migrant community should appropriately expect" (El Matrah 2009). In Australia's secular system, each and every religious and spiritual tradition can ensure their adherents apply the religious law and follow the practices of their religion, in so far as they do not transgress national or state law. Places of worship can be established, religious schools set up with government funding and assistance, (Bouma et al. 2010) counseling and community services provided on religious lines; radio stations and newspapers can be run by religious bodies for their followers; burial places will have sections for religious and ethnic groups; religious observances, in terms of prayer times and holy days are allowed under industrial relations and anti-discrimination legislation. In Australia, you can wear hijab, dishdasha, a Sikh

[79] See outline of the key arguments summarised above.

turban, tallit, nun's and monk's robes (Buddhist or Christian) mini-skirts or shorts; you can change religion, you can proselytize, you can contest the ideas of religion itself or challenge one in particular, and even make fun of religion. Jokes involving priests and rabbis abound. More importantly religious tribunals, or individuals depending on the faith tradition, can make decrees and rulings to bind their own adherents - who you can marry, whether your marriage has dissolved, what foods you eat, what amount of money you are required to give to your religious body, how you should dress and conduct relations with others. The state will not interfere, unless there is contravention of a law of Australia. Nor will the state fund your religious entity although a range of taxation benefits and other legal exemptions may be given. That has been the accepted position.

Legal obstacles

Provisions within the Australian *Constitution,* as noted earlier, create a significant roadblock to implementing a plural regime based on religious affiliation. Whilst it would be theoretically possible to amend the *Constitution* of Australia, this is a herculean task requiring a referendum in which the majority of Australians and the majority of voters in the majority of states support the change. Rarely are referenda successful. Just eight out of 44 referenda have succeeded and political consensus for the change is essential. A contentious issue such as legal pluralism along Singapore lines would be most unlikely to succeed.

Another constitutional issue is the de-establishment requirements in s. 116. This does not allow for one religion to be preferred over another, unlike s. 153 of the Singapore *Constitution* which provides that the legislature can make laws "regulating Muslim religious affairs and for constituting a Council to advise the President in matters relating to the Muslim religion", the Australian government has no such authority. Whilst the Australian and State governments can, and do, have advisory bodies, such as the Muslim Community Reference Group (MCRG) set up by the Howard government in 2005 (Muslim Community Reference Group 2006) and the government funded National Centre of Excellence in Islamic Studies[80] to train Islamic scholars and Imams in Australia, the regulation and

80 The National Centre for Excellence in Islamic Studies as a means to train Australian Imams was an initiative of the Howard government and was set up in 2007 during the time of the Rudd government. This training objective was eventually considered impractical within the Australian university environment. The Centre's federal funding ended in 2011.

establishment of an equivalent entity to MUIS for adherents of one religion would be unconstitutional.

Practical obstacles

Unlike Singapore where its Muslim minority shares the same Malay ethnicity and thus the same Malay language, culture, values and practices, Australia's Muslim population reflects the cultural diversity found across the Muslim world. Of course Muslims in Australia are united by a shared belief in Islam and identify with the concept of *ummah,* a worldwide community of believers, but as the Muslim diaspora in Australia has its origins in 80 different nations and today represents 50 different ethnicities and cultures, and speaks a variety of languages in addition to English, (now the first language of the 30%-40% born in Australia) it personifies the breadth of Australian multiculturalism. Some Muslims are descendants of 19th century settlers, others have recently arrived as immigrants or as refugees, some have fled repressive regimes whilst others have come for economic and family reasons retaining close attachments to their country of origin, some have come from Muslim monocultures, others from nations with religious and ethnic pluralism, (Ali 2011: 361) and there is also a growing number of local converts to Islam. This diversity supports the notion of 'Islams' rather than one Islam (Al-Azmeh 2009; Glenn 2004: 203; Black 2008). This is quite different to Singapore's relative homogeneity of the Malays, Sunni tradition, and Shafi'i school of law. Shafi'i has been dominant school of thought for centuries and continues to inform the jurisprudence of MUIS (AMLA s. 33) and the Syariah Court. Unlike Singapore, where 'traditionalism' has been the hallmark of its jurisprudence and court decisions,[81] Australia's eclectic Muslim population holds diverse jurisprudential and doctrinal allegiances ranging from "liberal, progressive, modernist, reformist, secular at one end through to moderate, traditional, orthodox in the mid-range and to conservative, extremist, radical, literalist, neo-revivalist or fundamentalist at the other end" (Black and Sadiq 2011: 386).

Given this pluralistic context, a formalised and officially recognised Syariah Court system in Australian would face practical obstacles in terms of the jurisprudence to be applied, the interpretative approach adopted, the persons entrusted with the role

[81] Traditionalism is discussed earlier in III. Also it has been defined as 'a dogmatic attitude that clings firmly to old ways, resisting innovations or accepting them only unwittingly'. See Abdul Rahman 2006: 416.

of adjudication, and how oversight and enforcement would occur. Such a court would need some degree of interpretative consistency. In Singapore, there is consistency as the "ordinarily the tenets of Shafi'i school" apply.[82] But which school of law should ordinarily apply in Australia - the one with the majority of followers, which would be Hanafi, or the one of the region, which would be Shafi'i, or should a Sharia Court just apply whatever the parties claim as their personal status law? This is not an issue that is unique to Australia, and scholars such as Yilmaz writing in the United Kingdom submit that a reformulated or composite form of Islam can emerge in Western and secular countries. Doctrinal difference can be overcome by using techniques such as *takhayyur* (Haj 2009: 150-151; Yilmaz 2003b; Muslim Arbitration Tribunal 2008) and *talfiq*. *Takhayyur* is selecting one juristic opinion irrespective of the school because it resolves an issue more fairly. It was a right given to an individual but in recent times has been used in Muslim countries legislating reforms particularly in family law.[83] *Talfiq* (meaning patchwork) allows various opinions to be combined to form a single new ruling. The resulting juristic fusion labelled *neo-ijtihad* could allow for a new form of Australian Islam to emerge, which attains unity from the current heterogeneity and divisions. This may be a laudable goal, however, it will take time and there are no guarantees as to what *neo-ijtihad* will produce. Whether the result is a traditionalist or a modernist interpretation of Islam will depend on who engages in the process. Which Australian scholars or which entity could assume authority for the collective *ijtihad* needed for an 'Australian Islam'? It would be more difficult than in England where there is a dominant ethnicity (South Asian) and school of law (Hanafi) and a concentrated Muslim community. Authority within the Islamic community in Australia is already factionalised and complex, marred by dissention and acrimonious disputes on leadership (Black and Hosen 2009a 415-416). With a

[82] AMLA specifies at s. 33(1) that 'the Majlis and the Legal Committee in issuing any ruling shall ordinarily follow the tenets of the Shafi'i school of law' unless that is contrary to public interest. In such situations the AMLA s. 33(2) provides that:

> the Majlis may follow the tenets of any of the other accepted schools of Muslim law as may be considered appropriate, but in any such ruling the provisions and principles to be followed shall be set out in full detail and with all necessary explanations.

[83] An example is in Malaysia where more extensive Maliki school grounds for fault (*fasakh*) divorce rather than restricted Shafi'i ones were adopted. See the *Family Law (Federal Territories) Act*, 1984, which has 12 grounds specified. This was done on the basis of *maslaha* (public interest).

range of representative bodies,[84] who speaks with collective authority and for whom on issues of Islam in Australia can be readily contrasted with Singapore where the one organisation, the MUIS, fulfils this role. However, whilst consensus of this type is necessary for court adjudications, a plurality of views and competing juristic visions can equally be seen as a healthy indication of freedom of religion and expression in a vibrant democracy.

5. Conclusion

Although Sharia is not recognised as a formal source of law in Australia and Muslims have made little headway in the quest for an official and government funded system of Sharia Courts,[85] legal pluralism does still operate in Australia but in the unofficial, informal and extra-judicial sphere. In this way, Muslims in Australia have the freedom to live their lives in accordance with Sharia, in so far as following a religious precept does not violate a law of Australia.[86] Or as Ali (2011: 371) points out, "a vast majority of Muslims don't pursue lives based on Shari'a" but are "beholden to multiple identities." A Muslim couple can marry according to Islamic law and have a valid *nikkah* which is also registered in accordance with the *Marriage Act 1961* (Cth).[87] Or they can choose just the Islamic marriage and not have it registered, or bypass a religious ceremony in favour of a secular one. Furthermore, they can cohabit without marriage

[84] For example, Australian Federation of Islamic Councils (AFIC), the Darulfatwa Islamic High Council, and National Council of Imams (ANIC), the Islamic Association of Australia; and a variety of state organizations including each of the state Islamic Councils and local *majlis ulama*, Imams, Sheiks. As well there a various Islamic Societies and Associations designed on ethnic lines. On the growth Islamic organisations and also ones with connections to international movements, such as *Al-Ikhwan al-Muslimum*: the Muslim Brotherhood, see Ali 2011: 363-365.

[85] In March 2012, Attorney General Nicola Roxon stated that: "there is no place for sharia law in Australian society and the government strongly rejects any proposal for its introduction, including in relation to wills and succession", (Karvellas 2012).

[86] For example, contracting an under age marriage or facilitating a forced marriage violates Australian law.

[87] Providing the ceremony was performed by a recognised marriage celebrant. Many Imams are recognized as celebrants.

altogether. Australian Muslims have choices, ones not available to a Muslim couple in Singapore who must solemnize their marriage according to Islamic law (Part IV AMLA), register it with the separate registering body for Muslims,[88] and risk criminal sanction if they were to live together without marrying. It is a criminal offence under AMLA for a Muslim to cohabit and live with a person outside of a registered Islamic marriage (AMLA s. 134[89]). Muslims in Australia are afforded the same relationship choices as are adherents of the other religions.

Whilst the Singapore model of constitutionally sanctioned legal pluralism manifested by the Syariah Court, a separate registration body, the Majlis (MUIS) with a Mufti and Legal Committee, has become a benchmark for other common law jurisdictions with Muslim minorities it is not one that could be readily or realistically replicated in the Australian context. The historical, cultural, demographic, sociological and legal settings mitigate against any similar entity being established in the near future. Crucial in this assessment is the difference between indigenous Malay homogeneity and the heterogeneity of Muslim Australia. It is accepted that for most Muslims Islam remains central to their identity in Australia, but that Muslim identity, for the reasons outlined above, is conceived in multifarious ways. One of larger immigrant communities in Australia is from Turkey,[90] a secular Muslim nation which does not have Sharia Courts. Since its founding as a secular Republic in 1923, Turks have resolved their

[88] Registrar of Muslim Marriages (ROMM) AMLA Part VI.

[89] AMLA s. 134 provides:

> (1) Any man who cohabits and lives with a woman, whether a Muslim or not, to whom he is not lawfully married, shall be guilty of an offence and shall be liable on conviction to a fine not exceeding $500 or to imprisonment for a term not exceeding 6 months or to both.
>
> (2) Any woman who cohabits and lives with a man, whether a Muslim or not, to whom she is not lawfully married, shall be guilty of an offence and shall be liable on conviction to a fine not exceeding $500 or to imprisonment for a term not exceeding 6 months or to both.

[90] Countries of birth data from ABA Census of Population and Housing 2006 shows that Lebanon has 8.9%, Turkey 6.8%, Afghanistan 4.7%, Pakistan 4.1% of the Australian Muslim population.

personal status matters quite differently from their fellow Muslim neighbours in Iraq, Iran and Syria and yet this does not make Turks 'lesser Muslims'. The same is true in Australia. The voluntary as opposed to mandatory application of Islamic law, allows Australian Muslims the choice, not only to follow a particular school of law, or to employ *takhyyur*, but to follow an interpretation of Islam that personally resonates. Progressive or liberal Muslims who accept modernist interpretations can follow that path, whilst traditionalist or textualist Muslims can adhere to the conservative perspective. This increases the internal pluralism in Australia. To give one institution a monopoly over interpretation and administration of Islam and Syariah law, as occurs in Singapore, would be counter-intuitive in Australia.

References

ABC NEWS ONLINE

2011 'Call for parts of Sharia law in Australia.' *ABC New Online*. 8 March 2011. http://www.abc.net.au/news/2010-03-08/call-for-parts-of-sharia-law-in-australia/354906. Last accessed 20 June 2012.

ABDUL RAHMAN, Noor Aisha Bte

2006 'Traditionalism and its impact on the administration of justice: the case of the Syariah court of Singapore' *Inter-Asia Cultural Studies* 5(3): 415-432.

2009 'Muslim personal law within the Singapore legal system: history, prospects and challenges.' *Journal of Muslim Minority Affairs* 29(1): 109-126.

AFIC (AUSTRALIAN FEDERATION OF ISLAMIC COUNCILS)

2011 'Embracing Australian values, and maintaining the rights to be different', Submission no. 81 to the Australian Parliament joint Standing Committee on Migration, 4 April.

AHMED, Imran

2010 *'Singapore's Islamic law and the inheritance imbroglio'*. The Grand Moofti Speaks. *9 April 2010. http://imranwrites.blogspot.com/2010/04/singapores-islamic-law-and-inheritance.html. Last accessed 20 June, 2012.*

AL-AZMEH, Aziz

2009 *Islams and Modernities*. London: Verso.

ALI, Jan A.

2011 'A dual legal system in Australia: the formalization of Shari'a.' *Democracy and Security* 7(4): 354-373.

ARSHAD, Raffia
2010 *Islamic Family Law*. London: Sweet and Maxwell.
AUSTRALIAN LAW REFORM COMMISSION
1986 *Recognition of Aboriginal Customary Laws,* ALRC Report 31. Canberra: AGPS.
BANO, Samia
2007 'Muslim family justice and human rights: the experience of British Muslim women.' *Journal of Comparative Law* 1(4): 1- 30
BAHRAWI, Nazry
2007 'Singapore: Can a woman head a Muslim household? *Women Living under Muslim Laws.* 18 August 2007. <http://www.wluml.org/node/4009>. Last accessed 20 June 2012.
BIN ABBAS, Ahmad Nizam
2012 'The Islamic legal system in Singapore.' *Pacific Rim Law and Policy Journal* 21(1): 163-187.
2011 'Overview of Islamic Judicial Structure in Singapore.' Unpublished.
BLACK, Ann
2008 'Accommodating Shariah law in Australia's legal system.' *Alternative Law Journal* 33(4): 214-219.
2010 'In the shadow of our legal system: Shari'a in Australia.' Pp. 239 -254 in Rex Ahdar and Nicholas Aroney (eds.), *Shari'a in the West.* Oxford: Oxford University Press.
BLACK, Ann and Nadirsyah HOSEN
2009a 'Fatwas: their role in contemporary secular Australia.' *Griffith Law Review* 18(2): 405-427.
2009b 'Fatwas and surgery: how and why a fatwa may inform a Muslim patient's surgical options' *Australian and New Zealand Journal of Surgery* 79(12): 866-871.
BLACK, Ann and Kerrie SADIQ
2011 'Good and bad Sharia: Australia's mixed response to Islamic law.' *UNSW Law Journal* 17(1): 383-412.
BOUMA, Gary D, Rod LING and Douglas PRATT
2010 *Religious Diversity in Southeast Asia and the Pacific.* Dordrecht: Springer.
BOYD, Marion
2004 *Dispute Resolution in Family Law: Protecting Choice, Promoting Inclusion.* Report to the Attorney-General of Ontario. http://www.attorneygeneral.jus.gov.on.ca/english/about/pubs/boyd/fullreport.pdf. Last accessed 21 June 2012.

BOWEN, Chris
2011 'The genius of Australian Multiculturalism.' Address to the Sydney Institute. 17 February 2011. http://www.minister.immi.gov.au/media/cb/2011/cb159251.htm. Last accessed 20 June 2012.

CAEIRO, Alexandre
2010 'Transnational ulama, European fatwas, and Islamic authority: a case study of the European Council for Fatwa and Research.' Pp. 121-141 in Stefano Allievi and Martin van Bruinessen (eds.), *Producing Islamic Knowledge: Transmission and Dissemination in Western Europe*. New York: Routledge.

CENTRE FOR MUSLIM MINORITIES AND ISLAM POLICY STUDIES
2009 'Muslim voices: hopes & aspirations of Muslim Australians.' *Department of Immigration and Citizenship*. http://www.immi.gov.au/living-in-australia/a-multicultural-australia/national-action-plan/_attach/muslim-voices-report.pdf. Last accessed 20 June 2012.

DAWSON, Benjamin and Steven THIRU
2007 'The Lina Joy case and the future of religious freedom in Malaysia.' *LAWASIA Journal* 2007: 151-162.

DEPARTMENT OF IMMIGRATION AND CITIZENSHIP
2011 *The People of Australia – Australia's Multicultural Policy*. http://www.immi.gov.au/living-in-australia/a-multicultural-australia/multicultural-policy. Last accessed 20 June 2012.

DEVINE, Miranda
2011 'Quest for Sharia law out of line.' *Herald Sun*. 19 May 2011. <http://www.heraldsun.com.au/opinion/quest-for-sharia-law-is-out-of-line/story-e6frfhqf-1226058532543>. Last accessed 20 June 2012.

DUNN Kevin
2005 'Australian public knowledge of Islam.' *Indonesian Journal for Islamic Studies (Studia Islamika)* 12: 1-32.

EL MATRAH, Joumanah
2009 'A Sharia tribunal is a contradiction of Islam.' *The Age*. 20 October 2009. <http://www.smh.com.au/opinion/society-and-culture/a-sharia-tribunal-is-contradiction-of-islam-20091020-h59c.html. Last accessed 20 June 2012.

ESSOF, Ismail
2011 'Divorce in Australia from an Islamic law perspective.' *Alternative Law Journal* 36(3): 182-186.

FAMILY LAW COUNCIL OF AUSTRALIA
2001 *Report on Cultural Community Divorce and the Family Law Act 1975: A*

Proposal to Clarify the Law. Report to the Attorney-General. < http://www.ag.gov.au/Documents/7000Cultural-Community%20 Divorce.pdf. Last accessed 20 June 2012.

GLENN, H. Patrick
2004 *Legal Traditions of the World.* 2nd edition, Oxford: Oxford University Press.

HAJ, Samira
2009 *Reconfiguring Islamic Tradition: Reform, Rationality, and Modernity.* Stanford: Stanford University Press.

HALLAQ, Wael B.
2009 *Introduction to Islamic Law.* Cambridge: Cambridge University Press.

HENNESSY, Annette
2007 'Rights of indigenous Australians – Queensland Murri court.' *Law Council of Australia, Rule of Law Conference.* http://www.lawcouncil.asn.au/fms/speeches/Rule%20of%20Law/Session %205%20Annette%20Hennessy.pdf. Last accessed 20 June 2012.

HOLE, Jacquelyn
2011 'Muslim Group want Sharia in Australia.' *ABC News Online.* 17 May 2011. http://www.abc.net.au/news/2011-05-17/muslim-group-wants-sharia-law-in-australia/2717096. Last accessed 20 June 2012.

HUMAN RIGHTS AND EQUAL OPPORTUNITY COMMISSION
2004 *ISMA - Listen: National Consultations on Eliminating Prejudice against Arab and Muslim Australians.* http://www.hreoc.gov.au/racial_discrimination/isma/report/pdf/isma_com plete.pdf. Last accessed 20 June 2012.

HUSSAIN, Jamila
2004 *Islam: Its Law and Society.* 2nd edition, Leichhardt: Federation Press.
2010 'More than one law for all: legal pluralism in Australia?' Paper presented at Fifteenth Annual Public Law Weekend, The Centre for International and Public Law, Australian National University, 4 September 2010. <http://law.anu.edu.au/cipl/Conferences&SawerLecture/2010/Hussain.p df. Last accessed 20 June 2012.

IBRAHIM, Heba
2011 'Multiculturalism and the Australian Muslim community: submission no. 341.' *The Australian Federation of Islamic Councils.*

ISLAMIC COUNCIL OF VICTORIA
2011 *Inquiry into Multiculturalism in Australia from the Islamic Council of Victoria,* Submission no. 81 to the Australian Parliament Joint Standing Committee on Migration, 11 March.

KERVALAS, Patricia

2011a 'Muslims to push for Sharia Law.' *The Australian*. 17 May 2011. http://www.theaustralian.com.au/national-affairs/muslims-use-multiculturalism-to-push-for-sharia/story-fn59niix-1226057100331. Last accessed 20 June 2012.

2011b 'Imam wants Sharia law here, but A-G says no way.' *The Australian. 18* May 2011. http://www.theaustralian.com.au/national-affairs/imam-wants-sharia-law-here-but-a-g-says-no-way/story-fn59niix-1226057823890. Last accessed 20 June 2012.

2012 'Roxon baulks at role for Sharia by Australian Muslims.' *The Australian*. 17 March 2012. http://www.theaustralian.com.au/national-affairs/roxon-baulks-at-role-for-sharia-by-australian-muslims/story-fn59niix-1226302118960. Last accessed 20 June 2012.

KILANI, Ahmed

2011 'Australian imams appoint a new mufti.' *Muslim Village*. 19 September 2011. http://muslimvillage.com/2011/09/19/australian-imams-appoint-a-new-mufti/. Last accessed 20 June 2012.

LAW COMMISSION

1972 *Report of jurisdiction in matrimonial causes*. Law Com. No.48. http://www.official-documents.gov.uk/document/hc5152/hc04/0464/0464.pdf. Last accessed 20 June 2012.

LAW REFORM COMMISSION OF WESTERN AUSTRALIA

2006 *Aboriginal Customary Laws*. Perth: Quality Press. <http://www.lrc.justice.wa.gov.au/2publications/reports/ACL/FR/Forepages.pdf>. Last accessed 20 June 2012.

LEONG, Wai Kum

2007 *Elements of Family law in Singapore*. Singapore: LexisNexis.

MERRITT, Chris

2011a 'It was a mistake to mention Sharia, admits Australian Islamic leader.' *The Australian*. 17 May, 2011. http://www.theaustralian.com.au/business/legal-affairs/it-was-a-mistake-to-mention-sharia-law-admits-australian-islamic-leader/story-e6frg97x-1226076664279. Last accessed 20 June 2012.

2011b 'No place in legal system for Sharia: Jim Speglman.' *The Australian*. 2 June 2011. http://www.theaustralian.com.au/business/legal-affairs/no-place-in-legal-system-for-sharia-spigelman/story-e6frg97x-1226067487968. Last accessed 20 June 2012.

2011c 'Debate on Shari'a a sign of a healthy democracy.' *The Australian*. 3 June, 2011. http://www.theaustralian.com.au/business/legal-affairs/debate-on-sharia-law-sign-of-healthy-democracy/story-e6frg97x-

1226068250656. Last accessed 20 June 2012.
2011d 'Sharia push surprises Muslim bodies.' *Hizb ut-Tahrir Australia*. 8 June 2011. http://archive.hizb-australia.org/local/3719-sharia-push-surprises-muslim-bodies. Last accessed 20 June 2012.

MOHAMAD, Maznah
2008 'Islam and family legal contests in Malaysia: hegemonizing ethnic over gender and civil rights.' Asia Research Institute Working Paper series no.109. Singapore: Asia Research Institute, National University of Singapore.

MUSLIM ARBITRATION TRIBUNAL
2008 *Family Dispute Cases*. http://www.matribunal.com/cases faimly.html. Last accessed 20 June 2012.

MUSLIM COMMUNITY REFERENCE GROUP
2006 'Building on Social Cohesion, Harmony and Security.' *Department of Immigration and Citizenship*. http://www.immi.gov.au/living-in-australia/a-multicultural-australia/mcrg report.pdf. Last accessed 20 June 2012.

PARKER, Natalie and Mark PATHE
2006 'Report on the review of the Murri court.' *Queensland Department of Justice and Attorney-General*. http://www.courts.qld.gov.au/ data/assets/pdf file/0020/90713/m-murri-court-report.pdf. Last accessed 20 June 2012.

PAYROW SHABANI, Omid A. (ed.)
2007 *Multiculturalism and Law: A Critical Debate*. Cardiff: University of Wales Press.

POYNTING, Scott, Greg NOBLE, Paul TABAR and Jock COLLINS
2004 *Bin Laden in the Suburbs: Criminalising the Arab Other*. Sydney: Sydney Institute of Criminology.

SAEED, Abdullah
2010 'Reflections on the establishment of Shari'a courts in Australia.' Pp. 223-238 in Rex Ahdar and Nicholas Aroney (eds.), *Shari'a in the West*. Oxford: Oxford University Press.

SAEED, Abdullah and Shahram AKBARZADEH (ed.)
2001 *Muslim Communities in Australia*. Sydney: UNSW Press.

TAN, Kevin Y.L.
2011 'Singapore: a statist legal laboratory.' Pp. 330-371 in Ann Black and Gary F Bell (eds.), *Law and Legal Institutions of Asia: Traditions, Adaptations and Innovations*. Port Melbourne: Cambridge University Press.

THE AGE
2006 'Sheikh Hilali is not fit to be the mufti of Australia' *The Age*. 29 October.

http://www.theage.com.au/news/editorial/sheikh-hilali-is-not-fit-to-be-the-mufti-of-australia/2006/10/28/1161749356027.html. Last accessed 20 June 2012.

VOYCE, Malcolm and Adam POSSAMAI

2011 'Legal pluralism, family personal laws and the rejection of Shari'a in Australia; a case of multiple or "clashing" modernities.' *Democracy and Security* 7(4): 338-353.

WEBER, David

2005 'Muslim leaders call for a Sharia divorce court.' The World Today, ABC Radio. 7 April 2005. http://www.abc.net.au/worldtoday/content/2005/s1340348.htm. Last accessed 20 June 2012.

YILMAZ, Ishan

2003a 'Non-recognition of post-modern Turkish socio-political reality and the predicament of women.' *British Journal of Middle Eastern Studies.* 30(1): 25-41.

2003b 'Muslim alternative dispute resolution and neo-ijtihad in England.' *Alternatives: Turkish Journal of International Relations* 2(1): 117-139.

2005 *Muslim Laws, Politics and Society in Modern Nation States: Dynamic Legal Pluralisms in England, Turkey, and Pakistan.* Aldershot: Ashgate.

ZWARTZ, Barney

2007 'Controversial Mufti attacks Australia in television interview.' *The Age.* 12 January 2007. http://www.theage.com.au/news/national/controversial-mufti-attacks-australia-in-tvinterview/2007/01/11/1168105116655.html. Last accessed 20 June 2012.

2008 'Australia's Muslims cool on change.' *The Age.* 9 February. http://www.theage.com.au/news/world/australias-muslims-cool-on-change/2008/02/08/1202234168549.html. Last accessed 20 June 2012.

SUBSTANTIVE EQUALITY AND MATERNAL MORTALITY IN NIGERIA

Ebenezer Durojaye

1. Introduction

> When women's lives are cut short or incapacitated as a result of pregnancy or childbirth, the tragedy cascades. Children lose a parent. Spouses lose a partner. And societies lose productive contributors... And as long as women remain disadvantaged in their societies, maternal and new-born health will suffer as well. But if we can empower women with the tools to take control of their lives, we can create a more supportive environment for women and children alike.[1]

It is a tragedy that in the 21st century, when man has explored the moon and other planets and made significant advancement in science and technology, women should continue to die during pregnancy and childbirth. Although recent studies show a significant decline in the number of maternal deaths worldwide (Horgan et al. 2010), nonetheless, it was still estimated that 287,000 women died during pregnancy and childbirth in 2010 (WHO et al. 2012: 22). Of these estimated numbers of maternal deaths, developing countries account for 99%, that is, about 284,000 (WHO et al. 2012: 22). It has further been shown that sub-Saharan Africa is the region bearing the greatest burden of maternal deaths, accounting for nearly three fifths (162,000) of all deaths. Moreover, the possibility of a woman dying

[1] Her Majesty Queen Al Abdullah of Jordan, 'Creating a Supportive Environment for mothers and newborns', cited in UNICEF (2009: 11).

during pregnancy or childbirth in Africa is put at about 1 in 39 compared with 1 in 3,800 in developed regions. In some countries such as Chad and Somalia, the risk of a woman dying during pregnancy and childbirth is higher at 1 in 15 and 1 in 16 respectively (WHO et al. 2012). For every one woman that dies during pregnancy or childbirth, 20 more are likely to suffer from life-long injuries (WHO 2005). On a daily basis, it is estimated that 1,000 women and girls lose their lives due to complications arising from pregnancy or childbirth.[2] Many of these women live in developing countries such as Asia and Africa. The situation is so appalling in Africa that governments were urged to declare maternal mortality a state of emergency in the region (African Commission 2008).

With about 640 deaths per 100,000 live births, Nigeria is said to have one of the highest maternal mortality ratios in the world (WHO et al. 2012: 22). Equally, the likelihood of a woman dying during pregnancy or childbirth is put at 1 in 29 compared to 1 in 8,900 in Malta (WHO 2012: 34). Other poor countries such as Lesotho and Swaziland have better maternal mortality ratios than Nigeria. Nigeria is said to have the second largest number of maternal deaths after India, accounting for about 40,000 deaths during pregnancy and childbirth each year. These two countries account for one third of all maternal deaths worldwide. Sadly enough, while deaths arising from childbirth or pregnancy have almost been eliminated in developed countries, many developing countries, including Nigeria, are still grappling with the challenge of maternal mortality. Indeed, maternal mortality represents one of the most telling evidence of inequity between rich and poor countries and urban and rural areas.

The truth remains that deaths arising from childbirth or pregnancy are preventable, but most countries in developing world have not shown enough commitment to addressing this challenge. Al Abdullah asked a rhetorical question: 'How can it be that in our age of modern advances and medical miracles we are still failing to safeguard women as they perpetuate the human race itself?' (UNICEF 2009: 28). There is no reason why women should continue to die in a bid to bring forth another life. For a country like Nigeria, which is endowed with natural and human resources and regarded as the largest exporter of oil in the region, it is almost inconceivable that maternal mortality remains a great threat to the lives and health of women. Worse still, Nigeria is regarded as one of the countries that has made

[2] See Mothers Day Everyday 'Global Maternal Mortality: Fact Sheet' available at http://mothersdayeveryday.org/docs/MDED FactSheet.pdf (Last accessed on 8 March 2012).

insufficient progress towards addressing maternal deaths with a view to meeting the target for the Millennium Development Goals (MDGs). This leaves much to be desired and merely exemplifies the little attention paid to women's health in the country.

Against this backdrop, this article examines the relevance of substantive equality in addressing maternal deaths in Nigeria. The article argues that aside from medical causes of deaths during pregnancy or childbirth, socio-cultural factors such as low status of women and lack of respect for their fundamental rights, often aggravate maternal deaths in Nigeria. While maternal deaths amounts to violations of women's rights to health and life, it is contended that the application of the concept of substantive equality, as opposed to formal equality, can be helpful in addressing some of the root causes of maternal deaths in the country. This may require the government to take some practical steps such as awareness campaigns, law reforms and gender-sensitive budgeting towards improving the health of women. The article points out that the tension between international human rights law, statutory law and customary law in a pluralist state may have serious implications for women's fundamental rights, particularly the right to health (Merry 2005). Therefore, the article argues that in accordance with its obligations under international and regional human rights instruments, the Nigerian government would need to pay more attention to promoting and protecting women's rights, including meeting their health needs.

2. The concept of Equality and Relevance for Women's Rights

The concept of equality is an important and fundamental principle essential in any democratic setting. Equality, as a 'treacherously simple concept' (Holtmaat 2004), is incapable of a precise definition. However, it is generally agreed that the notion of equality has a correlation with the principle of non-discrimination. Thus, an act of discrimination will lead to the violation of the right to equality (Shalev 2000: 38). The term 'discrimination' implies treating an individual or group of individuals differently from other members of society. While it is noted that not all discrimination will result in a violation of right, an unfair discrimination which may impugn the dignity of any individual will undoubtedly amount to a violation of right.

The classical conception of the notion of equality is often traced to Aristotle who argues that like should be treated alike and unlike in proportion to their differences (Aristotle 1976). This has given rise to a distinction between formal and substantive equality. Formal equality- often referred to as mathematical, absolute or numerical equality- merely treats every member of society in the same way without taking into cognizance their specific differences. It is aimed at promoting individual justice as the foundation for a moral claim to virtue and is dependent upon the notion that fairness requires consistent and equal treatment (Wesson 2007: 751). This type of approach is said to be blind to socio- economic disparities that may exist in every society. In other words, it does not take into cognisance the peculiar situation of vulnerable or marginalised members of society who have been historically disadvantaged either due to race, age or gender. Adherence to formal equality in the real sense does not guarantee true equality but disparity. Dworkin (1977: 37), warning Americans that sameness of treatment does not ensure true equality, opines that "we must take care not to use the Equal Protection Clause [of the 14th Amendment of the American Constitution] to cheat ourselves of equality".

The notion of formal equality is rooted in libertarianism. This idea supports the view that it is irrelevant to consider the socio-economic or physical differences in individuals in determining their access to social amenities or gain. At the centre of this argument is the fact that it is essential to retain formal equality if merit is to be maintained in a democratic society (McCrudden 1998: 543). It has further been argued that formal equality disfavours arbitrary decision processes, that is, when people or policies selectively disadvantage others based on irrelevant traits (Brest 1976: 2). In essence, the argument here is that formal equality avoids unnecessary and deficient considerations being introduced into decision-making process, thus, preventing irrational and unfair decisions, often based on uninformed criteria. In other words, formal equality is said to promote neutrality in decision-making. However, the so-called neutrality value canvassed by proponents of formal equality has been faulted as illusory and unrealistic (Fiss 1976: 135). This is because it is difficult, if not impossible, to argue that the law, legislature or judiciary is truly neutral to all parties.

On the other hand, the notion of substantive equality implies that every individual is treated in the same manner taking into consideration each individual's peculiar circumstances. In other words, substantive equality, as different from formal equality, aims at promoting social justice and egalitarianism in a society, particularly for the marginalised or vulnerable groups (Rawls 1971). This notion recognises the diverse and complex nature of a modern democratic setting and rejects the fallacy of the 'universal individual'. According to Albertyn and Goldblatt (1998: 250), 'a commitment to substantive equality involves examining the context of an alleged rights violation and its relationship to systemic forms of domination within a society'. Unlike formal equality, which fails to recognise personal idiosyncrasies, substantive equality admits of these personal idiosyncrasies and attempts at a pragmatic approach to accommodate them. For instance, if a deaf and dumb pupil were to be enrolled in the same school with other pupils who do not have similar problems, this will amount to upholding the notion of formal equality, which will be disadvantageous to the pupil in question. A substantive equality approach to this issue will require that such a pupil be accommodated in a special school where he/she will be able to cope effectively. In essence, the substantive equality approach strives toaddressing 'structural and entrenched disadvantage at the same time as it aspires to maximize human development' (Albertyn and Goldblatt 1998: 254).

An important aspect of the notion of substantive equality is that it aims towards equality of outcomes, which seeks to invest a certain moral principle into the equality approach. In essence, a substantive approach to equality may sometimes require the need for remedial actions to correct the injustice of the past or give more attention to the needs of the disadvantaged in society (Freedman 2001: 112). The non-discrimination provisions guaranteed in both the Convention on the Elimination of All Forms of Discrimination against Women (CEDAW)[3] and the Protocol to the African Charter on the Rights of Women (African Women's Protocol)[4] are good examples of the notion of substantive equality. According to CEDAW, discrimination against women includes:

> [A]ny distinction, exclusion or restriction made on the basis of sex which has the effect or purpose of impairing or nullifying the recognition, enjoyment or exercise by women, irrespective of their marital status, on a basis of equality of men and women, of

[3] CEDAW 1980. According to art 1 of CEDAW, discrimination is widely defined to embrace any distinction, exclusion or restriction made on the basis of sex which has the effect or purpose of impairing or nullifying the recognition, enjoyment or exercise by women on equal basis with their male counterpart.

[4] The Protocol of African Charter on Human and People's Rights on the Rights of Women in Africa adopted by the 2nd Ordinary Session of the African Union General Assembly in 2003 in Maputo CAB/LEG/66.6 (2003) entered into force 25 November, 2005. Art 1 of African Women Protocol defines discrimination against women as 'any distinction, exclusion or restriction or any differential treatment based on sex and whose objectives or effects compromise or destroy the recognition, enjoyment or the exercise by women, regardless of their marital status, of human rights and fundamental freedoms in all spheres of life'

> human rights and fundamental freedoms in the political, economic, social, cultural, civil or any other field.[5]

States parties to the treaty are, therefore, enjoined to take steps and measures to eliminate discrimination against women within their territories. Reaffirming the language of CEDAW, the Women's Protocol requires states to remove practices that discriminate against women and urges states parties to take all appropriate steps to eliminate social and cultural patterns and practices that are discriminatory to women.[6] It defines discrimination against women widely to include:[7]

> [Any] distinction, exclusion or restriction or any differential treatment based on sex and whose objectives or effects compromise or destroy the recognition, enjoyment or the exercise by women, regardless of their mental status, of human rights and fundamental freedoms in all spheres of life.

These definitions are important in holding states accountable for failure to address cultural practices that may exacerbate maternal deaths. Apart from the fact that Nigeria has ratified both the CEDAW in 1985 and the Protocol to the African Charter on the Rights of Women in Africa in 2004, it has further ratified other human rights instruments such as the International Covenant on Economic, Social and Cultural Rights, the International Covenant on Civil and Political Rights and the African Charter. The Committee on Covenant on Economic Social and Cultural Rights (ESCR) has noted that states are to integrate a gender perspective in policies, laws and programmes in order to advance the rights of the citizens. According to the Committee, a gender perspective recognizes that biological and socio-cultural factors play a significant role in influencing the health of men and women. It therefore urges states to proscribe discrimination in relation to health care services on various grounds including race, colour, sex, language, religion, political or other opinion, national or social origin, property, birth, physical or mental disability, health status (including HIV/AIDS), sexual orientation and civil, political, social or other status, which has the intention or effect of nullifying or impairing the equal enjoyment or exercise of the right to health.

---

[5] See art 1 of CEDAW above (note 3).

[6] See art 2 of the Women's Protocol note 4 above, which drew its inspiration from art 2 of CEDAW.

[7] *Ibid* art 1.

Also, the Human Rights Committee in its General Comment 18 has explained that equality together with non-discrimination constitutes a basic and general principle relating to the protection of human rights. In its General Comment 28, the Committee explains that all individuals are expected to enjoy the rights guaranteed in the ICCPR on an equal basis and in totality and that a state is in breach of the principle of equality whenever any person is denied the full and equal enjoyment of all rights. Thus, the Committee urges states to ensure equal enjoyment of all rights for men and women. It must be noted that 'non-discrimination and equality further imply that States must recognize and provide for the differences and specific needs of groups that generally face particular health challenges, such as higher mortality rates or vulnerability to specific diseases' (UNOCHR and WHO 2008: 7).

Historically, women in different societies across the globe have been treated less than human and subjected to all forms of discriminatory practices due mainly to patriarchal traditions and customary law. The situation is even more precarious for women in a pluralistic environment like Nigeria where statutory law operates side by side with customary or religious law. Cailleba and Kumar (2010) have argued that customary law may potentially limit human rights of women. Under patriarchy, women were denied their basic human rights and treated as less important than men. Moreover, they were merely assigned the roles of homemakers and child-bearers (Opara 1990; Mama 1997; Eboh 1998). Such a conservative approach was aided by the dichotomy of public and private spheres of life, which tended to shroud women's suffering and deprivation. Charlesworth et al. (1991: 6131) have contended that men have used this public/private dichotomy as a veritable weapon of women's oppression. Binion (1995: 627) also argues that this dichotomy represents the very face of patriarchy. Under this dichotomy, gender roles are constructed and women's subordination to men is cemented. The result is that men are seen as the all-knowing and all-powerful dictating the 'tune of gender music'. Thus, women's ability to enjoy their fundamental rights was invariably tied to the apron strings of men as either husband or father. In essence, the public/private dichotomy undermines women's equal status in society and perpetuates discriminatory practices against women.

Under the disguise of public/private dichotomy, women and girls are not expected to freely express their sexual desires. That privilege belongs to men alone, who not only determine when to have sex but can also flaunt their sexual desires. Women and girls are expected to repress their sexual desires and remain sexually passive. An attempt to act otherwise attracts public rebuke and condemnation. This same scenario is reinforced in the case of Nigeria. In many cultures in Nigeria, it is often believed that the home is a sacred place and that whatever transpires there is not subject to public scrutiny. Therefore, women generally, and young women in particular, have been subjected to various forms of abuses, including sexual abuse by their partners, husbands, fathers or close relatives (Effah-Chukwuma and Osakwe 2000: 2). Worse still, these abuses experienced by women are regarded as 'family affairs', which must not be reported to outsiders or even law enforcement agents.

Indeed, in exceptional cases where a woman is bold enough to report an act of domestic violence to the police, the police often advise that such matters should be settled amicably as it is a 'family issue' (Effah-Chukwuma and Osakwe 2000: 2). In other words, women and girls have had to stoically bear these violations of their rights in silence. Violations of women's rights in Nigeria take different forms including denial of inheritance rights, harmful widowhood practices, early or forced marriages and lack of access to sexual and reproductive health services. Under this oppressive and hostile environment, women and girls are unable to exercise control over their sexuality. This in turn makes it very difficult for women to seek sexual and reproductive health services.

In a nutshell, the public/private dichotomy is a potential threat to the exercise of women's sexual autonomy and the enjoyment of their sexual and reproductive well-being. This is because it exposes women and girls to violence and shields them away from the state's intervention. The fear of violence (actual or perceived) subdues women and girls and makes it difficult for them to exercise their free will or choices in sexual and reproductive health matters. Commenting on this situation, Cook and Howard (2007: 1041) have argued that developing an anti-discrimination theory can be useful in addressing the neglect of women's reproductive health and the detrimental impact of such neglect on the status of women in society. Reinforcing this argument, Loenen (1997: 407) has noted as follows:

> a meaningful and convincing interpretation of the concept of discrimination starts from its historical genesis as a principle directed at protecting groups which have suffered from *structural* disadvantage, from *patterns* of exclusion, and not just from some incidental impact... Sensitive groups thus need stronger protection against classifications with a negative impact... Such an asymmetrical conception of discrimination acknowledges that harm caused by measures which disadvantage vulnerable and subordinate groups is, indeed, a greater evil which merits more

> suspicion than measures which disadvantage powerful and otherwise privileged groups.

The foregoing observations on the plight of women in society are critical to the discussion of maternal deaths in Nigeria. Given that deaths during pregnancy or childbirth are preventable, there is no reason why women should continue to die in the thousands every year. It has been noted that 'death on this scale is not an inevitable danger of pregnancy and childbirth-it is a preventable loss of life and the tragic result of policy decisions that too often neglect, devalue and discriminate against women' (Center for Reproductive Rights 2005: 2). As it will be discussed below, some of the causes of maternal deaths in Nigeria are rooted in socio-cultural factors such as the low status of women and lack of respect for their fundamental rights. Moreover, the failure or inability of the Nigerian government to take drastic measures to address maternal deaths in the country merely testifies to the little regard the government has for the rights and worth of women.

It must be pointed out that section 42 of the Nigerian Constitution, which deals with non-discrimination is couched in a narrow language proscribing discrimination merely on grounds of sex, race, ethnic groups, religious or political beliefs. Unlike non-discrimination provisions in most human rights instruments, the section does not include the phrase 'other status', which has been interpreted broadly by some treaty monitoring bodies. In addition, section 42 of the Nigerian Constitution can be contrasted with the equality clause in section 9 of the South African Constitution of 1996, which prohibits discrimination on various grounds including, sex, gender, pregnancy, age, marital status and sexual orientation. Despite its narrow language, it is argued that the Nigerian provision deserves a generous and purposive interpretation to address gender inequality in the country.

Moreover, it should be noted that the notion of equality is intrinsically linked to the respect for human dignity. Therefore, failure to address the root causes of maternal deaths in Nigeria will amount to the violation of the right to dignity of women guaranteed under section 34 of the 1999 Constitution of the Federal Republic of Nigeria and other international and regional human rights instruments ratified by the country. The South African Constitutional Court in the *National Coalition of Lesbians and Gay* case has noted that 'Dignity is a difficult concept to capture in precise terms. At its least, it is clear that the constitutional protection of dignity requires us to acknowledge the value and worth of all individuals as members of our society'.[8] With regard to maternal deaths, Cook et al. (2001: 5)

[8] *National Coalition of Gay and Lesbians v Minister Justice South Africa*, CCT

have noted as follows:

> The failure to address preventable maternal disability and death represents one of the greatest social injustices of our times.... [W]omen's reproductive health risks are not mere misfortunes and unavoidable natural disadvantages of pregnancy but, rather, injustices that societies are able and obligated to remedy.

This would imply that the Nigerian government should be held accountable for incessant loss of women's lives during pregnancy and childbirth and is obligated to take necessary steps to address the social injustices women experience in the country on a daily basis.

3. Causes of Maternal Deaths in Nigeria

According to the World Health Organization, a maternal death is 'the death of a woman while pregnant or within 42 days of termination of pregnancy, irrespective of the duration and site of the pregnancy, from any cause related to or aggravated by the pregnancy or its management, but not from accidental or incidental causes' (WHO 1992). As stated earlier, deaths during pregnancy and childbirth are generally preventable and have almost been eliminated in developed countries. However, maternal mortality has remained one of the leading causes of death and morbidity among women in Africa (WHO et al. 2004: 6). The reasons why women die during pregnancy are well known, and include problems such as haemorrhage (25 per cent), unsafe abortion (13 per cent), eclampsia (12 per cent), infections (16 per cent) and, obstructed labour and other direct causes (16 per cent) (WHO 2005). Although these are the general causes of maternal deaths, the reasons women die from pregnancy may differ from one country to another (Center Reproductive Rights 2005; Center for Reproductive Rights 2007; Hailu et al. 2009). There are also indirect causes such as HIV/AIDS, malaria, anaemia and hepatitis (20 per cent). These complications can be addressed through provisions of emergency obstetric care services. But such services are generally unavailable in poor regions. Beyond the medical reasons, other reasons for deaths during pregnancy and childbirth include the three delays- delay in reaching treatment, delay in identifying the problem and delay in getting help.

11/98; [1999] (1) SA 6 (CC).

According to WHO (2006) it is estimated that 60 per cent of all deliveries take place outside health facilities and only about 60 per cent of births are attended to by skilled health care providers in developing countries. In Africa, the number of deliveries attended to by skilled health care providers is even less at about 47 per cent (WHO 2006: 18). For a country like Nigeria, the number of deliveries attended to by skilled medical personnel is disappointedly put at 37 per cent, lower than the average in the region (Bankole 2009: 4). More disappointedly, Nigeria is one of the countries thatis struggling to reduce maternal deaths as envisaged under goal 5 of the MDGs. As earlier noted, the maternal mortality ratio in Nigeria (640 deaths per 100,000 live births) is one of the highest in the world. Deaths during pregnancy occur due to a number of socio-cultural reasons including low status of women, early marriage and a general lack of respect for women's rights. In addition, corruption, misappropriation of resources and inadequate allocation of resources to the health sector often aggravate maternal mortality in the country.

Cook et al. (2003: 217) have noted that in assessing the human rights obligations of a state as regards sexual and reproductive health, attention must be given to three important elements which include clinical care; operation of the health care system and underlying conditions including social, economic and legal conditions of observance of human rights. These elements are equally useful in accessing a state's commitment to addressing maternal deaths. The discussion in this section will focus on three of such underlying conditions that contribute to maternal deaths in Nigeria, including low status of women, lack of sexual and reproductive health autonomy and poor allocation of resources to the health sector.

Due to the patriarchal nature of the Nigerian society, women have often been subjected to various forms of discrimination and human rights abuses. Moreover, because of cultural and religious practices, Nigerian women have almost been relegated to second-class citizens and have undergone horrifying experiences. These range from dehumanising widowhood practices, denial of inheritance rights to forced or early marriage (Ewelukwa 2002: 425; Iwobi 2008: 37). In addition, in some parts of the country, women may require the permission of their husbands to seek medical attention, including antenatal care. All these erode the dignity of women and invariably contribute to high maternal deaths in the country. For instance, when a woman is denied rights of inheritance, this may limit her economic opportunities, as she is likely to lack access to personal and real property. Given that most women are economically dependent on their partners, it may be difficult for women to afford medical treatment, including antenatal care. A report has shown that the reason why most women in the rural areas do not seek antenatal care is due mainly to lack of resources (Center for Reproductive Rights

2005).

Undoubtedly, cultural practices that prevent women from inheriting from their deceased husband or father is inconsistent with the notion of equality or non-discrimination guaranteed in international, regional human rights instruments that Nigeria has ratified. Moreover, as noted earlier, the Nigerian constitution prohibits discrimination on the grounds of sex in section 42. Unfortunately, the Nigerian Supreme Court has not developed a consistent approach to addressing this challenge. An opportunity for the Court to clarify its position on this issue was missed in the case of *Mojekwu v Iwuchukwu.*[9] In that case, the Nigerian Supreme Court was asked to consider the discriminatory nature of a customary practice that denies inheritance rights to a female child. The Supreme Court proceeded on the premise that customary laws were not generally discriminatory against women unless otherwise proved. Thus, the Court failed to appreciate the gender implications of customary laws for women's enjoyment of their fundamental rights. This approach of the Court is not only faulty, but also fraught with danger, especially when one bears in mind that men have almost always determined custom and tradition. While it is true that not all cultural practices are inimical to women's health and enjoyment of their fundamental rights, it is not in contention that some cultural practices perpetuate gender inequality and are potentially threats to women's rights.

Generally, women in Nigeria lack adequate access to sexual and reproductive health services and are unable to exercise their reproductive autonomy due mainly to pervasive discriminatory practices against them. Because of power imbalances and the belief that women are to be seen and not to be heard, women are unable to participate in making crucial decisions relating to their sexual and reproductive well- being. The existing patriarchal tradition and the social belief that children are crowns of a woman, often make it difficult for a woman to decide the timing and number of her children. Thus, in most cases a woman may be unable to negotiate contraceptive use or seek contraceptive services without the consent of her husband or partner. A 2009 report has shown that in 2003, only one out of four women of childbearing age in the country said they were involved in making decisions relating to their sexual and reproductive health (Bankole 2009: 14). In addition, young women and women in rural areas often lack adequate knowledge with regard to contraceptive services. These challenges usually contribute to high fertility rate in the country.

[9] *Mojekwu v Iwuchukwu* [2004] 4 SC (Part II) 1.

According to the 2008 Demographic Health Survey (DHS), the use of contraception has increased from 13 percent in 2003 to 15 percent in 2008, including a corresponding increase in the use of modern methods of contraception from 8 percent in 2003 to 10 percent in 2008. (National Population Commission and ICF Macro 2009). It states further that urban women are more than thrice as likely as rural women to use a method of contraception (26 and 9 percent, respectively). The DHS states further that about 20 per cent of adolescent women (majority of whom are unmarried) have an unmet need for contraception (Allan Guttmacher Institute 2004: 6). While on average Nigerian women want large families, about 20 per cent of married women still want to limit their family size or wait for some time before their next birth, but their contraceptive needs are unmet (National Population Commission and ICF Macro 2009). The consequences of the above scenario are grave for women's health in the country. Low contraceptive use among women, particularly young women, can lead to high fertility rate and incidence of unwanted pregnancies. At 2008, the total fertility rate in Nigeria was estimated at 5.7 births per woman. Although this is a modest decline from previous years, nonetheless, it remains somewhat high (National Population Commission and ICF Macro 2009). This tends to put the lives of Nigerian women in danger since there is a correlation between high fertility rate and maternal mortality (UNICEF 2010: 32).

One of the greatest challenges to meeting the health needs of women generally and maternal health in particular in Nigeria, is the problem of inadequate allocation of resources to the health sector. Although this problem affects health services generally, the impact is felt more as regards sexual and reproductive health issues. Over the years, the Nigerian government has exhibited a flagrant disregard to lives and well- being of its citizens, especially women, through its shoestring allocation to the health sector. Government's allocation over the years to the health sector has hovered around 4-5 per cent of the annual budget (Center for Reproductive Rights and Women Research Documentation Centre 2008: 4). Moreover, according to a World Bank Report (2010), the country's public health expenditure as percent of (GDP) was 2.12 in 2009 as against 1.90 reported in 2008, making it one of the countries that spent the lowest percentage on the health of its people in those years. Poor funding of the health sector has led to decay in government hospitals evident by acute shortage of medical supplies such as gloves, syringes, drugs, beddings and toiletries (Durojaye and Ayankogbe 2005: 187). The poor allocation of resources to health care services needed only by women would amount to an act of discrimination. For a country that is richly endowed with various natural resources, including oil, it is embarrassing that the health sector should remain in shambles. It must be recalled that at the Abuja Declaration (2001) African governments agreed to commit at least 15 per cent of their annual budgetary allocations to the health sector. Sadly, a recent report has shown that only two countries (Rwanda and South Africa) have fulfilled this promise (WHO 2011: 2).

4. Nexus between Legal Pluralism and Maternal Deaths in Nigeria

Legal pluralism has become an essential feature of many African countries that have undergone colonialism. It is often used to describe a situation where asubject matter or issue is regulated by multiple laws, norms or forums that co-exist within the same jurisdiction (International Council of Human Rights 2009: 41). Oba (2004: 113) has noted that legal pluralism is an important aspect of the Nigerian legal system. As a former colony of Britain, Nigeria adopts the common law legal system, which places emphasis on judicial precedent. However, in practice the country derives it sources of law from legislation, customary laws and Shari'ah. Although Islamic law and indigenous customary laws preceded the common law system, the latter by virtue of colonialism has tended to take preeminence over the former. The adoption of these three systems together in a diverse country with different ethnic groups and religious beliefs has implications for women's rights. It should be noted that Nigeria is a federation, therefore, each component state has powers to make laws While some statutory provisions such as the Constitution tend to give recognition to women's rights, customary laws and Shari'ah tend to perpetuate discriminatory practices against women. For instance, as noted above, the Constitution guarantees all individuals equal rights and freedoms and proscribes discrimination on grounds of sex, yet some cultural practices such as wife inheritance or primogeniture practiced in the Eastern part of the country- which denies women right of inheritance- seem to be inconsistent with the principles of non-discrimination and equality.

In addition, some provisions of Shari'ah as applicable in most parts of the northern region of the country perpetuate the low status of women. For instance, while sections 21 and 22 of the Child's Rights Act of 2003 prohibits early marriage by setting the marriageable age at 18, Islamic law (Shari'ah) applicable in the northern parts of the country allows for early marriage and prohibits adolescent girls from seeking contraceptive services. Child or early marriage is prevalent in the northern part of Nigeria as girls are married as young as 12 years or younger. When a girl is married at an early age, she is deprived the opportunity to be educated and develop mentally and physically and may be deprived of the means of livelihood. This clearly underpins the tension that may exist between statutory law and customary or religious law in a multi-cultural society like Nigeria.

The plural legal regime in Nigeria often creates confusion and uncertainty with regard to protecting women's fundamental rights and freedoms. Thus, there seems to be inconsistency and uncertainty in the application of this plural legal system. It has been noted that legal pluralism can potentially undermine women's rights to exercise free choices in matters that affect their sexual and reproductive well-being (Bond 2010: 5). The fact that maternal deaths in the northern parts of Nigeria, where Islamic law operates, are higher than any other parts of the country tends to lend credence to this assertion. Explaining the effects of the plural legal system on Nigerian women, Ewelukwa (2002: 446-447) asserts as follows:

> Fundamental contradictions inherent in the legal system - the coexistence of modern, statutory laws with traditional customary laws and practices – has created a complex and confusing legal regime under which women generally are denied adequate legal protection...Not surprisingly, many of the problems which are faced today in much of Africa 'are the product of trying to piece together, in a hasty fashion, not only the different legal systems but also fundamentally different conceptions of society and the family.

5. The Obligations of the Nigerian Government with regard to Maternal Mortality

Under international law, a state has the three-fold obligation with respect to the right to health, including women's health needs. These include the obligations to respect, protect and fulfil the right to health of women, particularly in the context of maternal mortality. The Committee on the Covenant on Economic, Social and Cultural Rights (ESCR 2000) has noted that governments' obligations as regards the right to health include ensuring availability of timely and appropriate health care services. Access to health care services must also be guaranteed to all on a non-discriminatory basis. As noted above, Nigeria has made commitments under international and regional human rights instruments with regard to safeguarding human rights of women. In addition, the country has affirmed different consensus statements or documents such as the International Conference on Population and Development (ICPD),[10] the Fourth World Conference on Women (FWCW)[11] also

[10] International Conference on Population and Development (ICPD) UN A/CONF.171 (13) 18 October 1994.

known as the Beijing Declaration, MDGs, and the Maputo Declaration on Operationalisation of Sexual and Reproductive health in Africa and the African Union initiated region-wide Campaign on Accelerated Reduction of Maternal Mortality in Africa (CARMMA).[12] These consensus statements or documents require that states must adopt measures towards protecting the rights of women and preventing deaths during pregnancy or childbirth.

The essence of a human rights-based approach to maternal mortality is to assess whether steps and measures taken by a state are consistent with its obligations under international law. More importantly, a rights-based approach pays attention to the issue of non-discrimination in provision of services especially as regards vulnerable and marginalised groups. In other words, it is not enough for a state to recognise that maternal mortality is a challenge, but such a state will be required to adopt appropriate and concrete measures that must address the root causes of maternal death, promote women's health and well-being and address gender inequality (Freedman 2001). Thus, the Nigerian government is required to take steps, including elimination of discriminatory practices against women, towards the prevention of maternal deaths in the country. It is important to note that states are not only expected to comply with the non-discrimination principles but are also expected to ensure the implementation of those principles within the state between private actors, thus invoking both negative and positive obligations (INTERIGHTS 2011: 20).

Obligation to respect

The obligation to respect is often described as a negative obligation, which requires states to refrain from interfering with the enjoyment of rights. It means that states must refrain from doing anything that will prevent an individual from enjoying his/her rights. In the context of maternal mortality in Nigeria, the existence of customary laws and practices, which render women subordinate to

[11] Fourth World Conference on Women Beijing held on 15 September 1995 A/CONF.177/20.

[12] This was launched in 2009 by African leaders. It focuses on three key areas: positive messaging; encouraging achievements and strides made in some countries in reducing maternal mortality and seeking to replicate them; and intensifying actions aimed at reducing maternal and infant mortality. The campaign aims to cut maternal mortality in countries with high rates.

men and expose them to sexual and reproductive ill-health, including morbidity and mortality arising from pregnancy and childbirth, could be interpreted as a breach of the obligation to respect. Despite the commitments made by the Nigerian government under international, regional and national law regarding the position of women, the status of women has not improved in the country. Moreover, the existence of a tripartite legal system in the country often compromises women's rights and makes it difficult for them to live on equal basis with men. This further perpetuates stereotypes and gives little regard to women's health and well-being. The failure of the Nigerian government to address this challenge is a breach of the obligation to respect women's rights.

In one of its Concluding Observations to Nigeria, the CEDAW Committee (2004) has expressed concerns with respect to the poor attention given by the Nigerian government to the sexual health needs of women and girls. The Committee (2008) has also expressed concern about the low rates of contraceptives usage leading to unwanted and unplanned pregnancies and the lack of sexuality education among young people, especially in the rural areas. Therefore, the Committee (2004) has urged the government to increase women's and adolescent girls' access to affordable and accessible health care services, including sexual and reproductive health services. It also urges the government to adopt adequate measures to increase knowledge of and access to contraceptive methods (CEDAW Committee 2008). This seems to be in line with the Committee's observation in General Recommendation 24 (1999), where states were urged to ensure that affordable and acceptable health services, including sexual and reproductive health services, are guaranteed to women and girls.

The Committee on ESCR has hinted that failure by a state to remove barriers to health care services and goods, for vulnerable and marginalized groups such as women, children, adolescents and those in rural areas, will amount to a breach of the state's obligation to realise the right to health of its citizens. In other words, physical accessibility to health care services must be assured to all women and girls, particularly those in rural areas. It should be noted that article 14 of the African Women's Protocol contains elaborate provisions relating to sexual and reproductive health of women. Article 14 guarantees all women the right to health, including sexual and reproductive health. This important article further provides that states should respect and promote a woman's right to control her fertility, decide the number and spacing of her children and choose any method of contraception.

More importantly, article 14 (2) (b) requires states parties to establish and strengthen existing pre-natal, delivery and post-natal health and nutritional services for women during pregnancy and while they are breastfeeding.[13] Also, the provision enjoins states parties to take appropriate measures to 'provide adequate, affordable and accessible health services, including information, education and communication programmes to women especially those in rural areas'.[14] The provisions of article 14 must be read together with article 2 of the Protocol, which proscribes discrimination against women in all facets of life. As noted earlier, the African Women's Protocol adopts a substantive equality approach to eliminating discrimination. Therefore, since Nigeria is a party to the Protocol, it is obligated to take adequate measures to remove all barriers, including cultural practices, to safe motherhood in the country.

Furthermore, both the ICPD and the Beijing Platform identify components of the right to the highest attainable standard of reproductive health from a woman's perspective.[15] They stress the importance of affordable, accessible and acceptable services throughout a woman's life cycle.[16] Acceptable services include gender-sensitive standards for the delivery of quality health care services, which must meet the peculiar needs of female adolescents.[17]Bearing these comments in mind, and taking into account the challenges facing women in the country, one may argue that the Nigerian government is not doing enough to remove barriers to safe-motherhood in the country.

Obligation to protect

This duty implies that governments must take necessary steps and measures to prevent a third party from interfering with the enjoyment of the right to health. In the context of maternal mortality, it would imply a government's obligation to ensure that third parties do not interfere with women's enjoyment of their sexual and reproductive health. Thus, as shown above, the challenges of socio-cultural

---

[13] African Women's Protocol (note 4).

[14] *Ibid* article 14 (2) (a).

[15] International Conference on Population and Development (note 10); Fourth World Conference on Women Beijing (note 11).

[16] *Ibid* para 25 and 223; para 92 and 106 (e) respectively.

[17] *Ibid* para 223 and 95; para 103,106(c) and 106(g) respectively.

factors, which contribute to high maternal mortality in the country, will amount to a breach of the obligation to protect women's right to health 9ceda Committee; 1999). Similarly, the negative attitudes of health care providers towards women attending antenatal care and barriers created by high cost of medical care, especially in rural areas, will constitute a breach of the duty to protect. A report has shown that women attending ante-natal care in Nigeria are sometimes forced to make unauthorised payments before they receive treatment (Center for Reproductive Rights and WARDC 2008). This often creates barriers for many women who are unable to make such payments. Thus, some of these women tend to shun treatment in public hospitals and resort to self-delivery or seeking help from untrained persons, thereby endangering their lives. In most cases, because of the poor facilities in public hospitals, some women are forced to attend private hospitals for delivery. For some women, (especially those in rural areas) who are unable to afford this treatment, there is the likelihood of being exposed to injury or death during childbirth. This amounts to failure on the part of the Nigerian government to protect women from discriminatory practices that may result in their death.

In one of its landmark decisions involving *Alyne da Silva Pimentel v Brazil*,[18] the CEDAW Committee has noted that 'lack of appropriate maternal health services has a differential impact on the right of life of women'. The Committee further notes that states have the obligation to guarantee all women of whatever racial, social and economic backgrounds to safe, timely, and non-discriminatory maternal health. This statement of the Committee is consistent with upholding the notion of substantive equality. The Committee reinstated the principle of due diligence to hold the Brazilian government responsible for its failure to regulate the activities of health providers in the country. It then found the Brazilian government in breach of its obligation under international law to ensure safe delivery for women. The decision in *Alyne v Brazil* is a clear indication of how a rights-based approach to maternal mortality can strengthen states' accountability at the national level. It also underscores the importance of international mechanisms in enhancing accountability where national mechanisms are unreliable, inefficient or non-existent (de Mesquita and Kismödi 2012: 79). More importantly, it demonstrates how a state may be in violation of its obligation to prevent discrimination in the delivery of health care services. The fact that the services not provided are only required by women is an indication of failure to fulfil women's rights to health and prevent inequality in access to health care service.

[18] Communication No. 17/2008.

In one of its Concluding Observations to the government of Nigeria, the CEDAW Committee (2008) has expressed serious concern 'about the persistence of entrenched harmful and cultural norms and practices, including widowhood rites and practices' and its implications for women's rights. In particular, the Committee has expressed concern about the link between harmful cultural practices and maternal deaths in the country. It therefore, urges the government of Nigeria, as a matter of priority to take decisive steps in order to address this situation.[19] These observations are consistent with ensuring gender equality and preventing women from discriminatory practices perpetrated by third parties. Indeed, they underscore the relevance of the substantive equality approach to preventing maternal deaths in the country.

Obligation to fulfill

This duty imposes obligations on a state to ensure that it has taken adequate measures, including budgetary, legislative and judicial, with respect to realising the right to health of its citizens. With regard to maternal mortality, the duty to fulfil requires a government to take steps and measures to ensure that access to sexual reproductive health services, particularly antenatal care services, are made available to women. The obligation to fulfil implies designing and implementing an appropriate legal framework that will address the incidence of maternal deaths. The Committee on ESCR, in General Comment 14 (2000), has explained that fulfilling the right to health requires a state to take a holistic approach. This will include realistic legal and policy frameworks that will assure health care goods and services to all, especially marginalised groups such as adolescents and women. Specifically, the Committee has noted that appropriate health care services must be provided to meet the peculiar needs of women.

It should be noted that the obligation to fulfil requires more than merely making laws and policies but also requires diligent implementation of those laws and policies. The Nigerian government has developed a number of policies and programmes in order to address the incidence of maternal mortality in the country. These include the National Policy on Health (Federal Ministry of Health 1998), the National Reproductive Health Policy (Federal Ministry of Health 2001), National Reproductive Health Strategic Framework (Federal Ministry of Health 2002), National Guidelines for Women's Health (Federal Ministry of Women

[19] *Ibid* paras 336-337.

Affairs 2002) and National Family Planning/Reproductive Health Policy and Standards of Practice (Federal Ministry of Health 2004), including a proposed bill on National Health. In addition, the government has embarked on different programmes aimed at reducing the incidence of maternal death in the country. These include a joint programme with the World Health Organization known as the 'Making Pregnancy Safer Initiative' launched in 2001; the establishment by the government in 2001 a multi-sectoral National Safe Motherhood Committee; and the establishment in 2005 of a Presidential Task Force on Maternal Mortality aimed at ensuring the realisation of MDG 5. Despite these efforts and initiatives the maternal mortality ratio in the country has remained high. The Nigerian government has not been able to translate this myriad of policies to positive results. The major challenge remains lack of political will and inadequate allocation of resources to the health sector.

While fulfilling the right to health requires a state to commit its resources towards the realisation of health care services to all, the Committee on ESCR realises that some states, due to lack of resources, may face the challenge of immediately realising the right to health for their citizenry. However, such states are required to take progressive steps towards realising this right. On the other hand, the Committee on ESCR (2000) notes that certain obligations relating to the right to health, such as ensuring access to medicines, goods and services (including contraception), access to minimum essential food, access to shelter, housing, sanitation and safe drinking water, equitable access to health facilities and prohibition of discriminatory practices with regard to health care services are core obligations, which are not subject to progressive realization. In other words, poor states would still be expected to demonstrate that they have applied their meagre resources judiciously towards realising the right to health of their citizens. In the Committee's view, the crucial point to consider in this respect is: whether a state is unable or unwilling (Committee on ESCR 2000).

For a country like Nigeria, which is regarded as the eighth largest oil producing nation in the world, it is almost inexcusable if not embarrassing, that the health system has become a charade due to poor funding. Despite the huge profit the country has made on sale of oil over the years, it has woefully failed to deliver a decent health care system (including sexual and reproductive health care services) to its citizens. Worst affected are vulnerable and marginalised groups such as women, children and adolescents. The government will need to allocate more resources to the health sector, especially maternal health care, in order to address the high maternal mortality ratio in the country. Certainly, the problem with Nigeria is not that of want of resources but rather a case of misplaced priorities and corruption on the part of its rulers (Nnamuchi; 2008: 1-42). It has been observed that to know the priority of a state, one needs to monitor what it spends its money on (Coen et al. 2004: 12; Fathalla et al. 2006: 2095-2100). Therefore, the Nigerian government will need to show more commitment to meeting the health needs of women by improving its allocation to the health sector, particularly sexual and reproductive health care services.

Some international and regional human right bodies have explained the importance of adopting a rights-based approach to maternal immortality. The International Human Rights Council (2009) in one of its resolutions has noted that death during pregnancy and childbirth violates women's rights to life, health, dignity and non-discrimination. In the same vein, the African Commission (2008) has noted that the incidence of maternal mortality in the region is a violation of women's fundamental rights and freedoms. More importantly, the CEDAW Committee (1999) in its General Recommendation 24 has noted that failure of a state to ensure access to health care services peculiar to the needs of women will amount to discrimination.

Furthermore, the CEDAW Committee (2008) in one of its Concluding Observations to the government of Nigeria has expressed grave concern as regards the high maternal mortality ratio in the country and lack of progress on the part of the government to address this challenge. The Committee has identified factors responsible for this situation to include 'unsafe abortions and inadequate post-abortion care, early and child marriages, early pregnancies, high fertility rates and inadequate family planning services, the low rates of contraceptive usage leading to unwanted and unplanned pregnancies, and the lack of sex education, especially in rural areas' (CEDAW Committee 2008).

Moreover, the Committee has expressed concern with regard to 'lack of access by women and girls to adequate health-care services, including pre-natal and post-natal care, obstetric services and family planning information, particularly in rural areas'.[20] The Committee therefore, calls upon the Nigerian government to 'improve the availability and affordability of sexual and reproductive health services, including family planning information and services'.[21] It also enjoins the government to adopt measures with a view to increasing knowledge of, and access to, affordable contraceptive methods, so that women and men can make informed

[20] *Ibid*.

[21] *Ibid* para 337.

choices about the number and spacing of children.

Following from the above and in the spirit of substantive approach to equality, it is clear that the Nigerian government will be required to enact appropriate laws that will remove barriers to quality sexual and reproductive health services for women and ensure non-discrimination and autonomy in reproductive decision-making to women and girls so as to guarantee safe pregnancy and childbirth (Center for Reproductive Rights 2005). Conversely the government will need to adopt measures that will facilitate access to school, for the girl-child, including knowledge on family planning services.

6. Conclusion

This article has discussed the importance of the notion of equality to advancing women's sexual and reproductive rights, particularly maternal health, in Nigeria. It has shown that the high maternal mortality in Nigeria can be attributed to entrenched patriarchal traditions, which perpetuate gender inequality and prevent women from enjoying their fundamental rights and freedom. This situation in turn prevents women from exercising their sexual and reproductive autonomy and conversely limits access health care services to them. Efforts aimed at addressing maternal deaths in Nigeria must necessarily be grounded in realising substantive equality for women in the country. Unless women are treated as human beings worthy of respect and dignity and not as second-class citizens, efforts to prevent women from dying during pregnancy and childbirth may remain ineffective. As Hunt and De Mesquita (2008: 11) correctly noted, the principles of equality and non-discrimination require a state to ensure women's enjoyment of the right to health on the basis of non-discrimination and equality. States must not only take steps and measures to prevent maternal deaths but must also prioritize measures towards those at risk of maternal deaths such as women in rural areas, women living in poverty, indigenous women and young women,

While it can be said that the Nigerian governments have taken steps and measures towards addressing maternal deaths in the country, these efforts have not been met with adequate allocation of resources to the health needs of women. In particular the government has failed to commit adequate resources to meeting the sexual and reproductive health of women. Therefore, in line with the government's commitment under the Abuja Declaration and other consensus statements, there is a need for the government to increase spending on the health sector generally and sexual and reproductive health in particular. More importantly, there is a need for the adoption of gender-sensitive budgeting, which must prioritise women's health needs in the country (Durojaye et al. 2010: 25).

In addition, there is a need for a reappraisal of the government's approach to addressing maternal deaths. This can be done through the adoption of remedial measures, which must address inequality in health care services and facilitate equal access to health care services for women, especially sexual and reproductive health services. Such measures should include properly monitored free maternal health care services for pregnant women, particularly those in rural areas. Moreover, the Nigerian government will need to enact appropriate laws that will advance women's rights and promote their sexual and reproductive autonomy. At the same time, the government will need to repeal existing customary laws and practices which have continued to perpetuate and exacerbate gender inequality and abuses of women's fundamental rights and freedoms.

References

AFRICAN UNION
2001 African Summit on HIV/AIDS, Tuberculosis and other Related Infectious Diseases, Abuja-Nigeria April 24-27 2001 OAU/SPS/ABUJA/3.

AFRICAN COMMISSION ON HUMAN AND PEOPLES' RIGHTS
2008 Resolution on maternal mortality in Africa, ACHPR/Res. 135 (XXXXIIII). http://www.achpr.org/sessions/44th/resolutions/135/. Last accessed July 4, 2012.

ALBERTYN, Cathi and Beth GOLDBLATT
1998 'Facing the Challenge of Transformation: Difficulties in the Development of an Indigenous Jurisprudence of Equality.' *South African Journal on Human Rights* 14: 248-276.

ALLAN GUTTMACHER INSTITUTE
2004 'Early Childbearing in Nigeria: A Continuing Challenge.' *Research in Brief Series*, No. 2. Africa.

ARISTOTLE
1976 *Nicomachean Ethics*. Translated by J.A.K. Thompson. London: Penguin.

BANKOLE, Akinrinola
2009 *Barriers to Safe Motherhood in Nigeria,* New York: Allan Guttmacher Institute.

BINION, Gayle
1995 'Human Rights: A Feminist Perspective.' *Human Rights Quarterly* 17:

509-526.

BOND, Johanna
2010 'Gender Discourse and Customary Law In Africa.' *Southern California Law Review* 83: 510-570.

BREST, Paul
1976 'In Defense of the Antidiscrimination Principle.' *Harvard Law Review* 90: 1-54.

CAILLEBA, Patrice and Rekha KUMAR
2010 'When customary laws face civil society organisations: Gender issues in Botswana.' *African Journal of Political Science and International Relations* 4(9): 330-339.

CRR (CENTER FOR REPRODUCTIVE RIGHTS)
2005 *Briefing Paper: Surviving Pregnancy and Childbirth: An International Human Right.* New York: Center for Reproductive Rights.
2007 *Failure to Deliver: Violations of Women's Human Rights in Kenyan Facilities*. New York: CRR.

CRR (CENTRE FOR REPRODUCTIVE RIGHTS) and WARDC (WOMEN ADVOCATES RESEARCH DOCUMENTATION CENTRE)
2008 *Broken Promises: Human Rights, Accountability and Maternal Death in Nigeria.* New York: CRR and WARDC.

CHARLESWORTH, Hilary, Christine CHIKIN and Shelley WRIGHT
1991 'Feminists Approaches to International Law.' *American Journal of International Law* 85: 613-645.

COEN, Amy, Geeta R. GUPTA, and Dina BOGECHO
2004 'Are We There Yet? Ten years down, ten to go in achieving reproductive rights and equality for women.' Pp. 12-17 in *Countdown 2015: Sexual and Reproductive Health and Rights for All* (Special Report on International Conference on Population and Development at Ten).

COOK, Rebecca, J., Bernard M. DICKENS, Andrew F. WILSON, and Susan E. SCARROW
2001 *Advancing Safe Motherhood through Human Rights*. Geneva: WHO.

COOK, Rebecca .J,Bernard M. DICKENS, and Mahmoud F. FATHALLA
2003 *Reproductive Health and Human Rights: Integrating Medicine, Ethics, and Law*. Oxford: Oxford University Press.

COOK, Rebecca J. and Susannah HOWARD
2007 'Accommodating Women's Differences under the Women's Anti-Discrimination Convention.' *Emory Law Journal* 56: 1039-1091.

DE MESQUITA, Judith B, and Eszter KISMÖDI
2012 'Maternal Mortality and Human Rights: Landmark Decision by United Nations Human Rights Body.' *Bulletin of the World Health Organization,*

Editorials 90: 79-79A.

DUROJAYE, Ebenezer and Olabisi AYANKOGBE

2005 'A Rights-Based Approach to HIV Treatment in Nigeria.' *African Human Rights Law Journal* 5: 287-307.

DUROJAYE, Ebenezer, Ilze KEEVY, and Olubayo OLUDURO

2010 'Gender Budgeting as a Tool for Advancing Women's Health Needs in Africa.'*European Journal of Social Science* 17: 18-27.

DWORKIN, Ronald

1977 *Taking Rights Seriously*. Harvard: Harvard University Press.

EBOH, Marie P.

1998 'The Woman Question: African and Western Perspectives.' Pp. 333-337 in E.C. Eze (ed.), *African Philosophy: An Anthology*. London: Blackwell Publishers.

EFFAH, *Joseph*ine and Ngozi OSARENREN

2001 *Beyond Boundaries: Violence against Women in Nigeria*. Lagos: Project Alert on Violence against Women.

EFFAH-CHUKWUMA, Josephine and Bridget OSAKWE

2000 *No safe haven: A Report of Attacks on Women in Nigeria*. Lagos: Project Alert on Violence Against Women.

EWELUKWA, Uche U.

2002 'Post-Colonialism, Gender, Customary Injustice: Widows in African Societies.' *Human Rights Quarterly* 24: 424-486.

FATHALLA, Muhammud F., Steven W. SINDING, Allan ROSENFIELD, Mohammed M. F. FATHALLA

2006 'Sexual and Reproductive Health for All: A Call for Action.' *The Lancet* 368: 2095-2100.

(FMOH) FEDERAL MINISTRY OF HEALTH

1998 *National Policy on Health*. Abuja: Federal Ministry of Health.

2001 *National Reproductive Health Policy*. Abuja: Federal Ministry of Health.

2002 *National Reproductive Health Strategic Policy*. Abuja: Federal Ministry of Health.

2004 *National Family Planning/Reproductive Health Policy and Standards of Practice*. Abuja: Federal Ministry of Health.

FEDERAL MINISTRY OF WOMEN AFFAIRS

2002 *National Guidelines for Women's Health*, Abuja: Federal Ministry of Women Affairs.

FISS, Owen M.

1976 'Groups and the Equal Protection Clause' *Philosophy and Public Affairs* 5: 107-177.

FREEDMAN, Lynn P
2001 'Using Human Rights in Maternal Mortality Programs: From Analysis to Strategy.' *International Journal of Gynaecology and Obstetrics* 75: 51-60.
FREDMAN, Sandra.
2003 'Beyond the Dichotomy of Formal and Substantive Equality: Towards a New Definition of Equal Rights.' Pp. 226-244 in Ineke Boerefijn, F. Coomans, J. Goldschmidt, R. Holdtmaat, R. Wolleswinkel (eds.), *Temporary Special Measures Accelerating De facto Equality of Women under Article 4 (1) of the UN Convention on the Elimination of All Forms of Discrimination against Women.* Oxford: Oxford University Press.
HAILU, Samuel, Fikre ENQUESELASSIE, and Yemane BERHANE
2009 'Health facility-based Maternal Death Audit in Tigray, Ethiopia.' *Ethiopia Journal of Health Development* 23: 115-119.
HOLTMAAT, Rikki
2004 'The Concept of Discrimination.' Paper delivered at the Academy of European Law Conference. Copy on file with the author.
HORGAN, Margret C., Kyle J. FOREMAN, Mohsen NAGHAVI, Stephanie Y. AHN, Mengru WANG, Susanna M. MAKELA, Alan D. LOPEZ, Rafael LOZANO, and Christopher MURRAY
2010 'Maternal Mortality for 181 Countries, 1980-2008: A Systematic Analysis of Progress towards Millennium Development Goal 5.' *The Lancet* 375: 1609-1623.
HUNT, Paul and Judith DE MESQUITA
2008 *Reducing Maternal Mortality: The Contribution of the Right to the Highest Attainable Standard of Health.* Essex: University of Essex.
INTERIGHTS
2011 *Non-Discrimination in International Law.* London: INTERIGHTS.
INTERNATIONAL COUNCIL FOR HUMAN RIGHTS
2009 *When Legal Worlds Overlap: Human Rights, State and Non-State Laws.*
Geneva: International Council for Human Rights.
IWOBI, Andrew U.
2008 'No Cause for Merriment: The Position of Widows under Nigerian Law.' *Canadian Journal of Women and Law* 20: 37-86.
LOENEN, Titia
1997 'The Equality Clause in the South African Constitution: Some Remarks from A Comparative Perspective.' *South African Journal on Human Rights* 13: 401-429.
MAMA, Amina A.
1997 'Heroes and Villains: Conceptualising Colonial and Contemporary Violence against Women in Africa.' Pp. 46-62 in M. J. Alexander and C.

T. Mohanty (eds.), *Feminist Genealogies, Colonial Legacies, Democratic Futures*. New York/London: Routledge.

MCCRUDDEN, Christopher

1998 'Merit Principles.' *Oxford Journal of Legal Studies* 18: 543-579.

MERRY, Sally

2005 'Human rights and global legal pluralism.' Pp. 215-222 in F. and K. von Benda-Beckmann and Anne Griffiths (eds.), *Mobile People, Mobile Law. Expanding Legal Relations in a Contracting World*. Aldershot and Burlington: Ashgate.

NATIONAL POPULATION COMMISSION (NPC) and INTERNATIONAL FINANCE CORPORATION MACRO (ICF)

2009 Nigeria Demographic and Health Survey 2008. Abuja: NPC & ICF.

NNAMUCHI, Obi

2008 'Kleptocracy and its many Faces: The Challenges of Justiciability of the Right to Health Care in Nigeria.' *Journal of African Law* 52: 1-42.

OBA, Abdumumuni

2004 'Lawyers, legal education and the Shari'ah courts in Nigeria.' *Journal of Legal Pluralism* 49: 113-161.

OFFICE OF THE UNITED NATIONS HIGH COMMISSIONER FOR HUMAN RIGHTS and WORLD HEALTH ORGAIZATION

n.d. *The Right to Health Fact Sheet No. 31*. Geneva: WHO.

OPARA, Chika

1990 'Hunters and Gatherers: Poetics as Gender Politics in Sam Ukala's the Slave Wife and the Log in your Eye.' *Review of English and Literary Studies* 7: 47-54.

RAWLS, John

1971 *A Theory of Justice*. Harvard: Harvard University Press.

SHALEV, Carmel

2000 'Rights to Sexual and Reproductive Health: The ICPD and the Convention on the Elimination of All Forms of Discrimination Against Women.' *Health and Human Rights* 4: 38-66.

TAMALE, Sylvia

2004 'Gender Trauma in Africa: Enhancing Women's Links to Resources.' *Journal of African Law* 48: 50-61.

UNITED NATIONS CHILDREN FUND (UNICEF)

2010 *State of the World's Children*. New York: UNICEF.

UNITED NATIONS COMMITTEE ON THE COVENANT ON ECONOMIC, SOCIAL AND CULTURAL RIGHTS (Committee on ESCR)

2000 The Right to the Highest Attainable Standard of Health; UN Committee on ESCR General Comment No 14, UN Doc E/C/12/2000/4.

UNITED NATIONS COMMITTEE ON THE ELIMINATION OF ALL FORMS OF DISCRIMINATION AGAINST WOMEN (CEDAW)

1980 Convention on the Elimination of All Forms of Discrimination Against Women, GA Res 54/180 UN GAOR 34th Session Supp. No. 46, UN Doc A/34/46 1980.

1999 Committee on CEDAW General Recommendation 24 on Women and Health. UN GAOR, Doc A/54/38 Rev 1.

2004 Concluding Observations: Nigeria. CEDAW/C/2004/I/CRP.3/Add.2 adopted at the 30th session of the Committee held on 30 January.

2008 Concluding Observations of the Committee on CEDAW: Nigeria. Forty-First Session, 30 June -18 July. CEDAW/C.NGA/CO/6

UNITED NATIONS HUMAN RIGHTS COUNCIL

2009 Human Rights Council Preventable Maternal Mortality and Morbidity and Human Rights. http://reproductiverights.org/en/document/preventable-maternal-mortality-and-morbidity-and-human-rights. Last accessed July 4, 2012.

UNITED NATIONS CHILDREN'S FUND (UNICEF)

2009 *State of the World's Children Report 2009: Maternal and Newborn Health*. http://www.unicef.org/sowc09/. Last accessed July 4, 2012.

UNITED NATIONS OFFICE OF THE HIGH COMMISSIONER FOR HUMAN RIGHTS (UNOCHR) and WORLD HEALTH ORGANIZATION (WHO)

2008 *Fact Sheet 33: The Right to Health.* Available at http://www.ohchr.org/EN/PUBLICATIONSRESOURCES/Pages/FactSheets.aspx. Last accessed on 4 July 2012.

WESSON, Murray R.

2007 'Equality and Social Rights: An Exploration in Light of the South African Constitution.' *Public Law* 4: 748-769.

WORLD BANK

2010 Trading Economics, 'Health expenditure; public (% of GDP) in Nigeria,' http://www.tradingeconomics.com/nigeria/health-expenditure-public-percent-of-gdp-wb-data.html. Last accessed 18 April 2012.

WORLD HEALTH ORGANIZATION (WHO)

1992 *The Tenth Revision of the International Classification of Diseases (ICD-10)*, Geneva: WHO.

2005 *The World Health Report 2005 – Make Every Mother and Child Count.* Geneva: WHO.

2006 *Skilled attendant at birth - 2006 updates*. Available at http://www.who.int/reproductivehealth/global_monitoring/skilled_attendant.html. Last accessed on 23 April 2012.

2011 *The Abuja Declaration: Ten Years On.* Geneva: WHO.

WORLD HEALTH ORGANIZATION (WHO), UNITED NATIONS CHILDREN'S FUND (UNICEF), UNITED NATIONS POPULATION FUND (UNFPA), WORLD BANK
2004 *Maternal mortality in 2000*: Estimates. Geneva: WHO.
2007 *Maternal Mortality in 2005*.Geneva: WHO.
2012 *Trends in Maternal Mortality: 1990 to 2010*. Geneva: WHO.

LEGAL PLURALISM INCARNATE: AN INSTITUTIONAL PERSPECTIVE ON COURTS OF LAW IN COLONIAL AND POSTCOLONIAL SETTINGS[1]

Ido Shahar

Introduction

Recent decades have witnessed a shift in the study of legal pluralism from a focus on legal pluralism in colonial and post-colonial settings, to a focus on legal pluralism in the Western, industrialized world (Merry 1988), and later on to legal pluralism stemming from globalization and trans-nationalism (see e.g.: Merry 2007; Tamanaha 2007, Berman 2007, 2009). And yet, legal pluralism in colonial and post-colonial settings is still one of the most prevalent and well-studied forms of this phenomenon. This form of legal pluralism was dubbed by Merry (1988: 872) 'classic', to denote the fact that it was the first type of legal pluralism to be studied systematically, and that it was in the context of colonial and post-colonial studies that the theoretical notion of legal pluralism was first developed.[2]

---

[1] Early versions of the article were presented at Tel Aviv University (in a seminar series on the Anthropology of Organizations) and at the workshop *Dynamics of Muslim Legal Pluralism under Colonial Rule* convened 9-10 December 2010 in Halle/Saale at the Institute of Oriental Studies of the Martin-Luther University (Halle-Wittenberg). I would like to thank the participants at these events for their helpful comments. My thanks go also to Gordon Woodman and Moussa Abou Ramadan for their valuable suggestions.

[2] For broad historical and conceptual discussions of legal pluralism, see: Griffiths 1986; Merry 1988; Woodman 1998; F von Benda-Beckmann 2002; Tamanaha 2007.

A situation of 'classic' legal pluralism occurs when a sovereign commands different bodies of law to different groups of the population according to their ethnicity, religion or geographic location. Surely, a wide variety of cases fall under this rubric.[3] Nevertheless, some general characteristics of 'classic' legal pluralism can be discerned:

1. This type of legal pluralism is usually the outcome of a colonial encounter in which a Western/colonial/statal body of law incorporates an indigenous/customary/religious body of law (Hooker 1975).

2. Since the incorporation of the indigenous/religious/customary body of law is always performed from a position of power, the status and jurisdiction of this body of law is determined by legal arrangements controlled by the colonial authorities. This is why the incorporated body of law always has, according to Hooker (1975), a 'servient' position vis-à-vis the 'dominant' position of the Western/colonial/statal body of law.[4]

3. The degree of state intervention in the 'servient' or subaltern body of law may range from the most minimal to the most extensive, and so does the degree of autonomy enjoyed by the courts that apply this incorporated body of law. Nevertheless, even when intervention is minimal (or allegedly minimal), the subservient body of law should not be seen as a pristine authentic remnant of a traditional legal system, representing the 'real' norms, values and ways of life of the indigenous culture. Rather, this body of law should be viewed as a product of the encounter between the colonized and the colonizer and of the asymmetrical

---

[3] Hooker's *Legal Pluralism: An Introduction to Colonial and New-colonial Laws* (1975) is still the most comprehensive review of "classic" legal pluralism in Asia and Africa. For a review of this type of legal pluralism in South America, see Sieder 2002.

[4] It is important to note, however, that the formal legal hierarchy of 'servient' and 'dominant' bodies of law does not always apply in concrete social situations. It may very well be that in specific contexts, the indigenous body of law would have the upper hand, in terms of the regulation of behavior, rather than the Western/colonial/statal body of law.

> power relations between them (see e.g.: Snyder 1981; Chanock 1985; Moore 1986; Merry 1991). Similarly, the courts that apply this subservient, incorporated body of law are usually 'hybrid institutions', combining different legal cultures (Santos 2006).

A vast body of literature dealing with classic legal pluralism has accumulated since the 1970s. Nevertheless, in this article I would like to point toward a significant lacuna in this body of research and attempt to redress it. Specifically, I highlight the lack of attention in this literature to the *organizational and institutional levels of analysis*, that is, to courts of law as organizations that operate within multiple organizational and institutional environments. Indeed, apart from a few notable exceptions (see e.g.: Moore 1973; K von Benda-Beckmann 1981; Spierz 1991; Santos 2006), most of the literature on classic legal pluralism – from the 1970s until this very day – has failed to consider these levels of analysis.

This article aims, therefore, to provide a fresh look at a well-studied phenomenon. It seeks to demonstrate that, by focusing on courts as organizations that are embedded within organizational and institutional contexts, one may gain new insights into classic legal pluralism. More specifically, I examine 'servient' or 'subaltern' courts in situations of classic legal pluralism and argue that these courts often operate within two different institutional fields: an indigenous one and a colonial/statal one. Each of the fields exerts different influences on these courts and places different demands on them. In terms of new institutional theory in organization studies (e.g.: Meyer and Rowan 1977; DiMaggio and Powell 1983; Scott 1995), these courts operate in an environment that is characterized not only by legal pluralism but also by institutional pluralism (Kraatz and Block 2008). Consequently, they develop pliable and dynamic legal cultures that reflect their bifurcated environment. In a sense, they embody the very essence of legal pluralism: they are shaped by the pluralistic nature of their environment, and at the same time they create and enact legally pluralistic arrangements through their rulings and practices. They represent, in other words, 'legal pluralism incarnate'.

To illustrate and develop this argument, the paper presents an empirical case study of sharī'a courts in present-day Israel. For the purposes of this research, I treat legal pluralism in contemporary Israel as 'colonial-like', that is, as similar to the legal pluralism we encounter in colonial and post-colonial settings. Many characteristics of classic legal pluralism can be identified in this case: The sharī'a body of law and the sharī'a court system have been incorporated into the Israeli legal system; within this system, sharī'a courts have been given jurisdiction over matters related to the personal status of one particular group, Muslim residents of Israel;[5] the Israeli sharī'a courts operate parallel to civil family courts, which undoubtedly occupy a more dominant position within the Israeli legal system, and their legal culture undeniably combines Palestinian-Islamic and Israeli elements (see Shahar 2000). Thus, although most scholars of post-colonialism would probably agree that the Israeli case differs from more 'ordinary' cases of colonial/post-colonial states,[6] the form of legal pluralism that can be observed in Israel today clearly belongs to the 'classic', post-colonial type.

I argue that Israeli sharī'a courts operate, simultaneously, in two different institutional fields. On the one hand, they belong to the field of Israeli state law, interact closely with other organizations in this field such as the High Court of Justice and the Ministry of Justice, and must gain legitimacy and acceptance within this field. On the other hand, they belong to the shar'ī (Palestinian) institutional field in Israel and the West Bank, interact with other organizations populating this field, and must adapt to its distinct norms, values and ideologies. I further contend that Israeli sharī'a courts cope with the contradictory pressures exerted by these two institutional fields by developing flexible, dynamic judicial policies and legal culture, which both reflect their pluralistic environment and reproduce it.

The article unfolds as follows. The next section briefly introduces the basic tenets of new institutional theory in organization studies and discusses the applicability of this theory to the study of legal pluralism. This is followed by a socio-legal review of Israeli sharī'a courts, their legal status, and the two different institutional fields within which they operate. The bulk of the analysis then dwells on two judicial reforms that were introduced into these courts in recent years, which are traced back to contradictory influences and pressures exerted within the two institutional fields. Finally, the empirical and theoretical implications of this research are elaborated.

---

[5] In fact, they also have jurisdiction in matters of personal status of foreign Muslim citizens sojourning in Israel, whose states also apply Islamic law in these matters.

[6] During the 1980s and 1990s, a lively academic debate took place among historians, sociologists, and political scientists concerning the identification of Zionism as a colonial movement and of Israel as a colonial state (see e.g.: Rodinson 1973; Schoenman 1988; Shafir 1996; Ghanem 1998). Referring to this debate extensively is beyond the scope of this paper, as for our purpose here it is sufficient to state that *legal pluralism* in Israel is indeed "colonial-like".

New Institutional Theory in Organization Studies and the Study of Legal Pluralism

New institutional theory has been one of the most influential organizational theories in the last four decades.[7] At its core lies an underlying skepticism toward atomistic explanations of social processes (Wooten and Hoffman 2008) and a belief that organizations, like individuals, are constituted through their embeddedness within broader systems of meanings and networks of relationships. Accordingly, a central construct in new institutional theory has been the notion of 'organizational field'. Each organization, according to new institutionalists, operates within one or more organizational fields, and cannot be understood outside of this context. An organizational field is defined as "a community of organizations that partakes of a common meaning system and whose participants interact more frequently and fatefully with one another than with actors outside of the field" (Scott 1995: 6).[8] Thus, for example, Israeli courts, as organizations, can only be understood in light of their relations with other organizations they interact with, and/or that are related to the Israeli legal system as a recognized area of institutional life. These may include other courts (e.g., magistrate's courts, district courts, the High Court of Justice, religious courts); state organizations such as the State Advocacy, the Ministry of Justice, and the Israeli parliament (the Knesset); state agencies outside the strict boundaries of the legal system that interact with it and affect it, such as the police, the prison administration; professional associations such as the Bar; and civil society groups such as human rights and women's rights organizations.[9]

---

[7] Indeed, its influence may also be detected in the law and society field of research (see e.g. Suchman and Edelman 1996). Several scholars applied the new institutional theoretical framework for the study of courts of law (e.g.: Epstein et al. 1989; Hall and Brace 1989; Brace and Hall 1995; Cohen 2002), yet, as far as I know, this approach was never applied in the context of legal pluralism.

[8] A different conceptualization was suggested by DiMaggio and Powell (1983: 148), who define an 'organizational field' as consisting of "those organizations that, in the aggregate, constitute a recognized area of institutional life: key suppliers, resource and product consumers, regulatory agencies, and other organizations that produce similar services or products". Obviously, there are no objective, absolute boundaries to organizational fields; rather, the demarcation of the boundaries in specific cases is relative and operational, and depends on both empirical investigation and the researcher's goals and perspectives.

[9] Researchers have often debated the relationship between the theoretical construct

A basic tenet of new institutional theory is that organizations within an organizational field are under constant pressure to conform to the rules and models that prevail within this field. Such conformism is necessary for an organization to gain legitimacy as a rational, effective and fair organization, whereas failure to conform to accepted rules, norms and models means loss of legitimacy. Since organizations depend on their environments for obtaining resources, they, or more precisely, the staff or the personnel working in them, cannot afford to lose their legitimacy in the organizational field.

According to DiMaggio and Powell (1983), organizations are therefore exposed to strong *isomorphic* pressures operating within the organizational field. They identify three different sources of isomorphism in organizational fields:

1. *Coercive isomorphism.* This kind of isomorphism results, according to DiMaggio and Powell, "from both formal and informal pressures exerted on organizations by other organizations upon which they are dependent and by cultural expectations in the society within which organizations function" (DiMaggio and Powell 1983: 67).

2. *Mimetic isomorphism.* This kind of isomorphism is based on imitation, and is intensified under conditions of uncertainty: "[W]hen organizational technologies are poorly understood, when goals are ambiguous, or when the environment creates symbolic

of 'organizational field' and other sociological notions of fields, especially that of Bourdieu (e.g.: Fourcade 2007; Emirbayer and Johnson 2008). Unlike Bourdieu's notion of field, the construct of 'organizational field' naturally focuses on organizations as predominant field actors. In recent years, however, this focus has somewhat eroded, and today the term 'institutional field' is often used interchangeably with 'organizational field' (as will also be done in this paper). Another major difference has to do with underlying assumptions concerning power and conflict: while for Bourdieu the field is a terrain of ongoing contestation and struggle for domination, early versions of new institutional theory tended to draw attention away from conflict within organizational fields. Instead, they were interested primarily in the processes whereby fields stabilize and coalesce around accepted, taken for granted structures, norms and 'rules of the game' (see Wooten and Hoffman 2008). This tendency has been somewhat mitigated, however, in recent new institutional literature (see e.g. Greenwood et. el 2008).

uncertainty, organizations may model themselves on other organizations" (DiMaggio and Powell 1983: 69). Such mimetic modeling occurs when other organizations in the organizational field are perceived as more legitimate or more successful.

3. *Normative isomorphism*. This kind of isomorphism is related to the diffusion of norms in organizational fields, and is attributed primarily to the presence of professionals and of professional networks in such fields. Professionals share common formal education and common codes of behavior, and are connected by professional networks that span organizational boundaries. They therefore constitute a significant conduit for the dissemination of rules, norms and cultural models between organizations.

DiMaggio and Powell contend that these isomorphic pressures push organizations pertaining to an organizational field towards becoming increasingly similar to one other; they also push the organizational field as a whole to homogenization and stabilization as it matures. Yet, what happens when an organization is active in more than one organizational field? This question has attracted growing attention among organizational scholars in recent years. Kraatz and Block (2008) observe that some organizations operate in environments characterized by 'institutional pluralism': they are active in multiple institutional spheres, are subject to multiple regulatory regimes, must conform to multiple normative orders, and are constituted by more than one 'institutional logic'. This situation poses many challenges in terms of the legitimacy of these organizations, their identity and status within the different organizational fields they belong to, and the consistency of their actions and policies.

New institutional theory provides us, therefore, with an interesting perspective and with useful analytical tools for studying courts of law in situations of legal pluralism, and especially for studying 'subaltern courts' in situations of 'classic' legal pluralism. How do such courts cope with their often multiple membership in more than one organizational or institutional field? How do they manage to maintain their legitimacy in two or more different fields, which may exert different and even contradictory demands and pressures? How does the pluralistic environment affect the judicial policies and decisions of these courts? And what legal and organizational cultures do these courts develop under such circumstances? In the pages below, I address these questions in a concrete socio-legal case study – that of sharīʻa courts in Israel.

Sharī'a Courts in Israel: An Overview[10]

The system of sharī'a courts in Israel consists of eight courts of first instance, which are spread in Palestinian-Muslim towns (Tayyibe, Bāqa al-Gharbiya, Nazareth) and in mixed Jewish-Palestinian cities (Jerusalem, Haifa, Jaffa, Beer-Sheva, Acre). In addition, a sharī'a court of appeals sits in Jerusalem. Except for the first instance court in Jerusalem, all other courts serve communities of Palestinian-Israelis, who are full citizens of Israel and dwell within the 1948 borders.[11] Israeli sharī'a courts are presided over by Muslim judges (qāḍīs), who are chosen by a public committee and appointed by the President of Israel. The courts conduct hearings and produce court records in Arabic, but their senior staff (the qāḍīs and the chief secretaries) must have good command of Hebrew as well, so that they can communicate with other governmental, municipal and professional functionaries.

The origins of the sharī'a court system in contemporary Israel are to be found in the legal systems of the late-Ottoman and Mandate periods. Indeed, one of the most significant vestiges of the Ottoman Empire in contemporary Israel is the preservation of a *millet*-like legal system in the domain of family law (Friedmann 1975: 206). The millet system of the Ottoman Empire was a system of 'classic' legal pluralism, under which some non-Muslim religious minorities (Jews and several Christian denominations) were granted extensive legal, religious and cultural autonomy. These religious communities were allowed to establish their own autonomous courts, which employed religious law, and which had jurisdiction in matters of personal status relating to their respective community members (Ursinus 1993; see also: Braude 1982; Davidson 1982).

Under the British Mandate in Palestine (1917-1948), the millet system was largely preserved. Nevertheless, Muslim sharī'a courts, which had previously been considered state courts, were now introduced as autonomous religious courts into the Millet-like personal status regime. This new arrangement was later inherited by

---

[10] For detailed discussions of Israeli sharī'a courts - their history, status and jurisdiction - see: Eisenman 1978; Layish 1965, 1971, 1975, 2006; Peled 2001a; Abou Ramadan 2008.

[11] The sharī'a court in West Jerusalem is unique in providing services to a population of non-citizens, namely, Muslim residents of East Jerusalem, which was occupied and annexed in 1967.

the state of Israel (see Layish 1965). Notably, until November 2001,[12] sharī'a courts had maintained greater jurisdiction than any other religious courts in Israel. They had enjoyed a virtual monopoly over the determination of the personal status of Israeli Muslim citizens - e.g., their identity as Muslims, bachelors, married, divorcees and parents of children.[13]

Like many other situations of classic legal pluralism, legal pluralism in Israel centers, therefore, on family law and personal status matters.[14] Another salient resemblance between the Israeli case and colonial/post-colonial cases is that the autonomous position granted to the subaltern body of law within the legal system is all but unlimited. Like the British colonial officers, who "generally recognized indigenous law, with the exception of laws that violated British law or were 'repugnant to natural justice, equity or good conscience'" (Merry 1991: 897), the Israeli parliament generally refrained from interfering with religious laws, unless their provisions were in direct contradiction to Israeli statutes (see Layish 2006). Indeed, although the Ottoman Law of Family Rights of 1917 (OLFR) and the Ottoman Law of Procedure for Sharī'a Courts[15] still apply to date in Israeli sharī'a courts, these laws have been curtailed to a significant extent by several Israeli statutes.

---

[12] On November 7, 2001, the Knesset passed Amendment No. 5 of the Family Courts Law, 5755–1995, which gave jurisdiction to the civil family courts in all matters of personal status affecting Muslims, except for marriage and divorce. By this Act, the Israeli legislator made the jurisdiction of sharī'a courts equal to that of the other religious courts in Israel. About the long political struggle that preceded the affirmation of this legislative amendment, see Shahar 2007.

[13] The jurisdiction of the sharī'a courts had been broad not only compared with that of Christian and Druze courts, but also compared with that of rabbinical courts (Layish 1965).

[14] Indeed, since colonial officers perceived personal status matters as most sensitive in terms of cultural identity (see Chanock 1985: 145), they were particularly inclined to incorporate religious/indigenous courts, dealing with these matters, into the colonial legal system. As noted by many observers, this policy characterized colonial rule in general (see, e.g.: Bohannan 1957: 72; Gluckman 1965: 64), and it is the main source of legal pluralism in post-colonial states until this very day (Hooker 1975; Benton 2002: 127).

[15] These sharī'a codes were promulgated by the Ottoman Empire at the very final moments of its existence. On OLFR, see Tucker 1996.

For example, the Israeli legislator, who was not indifferent to some elements of discrimination against women in sharīʿa courts, saw fit to criminalize certain acts that are sanctioned by the OLFR. Thus, Polygamy, unilateral repudiation of a wife without her consent, and marrying off a minor girl are all considered, according to Israeli Penal Law, as criminal offences, which are liable to severe punishments.[16] The Knesset also promulgated several statutes that were directed specifically to religious courts (e.g., The Succession Law [1965], The Spouses (Property Relations) Law [1973], The Prevention of Violence in the Family Law [1991]), and that are therefore applied in Israeli sharīʿa courts alongside the Ottoman sharīʿa codes.[17]

The relations between these highly diversified sources of law are far from being well-defined. Rather, they are characterized by ambiguity and equivocality. Consequently, the qāḍīs are able to employ the various sources of law at their disposal in a relatively free manner (see below). Like other subaltern courts in situations of classic legal pluralism, Israeli sharʿīa courts can therefore be described as 'hybrid institutions,' which employ norms and values originating from very different social philosophies. This 'norm pluralism' (Bowen 2003: 257) finds its expression in these courts' decisions.

Yet, as I aim to illustrate in this article, in order to better understand the hybrid character of these courts, it is not enough to analyze how they combine different bodies of laws and legal traditions. Rather, it is important to observe that they are located at the intersection of two different organizational fields, and thus operate within two different institutional settings. On the one hand, they belong to a broad organizational field - as defined above - which is structured around the Israeli state-legal system. On the other hand, and at the very same time, they belong to another organizational field, which is constructed around Palestinian-sharʿī

[16] Nevertheless, since the religious law itself has not been amended, such acts have become liable to civil and/or penal suits while still valid and approved by the religious law. See discussion of this issue below.

[17] See the website of the Israeli sharīʿa court system: http://www.justice.gov.il/MOJHeb/BatiDinHashreim/ The Israeli High Court of Justice has recently ruled that the Capacity and Guardianship Law (1962) is also applicable in sharīʿa courts (see, H.C.J 9740/05, X v. The Sharīʿa Court of Appeals in Jerusalem, P.D. 06(1) 1541 (2006); H.C.J 1129/06, X. v. The Sharīʿa Court of Appeals, P.D. 06 (2) 3313 (2006)). About these HCJ decisions, see also Abou Ramadan 2006.

organizations and institutions.

The first organizational field nurtures a strong Zionist, civil, and gender-equalizing ethos, which is very much alien to sharīʿa courts. Thus, although Israeli sharīʿa courts are part and parcel of this organizational field, their position within it is distinctly marginal: they are perceived as 'non-organic elements' in this field, and since they serve a population (Israeli Muslim-Palestinians) that is always looked upon with deep suspicion in the Israeli context, they are also suspicious in the eyes of most Israeli governmental functionaries.[18]

In comparison to the Israeli state-law organizational field, the second field - the Palestinian - sharīʿa organizational field - is not well-defined. It is constructed around institutions related to Islamic law, Islamic education and 'Islamic religious affairs' in Israel/Palestine, but since it includes institutions that operate in three distinct political environments (Israel, the West Bank and the Gaza Strip), its boundaries are rather blurred. This field, as I define it, includes Islamic institutions in Israel such as Israeli sharīʿa courts, sharīʿa colleges and universities,[19] muftis, imams and preachers (who may be regarded as religious institutions, not only as individuals), the waqf establishment in Israel, Islamic almsgiving associations and non-governmental Islamic organizations such as the Islamic movement in Israel.[20] It also includes, however, similar institutions that operate in the West Bank, in East Jerusalem and to some extent in the Gaza Strip as well.

[18] It is not surprising, therefore, that other actors within this field tend to refer to the rulings of Israeli sharīʿa courts with manifest suspicion. For example, in recent years, the National Insurance Institute has implemented a new policy with regard to children maintenance orders issued by sharīʿa courts: The Institute now demands that women who were awarded child maintenance payments in sharīʿa courts first present a court ruling confirming that they have custody over their children. The very fact that this measure was not implemented with regard to maintenance orders issued by other courts (e.g., family courts, rabbinical courts), reflects the distrust with which sharīʿa courts are regarded within the Israeli state-law organizational field.

[19] For example, the Umm al-Faḥm College of Preaching and Canonic Studies (*Kuliyyat Umm al-Faḥm li'l-Daʿwa wa'l-ʿUlūm al-Sharʿiyya*).

[20] On the Islamic Movement in Israel, see Meir 1998; Peled 2001b.

As shown by many scholars studying Palestinian society, following the 1967 war the national, familial and political ties between the Palestinians in Israel and their co-patriots in the West Bank and the Gaza Strip were reestablished (Rouhana 1989; Rekhess 1989; Smooha 1992). These ties were particularly firm in the case of Islamic religious services and Islamic institutions, as the development of such institutions within Israel was held at bay by the authorities until the late 1980s (Peled 2001a). Some of the leaders of the Islamic movement in Israel, for example, were educated in Islamic universities at the West Bank in the 1970s and 1980s, and still maintain very close relationships with various Islamic elements in the West Bank (see: Rekhess 1993; Louër 2007: 70, 158).

Likewise, Israeli qāḍīs maintain close relationships with their Palestinian and Jordanian counterparts. This is especially pronounced in Jerusalem, where many of the functionaries of the waqf establishment in *al-Ḥaram al-sharīf* (Temple Mount), serve as mediators and arbiters (*ahl al-khayr, muḥakkamin*)[21] on behalf of the Israeli shari'a court. Some of these people have even agreed to serve as marriage registrars (*ma'adhūnin*) by appointment of this court. The Israeli qāḍīs in Jerusalem do not hesitate to seek the advice of their Jordanian and Palestinian colleagues in the most prestigious cases which are brought to their deliberation (cases involving waqf disputes); and they tend to refer with pronounced respect to *fatwās* that were issued by the Jordanian-appointed (and later on, the Palestinian-appointed) mufti of Jerusalem.[22] It is not surprising, perhaps, that in recent years Israeli qāḍīs have become honored guests, regularly invited to participate in prayers on Muslim holidays and during the month of *Ramadan* at the *Ḥaram al-Sharīf* (Shahar n.d.).

We may therefore conclude that from the point of view of Israeli qāḍīs, the two fields - the Israeli state-law organizational field and the Palestinian-shar'ī organizational field - are both important and tangible. These two fields nurture, however, very different values, norms, bureaucratic traditions, organizational cultures and, of course, political inclinations. Whereas the organizational field associated with the Israeli state legal system is characterized by a strong Zionist,

[21] The role of these professional mediators is to intervene - by formal nomination of the qāḍī - in matrimonial disputes and to try and resolve them outside of the court (Layish 1975: 106).

[22] See for example, cases no. 985/2002; 112/1998; 404/1999, Israeli sharī'a court in Jerusalem.

civil, and gender-equalizing ethos, the shar'ī (Palestinian) organizational field is generally characterized by a national-Palestinian, religious-Islamic, and patriarchal ethos.[23]

This structural positioning of Israeli sharī'a courts at the intersection of two different organizational fields, poses exceptional challenges. Simply put, in order to continue functioning, the qāḍīs and personnel of these courts need to maneuver between the contradictory influences, pressures and expectations originating from the two opposing organizational fields to which these courts belong. To exemplify how such maneuvering may look, let us turn now to an analysis of two judicial reforms which have been introduced in these courts in recent years. At first glance, these two reforms - when viewed together - seem to indicate an incoherent judicial policy. However, I will show that they represent, in fact, a persistent effort to accommodate to conflicting demands exerted within two very different organizational fields.

The Judicial Policy of Israeli Sharī'a Courts: Coping with Contradictory Isomorphic Pressures

From the many judicial, procedural, and administrative reforms that have been implemented in the Israeli sharī'a courts in recent years (see Abou Ramadan 2003a, 2003b), I focus in this section on two specific judicial reforms: a reform in maintenance claims and a reform in the treatment of Israeli statutes. My discussion of these reforms is based on an analysis of sharī'a courts' decisions, especially those issued by the sharī'a court of appeals, as well as on fieldwork that I conducted in the Israeli sharī'a court in West Jerusalem during the years 2000-2004.

[23] This is not to say, however, that these organizational fields should be seen as monolithic, well-defined and static. Undoubtedly, each of these fields comprises not only diverse organizations, but also diverse legal philosophies, bureaucratic traditions, and political tendencies. And yet, as assumed by new institutional theorists, these organizational fields are characterized by 'dominant' or commonly accepted 'institutional logics,' and organizations that belong to them are expected to conform to these commonly accepted logics.

(a) Reform in Maintenance Claims

In the mid-1990s, the Israeli sharīʻa court system found itself under mounting pressures: voices - originating primarily from liberal and feminist circles in Israeli society - began to express public criticism of the sharīʻa courts. Specifically, they called for the equalization of the status of Muslim women to that of Jewish, Christian and Druze women. These feminist activists argued that Muslim women were discriminated against, since unlike women from other religious communities, they were not allowed to file maintenance suits against their husbands in civil courts, and had no choice but to appeal to sharīʻa courts. This limitation, in their view, prevented Muslim women from improving their position within the traditional patriarchal family (see e.g. Ibrahim 1993: 26-27).

Blaming the qāḍīs presiding in shariʻa courts for being 'conservative', and viewing the procedural and material laws employed by sharīʻa courts as inherently discriminatory against women (Bishara and Toma-Suliman 1997), feminist activists demanded that jurisdictions in matters pertaining to the personal status of Muslims be conferred upon civil family courts. In other words, they demanded that the jurisdiction of sharīʻa courts be reduced and equalized to the jurisdiction of the other religious courts in Israel. Several women's organizations and civil rights organizations had joined hands in this struggle, and by 1995, a 'Working Group for Equality in Personal Status Issues' had been established.[24]

This ad-hoc coalition of civil society organizations waged a public and political campaign promoting its cause. The group initiated a bill for the amendment of the Family Courts Law, [25] with the purpose of granting Muslim women the option of recourse to civil family courts in maintenance suits, as well as in all other matters of personal status except for marriage and divorce.[26] This enterprise was met with

[24] This working group consisted of the following organizations: Women Against Violence; The Association for Human Rights in Israel; The Arab Association for Human Rights; Al-Ṭufūla: Pedagogical and Multipurpose Women's Center; Israel's Women Network; Shatil: Equal Access Project; Al-Siwar: Arab Feminist Movement in Support of Victims of Sexual Violence; Haifa Women's Shelter; The Association for Nurturing Family Relations; The Social Workers' Association.

[25] See report in the website of the Association for Human Rights in Israel. Available at: http://www.acri.org.il/he/?p=5593 (Accessed 20.7.2012).

[26] In a clarification annexed to the legislative bill, the drafters presented statistical data from the database of the National Insurance Institute, which indicated that the

fierce opposition on the part of Israeli qāḍīs. Realizing the danger for sharī'a rule, and aiming to prevent any detraction of their status and authority, the qāḍīs - led by the charismatic president of the sharī'a court of appeals, Aḥmad Naṭūr[27] - initiated a legal reform of their own.

Striving to take the sting out of the bite of the feminist-liberal initiative, qāḍī Naṭūr sought a method that would yield a systematic increase in the sums of maintenance payments adjudicated in shari'a courts. The solution he found was to initiate a reform that transferred the authority to determine the sums of maintenance from appointed informants (*mukhbirūn*) to the qāḍīs themselves. Instead of relying on informants for the purpose of gathering information concerning the husband's financial state, as the OLFR provisioned,[28] Naṭūr suggested that the qāḍīs themselves determine the sums of maintenance payments, relying, for that purpose, on official state documents such as income tax and national insurance forms.

Interestingly, in order to achieve this reform, the qāḍīs made a creative use of a unique judicial mechanism: the legal circular (*marsūm qāḍā'ī*).[29] All the qāḍīs holding office in Israeli sharī'a courts signed the circular, thereby committing themselves to apply the procedural reform that it suggested. It seems, however, that the qāḍīs committed themselves not only to the procedural reform, but also to the notion of allotting more generous sums as maintenance payments to women. In the

sums of wives' maintenance and child maintenance payments adjudicated by sharī'a courts are significantly lower than the sums adjudicated by family courts. They therefore concluded that to improve the status of Muslim and Christian women, it is mandatory to grant these women better access to civil family courts. The implicit underlying assumption was that substantial and comprehensive legal equality between men and women can only be achieved in the civil courts, and not in the patriarchal sharī'a courts (a bill draft prepared by the Working Group for Equality in Personal Status Issues, no author, no date is mentioned).

[27] On the growing influence of qāḍi Natūr in the sharī'a court system, see Abou Ramadan 2003b.

[28] Article 31 of the OLFR.

[29] The circular, titled '*marsūm qāḍa'i Raqam 2: Wazifat al-Mukhbirin fī Qāḍaya al-Nafaqa*' was published in 1995. Available at: http://www.justice.gov.il/NR/rdonlyres/1A2E05D7-6731-4804-B28A-D52B6350CD13/0/MRASEEM02.pdf (Accessed: 17.3.2012).

years following the promulgation of the circular, a 50% rise in the sums of maintenance has been noted in the sharī'a court in West Jerusalem.[30] Indeed, a report issued by the National Insurance Institute in 2003 further supports these findings, and shows that a similar process took place at the national level as well. According to the data gathered by the National Insurance Institute, in 2002 sharī'a courts granted women higher maintenance sums than any other court system in Israel - higher even than civil family courts.[31] Nevertheless, despite the impressive efforts made by the qāḍīs, and despite the substantial increase in the average maintenance sums determined by sharī'a courts, the 'legislation train' did not stop, and the amendment to the Family Court Law passed in the Knesset in November 2001.[32]

For our purpose, however, the most important aspect of this episode is the direct link between the pro-women judicial reform initiated by the qāḍīs and the pressures exerted on sharī'a courts within the Israeli state-law organizational field. The judicial reform led by qāḍī Naṭūr was a direct response to a threat to the status of Israeli sharī'a courts within this field, i.e., to the threat that their jurisdiction would be reduced. This threat was created by civil society organizations, which also belonged to the Israeli state-law organizational field, as this field was defined above. These organizations - most of which were dominated by liberal circles in Jewish Israeli society - tried to mobilize this field, and eventually the Knesset, for improving the status of women in Israeli sharī'a courts. Put differently, they sought to harness the coercive power of the state for promoting their agenda.

To prevent this danger, sharī'a courts had to accommodate to the dominant norms,

---

[30] My data is based on a sample of maintenance files that were adjudicated by the sharī'a court in West Jerusalem between the years 1994-1998. The sample includes: 6 files from 1994; 5 files from 1995; 5 files from 1996; 8 files from 1997; 6 files from 1998. I do not have systematic estimates of the maintenance sums adjudicated by other sharī'a courts in Israel, but I was told (proudly) by qāḍī Naṭūr, who was the leading author of the legal circular, that the sums of maintenance payments have increased significantly following the issuance of the circular (interview with qāḍī Naṭūr, January 1998). It is therefore reasonable to assume that the same rise in maintenance payments also occurred in other courts (see also Reiter 1997: 226).

[31] See Toledano 2003: 19, table 12.

[32] For a much more detailed discussion of this episode and of this legal circular, see Shahar 2007.

values and logics of the Israeli state-law organizational field, and especially to its gender-equalizing ethos. This sort of adjustment was deemed necessary for sharīʿa courts to maintain their legitimacy and status within this field. Moreover, to achieve this goal these courts had to become more similar to the civil family courts, which are more central actors in this field and which better represent its ethos. In terms of new institutional theory, processes of mimetic isomorphism also contributed, therefore, to the pro-women judicial reform initiated by Israeli sharīʿa courts. These courts were pushed to imitate civil family courts and to determine similar maintenance sums to women, as a means for gaining legitimacy within the Israeli state-law organizational field. The fact that even this incredibly effective internal reform could not prevent the diminution of sharīʿa courts' jurisdiction testifies, perhaps, to the relatively marginal position of these courts in the state-law organizational field, and to their relative lack of political power.

(b) Taking 'Earthly Laws' Out of Sharīʿa Courts' Rulings

During the second half of the 1990s – at about the same time that the sharīʿa court system had been entangled in the bitter struggle described above, and not at all unrelated to this struggle – the sharīʿa court of appeals had begun promoting a surprising new judicial policy. Under the leadership of qāḍī Naṭūr, the sharīʿa court of appeals embarked on an effort to distance the sharīʿa court system from Israeli law. In numerous appellate decisions, phrased in sharp rhetoric, the sharīʿa court of appeals admonished the first instance sharīʿa courts for relying in their judgments on Israeli law. Thus, for example, qāḍī Naṭūr stated, with regard to a decision concerning temporary maintenance:

> [I]t should be mentioned that the civil law that the lower court draws on, with regard to temporary maintenance, is unrelated to the law applied by sharīʿa courts. The lower court ruling does not apply to Muslims, given that the sharīʿa court is prohibited from ruling in accordance with laws that are not grounded in Islamic law, and must only rule in accordance with the sharīʿa law.[33]

And in another decision, dealing with the Capacity and Guardianship Law:

---

[33] Case no. 191/1997, the Israeli sharīʿa court of appeal, quoted in Abou Ramadan 2003b: 277.

> The sharī'a courts must not rely on the Capacity and Guardianship Law, 1962 [...] the noble sharī'a constituted a complete judicial system before [this law was promulgated], and will remain such after [it will change or disappear]. The sharī'a does not require any positive secular rules.[34]

This new emphasis on Islamic sources - and only on Islamic sources - stands in sharp contrast to the judicial policy of previous generations of Israeli sharī'a judges, who had no inhibitions with regard to reliance on Israeli statutes (Layish 1975).

These new directives to first instance sharī'a courts resulted in substantial confusion, and yet this did not deter the sharī'a court of appeals, which was determined, so it seems, to create a symbolic - if not real - buffer between the sharī'a court system and Israeli law. This policy was taken one step forward when the sharī'a court of appeals directed qāḍīs that even when they find out, during their hearings, that litigants had violated Israeli statutes, they should avoid mentioning these violations in their rulings.

To better understand the meaning of this last reform, some background information is necessary. Until the late 1990s, when Israeli qāḍīs had encountered a case of polygamous marriage or of marrying off a minor girl, they naturally ratified these marriages, as these are perfectly legitimate practices according to the Ottoman sharī'a code.[35] Nevertheless, they also added a note to the file, stating that a felony had been committed.[36] Moreover, the file was sent to the sharī'a court

---

[34] Case no. 55/2001, quoted in Abou Ramadan 2003b: 278. For similar statements, see also cases no. 294/1998; 194/1999.

[35] The OLFR determines that a man is allowed to marry up to four wives at the same time (article 14), and that a guardian may marry off a girl 15 years of age (article 35). If it can be proved that the girl is mature enough, it is allowed to marry her off from the age of 11.

[36] As mentioned above, such social practices were criminalized by the Israeli legislator. A Muslim man who wishes to marry more than one wife, or to marry off his minor daughter, or, to mention another such category - to repudiate his wife without her consent for divorce, may certainly do so, and this act will be valid from a religious (and legal) point of view. Nevertheless, by performing any of these acts, this man takes the risk that the Israeli prosecution service will prosecute him for a criminal offence.

administration for further handling.[37] As described above, since the mid 1990s, the Israeli sharī'a court of appeals has determined in several decisions that it is not for the sharī'a courts to make any notes or indications concerning violations of Knesset legislation. In line with its directives concerning the prohibition of reference to Israeli statutes, the sharī'a court of appeals stressed that the only duty of sharī'a courts is to rule according to Islamic principles. Thus, as long as sharī'a rules had not been violated, any offence against "earthly" legislation was of no interest to these courts.[38]

This new policy, which was, again, in total contradiction to previous practices, emphasizes the far-reaching judicial agency enjoyed by the qāḍīs presiding in Israeli sharī'a courts. For the purposes of this paper, however, the question 'how was such a reform introduced?', is less interesting than the question 'why was it introduced?'

The answer to this latter question, I argue, is that this reform constitutes an attempt, led by the Israeli sharī'a court of appeals, to gain support and legitimacy in the shar'ī (Palestinian) organizational field. I contend that there is a close link between the pressures exerted on Israeli sharī'a courts in the state law organizational field during the mid-1990s and the (almost) unconcealed efforts made by the sharī'a court of appeals to gain status and legitimacy in the opposing, shar'ī (Palestinian) field. In other words, the more alienated Israeli sharī'a courts became within the Israeli field, the more prone they were to seek legitimacy and support within the shar'ī (Palestinian) organizational field.

Admittedly, gaining legitimacy in this latter field was not a trivial task for Israeli sharī'a courts. During the 1970s and 1980s, these courts were usually seen by Islamic elements - even within Israel - in highly critical terms,[39] and all the more

[37] Moreover, until 1998 Israeli sharī'a courts used to issue an annual report on cases in which offences against state law had been committed. It is noteworthy, however, that legal procedures had almost never been taken in such cases (see Shahar 2004: 204-205).

[38] See, for example, Sharī'a Court of Appeals Files: 128/1997; 9/1999; 263/2003.

[39] See, for example, the harsh criticism expressed by Shaykh Hāshim 'Abd al-Raḥman, speaker of the Islamic Movement in Israel, concerning the fact that qāḍis presiding in Israeli sharī'a courts lack Islamic education (*Ṣawt al-Ḥaqq wa'l-Ḥūrriyya*, 1/7/1994, 28). See also: Landau 1969: 10; Dumper 1994; Peled 2001b: 121.

so in the eyes of non-Israeli constituencies. Until the 1990s Israeli sharī'a courts were perceived as 'contaminated' courts, guilty of collaboration with the Zionist regime and of the corruption of Islamic law. A good illustration of the hostility toward Israeli sharī'a courts in the shar'ī (Palestinian) organizational field can be found, I believe, in a fatwā[40] that was issued in the mid-eighties by the late sheikh Sa'd al-dīn al-'Alamī, the acting Jordanian qāḍī al-quḍā' (chief qāḍī) and the Mufti of Jerusalem. This man - surely, a respectable and highly esteemed functionary, who held a senior position in the shar'ī (Palestinian) field - issued a fatwā that literally permitted the killing of the president of the Israeli sharī'a court of appeals, sheikh Tawfīq 'Asliyya, who was allegedly guilty of selling waqf property to Israeli official and semi-official elements.[41]

It may be argued, therefore, that Israeli sharī'a courts suffered from a chronic lack of legitimacy in the shar'ī (Palestinian) organizational field. Seeking to improve their reputation within this field, Natūr and the other qāḍīs did exactly what new institutional theorists would predict them to do under conditions of uncertainty and loss of legitimacy: they imitated other, more prestigious organizations in the field, and tried to implement practices which were perceived in the field as worthwhile and normative. Indeed, it appears that this exact policy - a refusal to indicate offenses against civil statutes - had been exercised before in this field. Specifically, after the Israeli occupation of 1967, the Jordanian sharī'a courts in the West Bank declared that they would not cooperate with the Israeli authorities. Whereas prior to the occupation these courts used to inform the Jordanian authorities of breaches of civil statutes that came to light during shar'ī proceedings,[42] after the occupation they refrained from such action, to avoid Israeli

[40] An opinion or a ruling issued by an Islamic jurisconsult (muftī) on a point of Islamic law.

[41] I was unable to locate this fatwā, but I heard this story on two different occasions from two different informants. One of the informants even claimed that following the issuance of this fatwa, close quarters protection was provided to sheikh 'Asliyya by the Israeli General Security Services. At the same time, other informants were unable to remember such a fatwā, and raised doubts concerning the authenticity of this story. For a critical discussion of the role played by Israeli qāḍīs in selling waqf property to Jewish elements, see Dumper 1994: 32.

[42] Like the Israeli law, the Jordanian law criminalized certain offenses arising from family law (e.g., non-registration of a divorce pronounced out of court; involvement in the marriage of an under-aged woman). See Welchman 2000: 73-74, n. 136.

persecution of litigants (see Welchman 2000: 73-74).

The directives of the Israeli sharīʻa court of appeals to stop referring to Israeli statutes and to stop acknowledging offences against these statutes should be seen, therefore, as a case of mimetic isomorphism, designed to increase the legitimacy of Israeli sharīʻa courts in the sharʻī (Palestinian) organizational field. Indeed, this policy appears to have been quite successful: since the mid 1990s, slowly but confidently, the reputation of Israeli sharīʻa courts - and particularly of the sharīʻa court in West Jerusalem - has improved, and these courts gained considerable legitimacy within the sharʻī (Palestinian) field.

A good indication of this improved position can be found in another fatwā, which was again issued by the Muftī of Jerusalem (this time it was sheikh ʻAkrama Ṣabrī). In this fatwā (which in fact brings us back to the previously discussed reform), the Muftī responded to a query (*istiftā'*) asking for his opinion on the proposed legislation amendment that threatened to reduce the jurisdiction of Israeli sharīʻa courts. The muftī's opinion was clear-cut:[43]

> Matters of personal status - which include in addition to the issue of waqf such issues as marriage and divorce, maintenance, guardianship, bequests and so forth - belong to the domain of acts of worship (*ʻibadāt*). Therefore Muslims are forbidden to act in discordance [with sharīʻa rules] in these matters. A Muslim must perform God's directives with regard to maintenance or bequests, just as he must perform God's directives with regard to the duties of prayer, alms giving and the Hajj, even if he lives in a non-Muslim state. [....] The implementation of non-Islamic laws in matters of personal status is hence considered a direct assault on the realm of worship [...] and therefore it is forbidden for Muslims to resort to courts which adjudicate in these matters in a non-Islamic manner. What we need is to safeguard the sharīʻa courts, and to invest effort in broadening their jurisdiction so that it will include all aspects of life, and not in reducing it.[44]

[43] I am thankful to Dr. Moussa Abou Ramadan, who brought this fatwā to my attention and provided me with a facsimile copy of it.

[44] The istiftā' was posed in July 21, 2001, by Zahī al-Majīdāt, a lawyer, who is also Secretary of the Mizzān Association - an association affiliated with the Islamic Movement in Israel. The fatwā was issued ten days later, in July 31.

Fatwās issued by this muftī have no legal standing in Israel, as he is not recognized by the Israeli legal system. His unequivocal stand in support of the Israeli qāḍīs therefore had no effect whatsoever on the legislation process, and the bill indeed passed in the Knesset a few months after this fatwā had been issued. Nevertheless, the Israeli qāḍīs could probably find some comfort in the implicit - yet clear - message that the fatwā conveyed: The muftī regards Israeli sharī'a courts as legitimate tribunals, which appropriately implement the sacred laws of the sharī'a. Undoubtedly, in terms of their legitimacy in the shar'ī (Palestinian) field, the Israeli courts have gone a long way. Whereas only 15 years earlier the muftī of Jerusalem issued a fatwā permitting the assassination of the president of the Israeli sharī'a court of appeals, this new fatwā fully acknowledged the legitimacy of these courts as esteemed sharī'a courts.

Conclusion

The institutional-organizational level of analysis has rarely been visited by scholars of legal pluralism. The prime purpose of this article was therefore to demonstrate the usefulness of an organizational-institutional perspective on legal pluralism. I contend that a great deal of the 'dynamics of legal pluralism' (Yilmaz 2005; F and K von Benda-Beckmann 2006) takes place in organizational arenas such as courts of laws and other mechanisms of dispute resolution, and that in order to better understand these dynamics we must direct scholarly attention to these loci of pluralism. Furthermore, we may draw, for that purpose, on theories and analytical tools developed in the field of organization studies.

To illustrate that, the article has dwelt on the empirical case study of sharī'a courts in contemporary Israel. I have shown that these courts operate, at one and the same time, within two different organizational fields: an organizational field structured around Israeli state-law, and an organizational field structured around shar'ī (Palestinian) institutions. These courts can therefore be described as "pluralistic organizations" (Kraatz and Block 2008), in the sense that they operate within a pluralistic, complex and bifurcated institutional environment. As such, they are exposed to very different, and often contradictory, influences and demands originating from the two organizational fields they belong to. While they need to maintain their legitimacy in both of these fields, any accommodation to the norms and expectations in one field might risk their status in the other. I contend that this situation is not unique to Israeli sharī'a courts, but rather is characteristic of many subaltern courts under conditions of classic legal pluralism. We can therefore generalize - to an extent - from the case of Israeli sharī'a courts to other similar 'hybrid' courts.

How do such subservient courts cope with their pluralistic environment? How do they handle the conflicting demands and expectations directed towards them? While they cannot exit any of the organizational fields they partake in, they can certainly maneuver between them as the need arises.[45] The case study of Israeli sharī'a courts illustrates how this maneuvering may look. It appears that these courts maneuver between the two organizational fields in a way that is reminiscent of the maneuvering of individual litigants, who switch between one normative order and another. Thus, just like individual actors, who in their search for normative anchors may choose from among the various normative orders available to them (Pospisil 1978: 102-3; see also Benton 2002), or in their search for favorable judgments may shop for a forum (K von Benda-Beckmann 1981) - just like them, "pluralistic courts" in situations of classic legal pluralism appear to be able to shift, in their quest for legitimacy and resources, from conformity to one organizational field to conformity to the other.

This maneuvering capacity turns pluralistic organizations into exceptionally dynamic, adaptive and pliable organizations (Kraatz and Block 2008). Indeed, as I have tried to show in this article, the Israeli sharī'a courts have developed a dynamic legal culture, which may be described as a "culture of change" - a culture that embraces adaptations, organizational transformations and reforms, and which views them in highly positive terms.

We may further speculate that in the context of legal pluralism, the inherent dynamism of such pluralistic courts is an important source of social change, far beyond the courts themselves. Since these courts serve as meeting points between cultures, normative orders and social practices, as well as between 'the state' and its subjects, they transfer their dynamism farther on. Such courts - with their highly transformative judicial policies, which continuously fluctuate between normative orders and between institutional logics - both *constitute* legal pluralism and *are constituted* by it.

This dynamism, however, does not come cheap. From the point of view of the

[45] In fact, as argued by Kraatz and Block (2008: 244), this ability to maneuver between conflicting demands is a critical organizational capability of pluralistic organizations.

pluralistic court (or more accurately, from the point of view of its staff), there are two noticeable drawbacks for this positioning betwixt and between organizational fields. First, pluralistic organizations, which "play simultaneously in two games, with two different sets of rules", to use a metaphor suggested by Kraatz and Block (2008: 243), might end up marginalized on both game boards. In other words, they might suffer from low status and weak legitimacy in both organizational fields. This might occur if an act of conformity with the demands originating from one field entails an estrangement from the other. In such cases, the pluralistic organization, which by definition needs to fluctuate between opposing demands, will inevitably be seen in both organizational fields as a dubious organization. Moreover, as argued by new institutional theorists, the weaker the legitimacy of an organization, the stronger its tendency to adapt to the rules and requirements set by its environment (Scott and Mayer 1991). Thus, the pluralistic organization may find itself in a vicious circle: the more it is marginalized within its surrounding organizational fields, the more exposed it is to contradictory isomorphic pressures; and the more it strives to conform to these contradictory pressures, the more marginalized it is.

The second price to be paid for "excessive" dynamism has to do with the danger of losing one's organizational integrity. Indeed, the conspicuous dynamism displayed by Israeli sharī'a courts was perceived as irrational, incoherent and arbitrary not only by some academic critics of this system,[46] but also by some of my interlocutors during my fieldwork at the West Jerusalem first instance court. This is what one of the lawyers, working regularly in this court, had to tell me in this regard:

> Here [in the Israeli shari'a court] you have no order (*ni[illegible]m*). One day is like this, and the other day like that. One day they say that civil laws apply here, the other day they say they don't apply. This is no way to run a court (conversation with N.S, June 8, 2004).

From a new institutional perspective, however, the judicial policy of Israeli sharī'a courts is far from being erratic or irrational. Rather, their policy is perfectly explainable in the context of their pluralistic legal and organizational environment, and of their simultaneous belonging to two different organizational fields. New institutional theory thus helps to identify the organizational motives and the

---

[46] See, for example, Abou Ramadan 2003a, 2003b.

organizational mechanisms that bring about this far reaching judicial dynamism - and here lies its explanatory power.

As I tried to illustrate by introducing this case study, shifting our attention from the normative-orders level of analysis to the institutional-organizational level of analysis, may break new grounds in research into legal pluralism. Indeed, it may take our analysis of legal pluralism a step further than simply denoting the plurality of normative orders or acknowledging the hybridity of legal institutions, and into the realm of causational explanations. This move may provide us, therefore, not only with insights into concrete empirical cases, but also, at last, with an adequate answer to the generation-old quandary concerning the theoretical utility of the concept legal pluralism (see e.g.: Twining 2000: 87; Teubner 1997; Tamanaha 1993).

References

ABOU RAMADAN, Moussa

2003a 'Transition from Tradition to Reform: The Shari'a Appeals Court Rulings on Child Custody.' *Fordham International Law Journal* 26(3): 595-655.

2003b 'Judicial Activism of the Shari'a Appeal Court in Israel 1994-2001: Rise and Crisis.' *Fordham International Law Journal* 27(1): 254-303.

2006 'Islamic Legal Reform: The Alimony of Muslim Wife in the Shari'a Court of Appeals.' *HAWWA: Journal of the Women of the Middle East and the Islamic World* 4(1): 29-75.

2008 'Notes on the Anomaly of the Sharīʻa Field in Israel.' *Islamic Law and Society* 15: 84-111.

BENDA-BECKMANN, Franz von

2002 'Who's Afraid of Legal Pluralism?' *Journal of Legal Pluralism* 47: 37-82.

BENDA-BECKMANN, Franz von, and Keebet von BENDA-BECKMANN

2006 'The Dynamics of Change and Continuity in Plural Legal Orders.' *Journal of Legal Pluralism* 53-4: 1-44.

BENDA-BECKMANN, Keebet von

1981 'Forum Shopping and Shopping Forums - Dispute Settlement in a Minangkabau Village in West Sumatra.' *Journal of Legal Pluralism* 19: 117-153.

BENTON, Lauren

2002 *Law and Colonial Cultures: Legal Regimes in World History, 1400-1900.* New York: Cambridge University Press.

BERMAN, Paul S.
2007 'Global Legal Pluralism.' *Southern California Law Review* 80: 1138-255.
2009 'The New Legal Pluralism.' *Annual Review of Law and Social Sciences* 5: 225-242.

BISHARA, Suhad and Aida TOMA-SULIMAN
1997 'Personal Status and Family Laws.' Pp. 66-73 in *NGO Report: The Status of Palestinian Women Citizens of Israel*, The Working Group on the Status of Palestinian Women in Israel. Available at http://www.arabhra.org/HraAdmin/UserImages/Files/CedawReport1997English.pdf. Last accessed on 20.7.2012.

BOHANNAN, Paul J.
1957 *Justice and Judgment among the Tiv*. London: Oxford University Press.

BOWEN, John R.
2003 *Islam, Law and Equality in Indonesia: An Anthropology of Public Reasoning*. Cambridge: Cambridge University Press.

BRACE, Paul and Melinda G. HALL
1995 'Studying Courts Comparatively: The View from the American States.' *Political Research Quarterly* 48(1): 5-29.

BRAUDE, Benjamin
1982 'Foundation Myths of the Millet System.' Vol. 1, Pp. 69-88 in Benjamin Braude and Bernard Lewis (eds.), *Christians and Jews in the Ottoman Empire*. New York and London: Holmes and Meier Publishers.

CHANOCK, Martin
1985 *Law Custom and Social Order: The Colonial Experience in Malawi and Zambia*. Cambridge: Cambridge University Press.

COHEN, Jonathan, M.
2002 *Inside Appellate Courts: The Impact of Court Organization on Judicial Decision Making in the United States Courts of Appeal*. Ann Arbor: The University of Michigan Press.

DAVIDSON, Roderic H.
1982 'The *Millets* as Agents of Change in the Nineteenth-Century Ottoman Empire.' Vol. 1, pp. 319-337 in Benjamin Braude and Bernard Lewis (eds.), *Christians and Jews in the Ottoman Empire*. New York and London: Holmes and Meier Publishers.

DIMAGGIO, Paul J. and Walter W. POWELL
1983 'The Iron Cage Revisited: Institutional Isomorphism and Collective Rationality in Organizational Fields.' *American Sociological Review* 48: 147-160.

DUMPER, Michael
1994 *Islam and Israel: Muslim Religious Endowments and the Jewish State*. Washington, D.C.: Institute for Palestine Studies.
EISENMAN, Robert H.
1978 *Islamic Law in Palestine and Israel*. Leiden: Brill.
EMIRBAYER, Mustafa and Victoria JOHNSON
2008 'Bourdieu and Organizational Analysis.' *Theory and Society* 37 (1): 1-44.
EPSTEIN, Lee, Thomas G. WALKER and William J. DIXON
1989 'The Supreme Court and Criminal Justice Disputes: A New Institutional Perspective.' *American Journal of Political Science* 33: 825-841.
FOURCADE, Marion
2007 'Theories of Markets and Theories of Society.' *American Behavioral Scientist* 50: 1015-1034.
FRIEDMANN, Daniel
1975 'The Effect of Foreign Law on the Law of Israel: Remnants of the Ottoman Period.' *Israel Law Review* 10: 192-206.
GHANEM, As'ad
1998 'State and minority in Israel: The case of ethnic state and the predicament of its minority.' *Ethnic and Racial Studies* 29: 428-448.
GLUCKMAN, Max
1965 *The Ideas in Barotse Jurisprudence*. New Haven: Yale University Press.
GREENWOOD, Royston, Christine OLIVER, Kerstin SAHLIN and Roy SUDDABY (eds.)
2008 *The Sage Handbook of Organizational Institutionalism*. LA, London, New Delhi and Singapore: Sage.
GRIFFITHS, John
1986 'What Is Legal Pluralism?.' *Journal of Legal Pluralism* 24: 1-55.
HALL, Melinda, G. and Paul BRACE
1989 'Order in the Court: A New Institutional Approach to Judicial Consensus.' *Political Research Quarterly* 42: 391-407.
HOOKER, M. Barry
1975 *Legal Pluralism: An Introduction to Colonial and Neo-Colonial Laws*. Oxford: The Clarendon Press.
IBRAHIM, Ibtisam
1993 *The Status of Arab Women in Israel*. Jerusalem: Sikkuy [in Hebrew].
KRAATZ, Matthew S. and Emily S. BLOCK
2008 'Organizational Implications of Institutional Pluralism.' Pp. 243-275 in Royston Greenwood et al. (eds.), *The Sage Handbook of Organizational Institutionalism*. LA, London, New Delhi and Singapore: Sage.

LANDAU, Jacob M.
1969 *The Arabs in Israel*. Oxford: Oxford University Press.
LAYISH, Aharon
1965 'Muslim Religious Jurisdiction in Israel.' *Asian and African Studies* 1: 49-79.
1971 'Qāḍīs and Shari'a in Israel.' *Asian and African Studies* 7: 237-272.
1975 *Women and Islamic Law in a Non-Muslim State*. Jerusalem: Israel University Press.
2006 'Adaptation of a Jurists' Law to Modern Times in an Alien Environment: The Case of the Shari'a in Israel.' *Die Welt Des Islams* 46: 168-191.
LOUËR, Laurence
2007 *To Be an Arab in Israel*. New York: Columbia University Press.
MEIR, Thomas
1998 *The Resurgence of the Moslems in Israel*. Givat Haviva: Center for Arab Studies.
MERRY, Sally E.
1988 'Legal Pluralism.' *Law and Society Review* 22(4): 869-896.
1991 'Law and Colonialism.' *Law and Society Review* 25(4): 889-922.
2007 'International law and sociolegal scholarship: towards a spatial global legal pluralism.' *Studies in Law, Politics and Society* 41:149–68
MEYER, John W. and Brian ROWAN
1977 'Institutionalized Organizations: Formal Structure as Myth and Ceremony.' *American Journal of Sociology* 83(2): 340-363.
MOORE, Sally F.
1973 'Law and Social Change: The Semi-Autonomous Social Field as an Appropriate Subject of Study.' *Law and Society Review* 7: 719-746.
1986 *Social Facts and Fabrications: Customary Law on Kilimanjaro, 1880-1980*. Cambridge: Cambridge University Press.
PELED, Alisa, R.
2001a *Debating Islam in the Jewish State: The Development of Policy Toward Islamic Institutions in Israel*. New York: SUNY Press.
2001b 'Towards autonomy? The Islamist movement's quest for control of Islamic Institutions in Israel.' *The Middle East Journal* 55(3): 378-398.
POSPISIL, Leopold
1978 'The Structure of Society and its Multiple Legal Systems.' Pp. 96-109 in Philip H. Gulliver (ed.), *Cross-Examinations: Essays in Memory of Max Gluckman*. Leiden: E.J. Brill.
REITER, Yitzhak
1997 'Qāḍīs and the Implementation of Islamic Law in Present Day Israel.' Pp. 205-231 in Gleave and Eugenia Kermeli (eds.), *Islamic Law: Theory and*

Practice. London and New York: I.B. Tauris.
REKHESS, Elie
1989 'Israeli Arabs and the Arabs of the West Bank and Gaza: Political affinity and national Solidarity.' *Asian and African Studies* 23:119-54.
1993 'Resurgent Islam in Israel.' *Asian and African Studies* 27: 191-210.
RODINSON, Maxime
1973 *Israel: A Colonial Settler State?* New York: Monad Press.
ROUHANA, Nadim
1989 'The Political Transformation of the Palestinians in Israel: From Acquiescence to Challenge.' *Journal of Palestine Studies* 18(3): 38-59.
SANTOS, Boaventura de Sousa
2006 'The Heterogeneous State and Legal Pluralism in Mozambique.' *Law and Society Review* 40: 39-75.
SCHOENMAN, Ralf
1988 *The Hidden History of Zionism*. Santa Barbara: Veritas Press.
SCOTT, Richard W. and John W. MAYER
1991 'The Organization of Societal Sectors: Propositions and Early Evidence.' Pp. 108-140 in Walter W. Powell and Paul D. DiMaggio (eds.), *The New Institutionalism in Organizational Analysis*. Chicago: The University of Chicago Press.
SCOTT, Richard W.
1995 *Institutions and Organizations*. CA, Thousand Oaks: Sage.
SHAFIR, Gershon
1996 'Zionism and Colonialism: A Comparative Approach.' Pp. 227-244 in M. N. Barnett (ed.), *Israeli in Comparative Perspective*. Albany: SUNY Press.
SHAHAR, Ido
2000 'Palestinians in Israeli Courts: Culture, Control, and Resistance in the Shari'a Court of West Jerusalem.' Unpublished Master's thesis, The Hebrew University of Jerusalem [in Hebrew].
2004 'Modernizer and Guardian of Tradition: The Shari‘a Court and Women's Status.' *Hamizrah Hehadash* 44: 195-211 [in Hebrew].
2007 'Legal Reform, Interpretive Communities and the Quest for Legitimacy: A Contextual Analysis of a Legal Circular.' Pp. 198-227 in Ron Shaham (ed.), Law, Custom and Statute in the Muslim World: Studies in Honor of Aharon Layish. Leiden: Brill.
n.d. 'A Tale of Two Courts: How Organizational Ethnography Can Shed New Light on Legal Pluralism.' *PoLAR* (forthcoming).
SIEDER, Rachel (ed.)
2002 *Multiculturalism in Latin America: Indigenous Rights, Diversity and*

Democracy. Houndmill and N.Y.: Palgrave and MacMillan.

SMOOHA, Sami

1992 *Arabs and Jews in Israel: Change and Continuity in Mutual Intolerance*. Boulder, Co: Westview.

SNYDER, Francis G.

1981 'Colonialism and Legal Form: The Creation of 'Customary Law' in Senegal.' *Journal of Legal Pluralism and Unofficial Law* 19: 49-76.

SPIERTZ, Joep H. L.

1991 'The Transformation of Traditional Law: A Tale of People's Participation in Irrigation Management on Bali.' *Landscape and Urban Planning* 20: 189-196.

SUCHMAN, Mark and Lauren B. EDELMAN

1996 'Legal Rational Myths: The New Institutionalism and the Law and Society Tradition.' *Law and Social Enquiry* 21:903-966.

TAMANAHA, Brian Z.

1993 'The Folly of the "Social Scientific" Concept of Legal Pluralism.' *Journal of Law and Society* 20: 192-217.

2007 'Understanding Legal Pluralism: Past to Present, Local to Global.' *Sydney Law Review* 30: 375-411.

TEUBNER, Gunther

1997 'Global Bukowina: Legal Pluralism in the World Society.' Pp. 3-28 in Gunther Teubner (ed.), *Global Law Without a State*. Brookfield: Dartmouth.

TOLEDANO, Esther

2003 'Periodic Report on Women Granted Maintenance Payments by The National Insurance Institute in 2002.' Jerusalem: The National Insurance Institute, publication no. 185 [in Hebrew]. Available at http://www.btl.gov.il/SiteCollectionDocuments/btl/Publications/seker_185.pdf. Last accessed: 17.6.2012.

TUCKER, Judith E.

1996 'Revisiting Reform: Women and the Ottoman Law of Family Rights, 1917.' *Arab Studies Journal* 4: 4-18.

TWINING, William

2000 *Globalisation and Legal Theory*. Cambridge: Cambridge University Press.

URSINUS, Michael O. H.

1993 'Millet.' Pp. 61-64 in C.E. Bosworth et al. (eds.), *Encyclopaedia of Islam,* 2nd ed. (*EI2*), Vol. 7.

WELCHMAN, Lynn

2000 *Beyond the Code: Muslim Family Law and the Shari'a Judiciary in the*

Palestinian West Bank. The Hague, London, Boston: Kluwer Law International.

WOODMAN, GORDON R.

1998 'Ideological Combat and Social Observation: Recent Debates about Legal Pluralism.' *Journal of Legal Pluralism* 43:21-59.

WOOTEN, M. and Andrew J. HOFFMAN

2008 'Organizational Fields: Past, Present and Future.' Pp. 130-148 in in Royston Greenwood et al. (eds.), *The Sage Handbook of Organizational Institutionalism*. LA, London, New Delhi and Singapore: Sage.

YILMAZ, Ihsan

2005 *Muslim Law, Politics and Society in Modern Nation States: Dynamic Legal Pluralism in England, Turkey and Pakistan*. Aldershot and Burlington: Ashgate.

HALACHA, THE 'JEWISH STATE' AND THE CANADIAN *AGUNAH*: COMPARATIVE LAW AT THE INTERSECTION OF RELIGIOUS AND SECULAR ORDERS

Pascale Fournier[1]

Introduction

Let us imagine Sarah, 40, who has been married to Joseph, 45, for over 15 years. They have a 10 year old adoptive child from Israel whom they raised together in Canada. Sarah has graduated from the University of Toronto in Political Science and Women's Studies and has recently been promoted as a tenured professor at York University. Joseph, on the other hand, has never liked school very much and, after college, became an automobile mechanic. In the last three years, Sarah and Joseph have been separated and have obtained a civil divorce in Montreal.[1]

[1] I thank the Social Sciences and Humanities Research Council of Canada and the Québec Bar Foundation for supporting this project and Pascal McDougall, Glenys Stevenson, Merissa Lichtsztral and Leehee Goldenberg for their invaluable contributions. I thank Robert Leckey, Roderick A. Macdonald and Yüksel Sezgin for close readings and precious insights and the anonymous peer-reviewers for their useful comments. I also thank Prakash Shah and Marie-Claire Foblets for their support. I have benefitted from presenting earlier versions of this paper at the Université Libre de Bruxelle's *Colloque international sur l'accomodement raisonnable de la religion en Belgique et au Canada* in Brussels, Belgium ('Le sacré reconsidéré: enjeux de citoyenneté et d'accessibilité à la Justice pour les

However, Joseph refuses to grant Sarah a *get*, the Jewish divorce which can effectively only be granted by the husband.[2] Joseph is more than happy to retaliate for the humiliation he suffered, having had to sell his house following divorce. He has vowed never to grant Sarah a religious divorce and to leave her as an *agunah*, a chained wife. Last year, Sarah met David, another modern Orthodox man, and they now want to marry and have a child together. However, being an *agunah*, Sarah cannot remarry according to *halacha* (Jewish law) (Cohn 2004: 66) and she cannot have legitimate children in the eyes of her religious community. Any children she may bear with her partner will be considered a *mamzer* (pl. *mamzerim*, bastard children) and will be "effectively excluded from Judaism" (Nichols 2007: 155). The *mamzer* status continues on for generations down the

femmes religieuses au Canada'), at Harvard Law School's *Global Legal Education Forum* in Cambridge, MA ('Teaching Across Systems and Borders: Rethinking the Religious/Secular Divide in Legal Thought'), at the University of Toronto Munk School of Global Affairs conference *The Politics of Islam in Western Europe* ('Navigating the Secular/Religious Divide: Muslim Women Divorcing in Western Europe'), at the Réseau hispano-canadien d'experts en immigration (RHICEIN)'s event *Espagne, Canada, État des savoirs sur le statut des immigrés* in Madrid, Spain ('Droit constitutionnel canadien et liberté de religion: de la Cour suprême aux acteurs sociaux'), and at the Oñati International Institute for the Sociology of Law workshop *Legal Practice and Accommodation in Multicultural Europe*, convened in Oñati, Spain by Marie-Claire Foblets and Prakash Shah ('Calculating Claims: Jewish and Muslim Women Navigating Religion, Economics and Law in Canada').

[2] The authority to divorce is found in the Torah at verse 24:1 in the book of Deuteronomy, which was interpreted as bestowing on the husband the exclusive privilege to enact divorce (Kaplan 2004: 61). My fictitious character Sarah might not be considered an *agunah* according to a strict Jewish legal definition of the term, i.e. as someone who fits the narrow (mostly fault-based) grounds entitling a spouse to have the divorce compelled by the rabbinical courts but does not obtain divorce. For a summary exposition of religious grounds to compel divorce see *infra* part V. For an exposition of this narrow definition of the *agunah* problem, see Broyde (2001: 10). I have included such a contested example of an *agunah* woman on purpose, to plead for a wider definition of the *agunah* as encompassing all forms of divorce refusal. This definition aligns with that of Justice Rosalie Abella, herself a Jewish woman, writing for the Supreme Court of Canada in *Bruker v. Marcovitz*.

line and *mamzerim* are only permitted to marry each other (Rayner 2001: 43).[3] In fact, Sarah is still considered religiously married to Joseph, notwithstanding her civil divorce (Bitton 2009: 117-118; Biale 1984: 102).

Sarah's existence is now split in two. In her 'secular' life, she is financially autonomous, having bought her own apartment and settled her financial disputes with Joseph. According to her tax forms, she is single. However, in the eyes of her synagogue, her Orthodox Jewish neighbours and her religious family, she is still considered married. This schizophrenic state of affairs is an important phenomenon in Israel and in countries of the Diaspora, where many women "fall between the cracks of the civil and religious jurisdictions" (Shachar 2008: 576), with the isolation and economic hardships this situation often entails. In Canada, this issue has reached the Supreme Court in the landmark *Bruker v. Marcovitz* case.

Both Israel and Canada, like other polities, have adopted State mechanisms to sanction *get* refusal and alleviate the "plight of the *agunah*" (Breitowitz 1992, 1993: 277; Hacohen and Greenberg 2004: 14). The Canadian responses, which stem from civil law and reach out into the religious sphere, take the form of judicial enforcement of contractual agreements related to the *get* and of sanctions against refusing husbands engaged in (civil) procedures under the *Divorce Act*. The Israeli legislation, the so-called *Sanctions Law*, provides for sanctions of *get* refusal and grants disciplinary power to (religious) rabbinical courts that adjudicate divorces. In this article, I unpack the functioning of the Israeli and Canadian State law solutions to this social problem by presenting the results of two years of fieldwork and interviews with Jewish women in Canada and Israel. I analyse how both legal systems operate and investigate the underground voices of Jewish women who navigate between the religious and the secular spheres upon divorce. After having exposed my methodological postures and approaches, I present for each country the 'official' legal response and the 'unofficial' socio-legal phenomena, which lie beneath the surface. In the context of Jewish divorce, it seems clear that the Canadian civil state remedies are influenced by a web of alternative community responses and recourses that are available to women and

[3] Men, on the other hand, are not subject to these consequences. Indeed, a man's marriage with another woman in the absence of a *get* is halachically valid and that man's children are legitimate. He is not considered to have committed adultery, but merely to have contravened a rabbinical decree prescribing monogamy (Nichols 2007: 155).

that at times render ineffective the civil remedies. For instance, contractual clauses such as the one at issue in *Bruker v. Marcovitz* may be inefficient and scarcely used, given that there already exists a customary Jewish marriage contract, the *ketubah* and that the latter is held to be unenforceable by civil courts. Moreover, the *Divorce Act* recourses' efficiency is circumvented if Jewish legal subjects do not see in civil courts a meaningful solution to their problem, but instead go to community members and institutions who can provide them assistance and support. Quite similarly, Israel's *Sanctions Law*, while attractive to some Jewish women of the Diaspora, is also hopelessly ensnared in informal practices of rabbinical court judges, police, and rabbinical advocates. In fact, my interviews and the socio-legal literature reveal that the indeterminacy of (religious) adjudication simultaneously accounts for the shortcomings of the *Sanctions Law* and provides means for Jewish women to strategically manipulate it to their advantage.

This complexification of State law, which I investigate on both the Canadian and Israeli fronts, is meant to build on burgeoning literature on the subject of the interaction between secular state law and 'unofficial' religious norms (Moon 2008a; Grillo et al. 2009; Foblets et al. 2010; Nichols 2011; Maclean and Eekelaar n.d.). In so doing, I want to stress that no policy response can ignore non-State normative commitments and community affiliations, as the latter often explain the shortcomings of State law and might even provide inspiration for alternative strategies for women and legal practitioners in minority communities. I thus seek to further a new pragmatic approach to the practice of law, one that takes into account the relevance of *everyday* normativity and its potential usefulness to alleviate the 'plight of the *agunah*'.

Interviews, Stories and Pluralities: Notes on Field Research

This analysis is based on my field-work in Canada and Israel, during which I interviewed twelve Jewish women who had experienced difficulties in obtaining a *get* from their husbands and had used all kinds of strategies to break away from a marriage that they no longer wished for themselves and their children.

The Canadian fieldwork included visits to synagogues, discussions with practicing and non-practicing Jewish men and women, rabbis and other religious experts, as well as formal interviews conducted in Toronto, Montreal and Ottawa, with six Jewish women. The women were chosen from a variety of denominations and socio-economic backgrounds. They had all been married and were civilly or religiously divorced, or both, and were thus able to provide qualitative accounts of the socio-legal interplay between the secular State and religious law.[4]

Through my fieldwork in Israel, I informally questioned activists, rabbinical advocates, lawyers, and academics, and conducted formal interviews with six Jewish women from different towns and cities across Israel. Four women were already divorced and two were struggling to obtain their *get*. Four of these women had the Israeli *Sanctions Law* applied against their husbands because the latter were refusing to grant the *get*. The women had the *Sanctions Law* enforced by a rabbinical court, in a process whereby their husbands were either put in jail, had their driver's licenses taken away, had their passports confiscated and/or were disqualified from certain honours in the synagogue. The interviews were conducted with a Hebrew-English translator. Four interviews were held in Hebrew (with the translator asking the questions under the supervision of a research assistant who understands Hebrew) and two were held in English in one-on-one conversations.

I must insist that this research is not quantitative in nature, but qualitative. Even though I sometimes make quantitative assessments of the participants' circumstances to reflect on other quantitative data, I am acutely aware of the limitations of my methodological approach. This qualitative research cannot cover every Jewish community and the participants are not necessarily representative of all Jewish communities in Canada or Israel. Therefore, this data must be treated with caution, as a method to reflect the subjective and individual experiences of Jewish women who go through divorce. In this endeavour, I use a 'story-telling' (Van Praagh 1999; Campbell 2009) approach to the field to depict the ways in which legal agents navigate the socio-economic endowments that community life produces. If it is indeed difficult to draw policy conclusions from mere stories (Fajet 1994), I have nevertheless tried to combine my intimate portraits with empirical data, case-law analysis and socio-legal literature, to draw some general conclusions from these years of fieldwork. However, I also use the story-telling approach, which has important historical origins in feminist jurisprudence (Bartlett 1990) and critical race theory (Delgado 1993), based on the idea that "law can never rest on a complete picture of reality, but it can acquire a fuller, more accurate vision by accumulating stories that widen the horizon" (Baron 1994: 284). In this sense, qualitative interview analysis brings new, marginalized accounts of the socio-legal processes as they are experienced by Jewish women and thus builds on existing scholarship from its margins.

[4] For extensive analysis of the findings of this fieldwork, see Fournier (2012).

In addition to providing fragments of untold knowledge about Canadian and Israeli legal systems, my methodology provides me with an opportunity to put to the test a legal pluralist methodology, and to show its relevance to two countries as seemingly diverse as Canada and Israel. Rather than an exhaustive empirical account, my article can thus be viewed as an invitation into uncharted territory. Specifically, my study the *agunah* problem will allow me to illustrate and introduce *critical* legal pluralism (Kleinhans and Macdonald 1997), an approach whose main impetus is, as put by one critical legal pluralist scholar, to unveil "how apparently marginalized actors [...] might at once be both influenced by and pivotal in shaping the normative frameworks by which they live" (Campbell 2008: 123). The Canadian manifestation of this movement has been headed by Roderick A. Macdonald, who has attempted to build on classical legal pluralism's impetus to look beyond state law (F and K von Benda-Beckmann 2006; Griffiths 1986; Merry 1988). *Critical* legal pluralism understands the law as encompassing "how legal subjects understand themselves and the law" (Kleinhans and Macdonald 1997: 36). For *critical* legal pluralists, "law arises from, belongs to, and responds to everyone" (Macdonald 2002: 8). This outlook led me to analyse Israeli law through the eyes of *agunah* women. Indeed, my encounters underline "the relevance of first-person accounts [...] to developing a fuller sense of the law" (Campbell 2009: 191). With this methodological posture, I aim to go beyond conventional feminist accounts of the *agunah* problem (Stopler 2004; Shalev 1995: 92) towards portraits of women moving through secular and religious divorces as social agents (Korteweg 2008). Specifically this article is inspired by a particular form of *critical* legal pluralism, which "dissociates the law from the State without giving up on its institutional autonomy and differentiation from other normative orders" (Melissaris 2004, 2009: 60). My qualitative fieldwork reintroduces the multiple sites of regulation of Jewish divorce, establishing the *everyday life*[5] normativity of Canadian and Israeli Jewish communities as a challenging and important focus for contemporary legal practice. By casting the Jewish community institutions and the way Jewish women navigate through them as *spatial* layers of legal pluralism (Manderson 2005) in Jewish communities, I aim to steer the research agenda in a direction that paints a clearer picture of some social processes that affect State law's effectiveness in alleviating the plight of the *agunah*.

[5] On the implications of this concept in several strands of legal pluralist scholarship see Sarat and Kearns (1993); Macdonald (2002); Ewick and Silbey (1998); Merry (1986); Sarat (1990).

'Official' Stories: the Canadian *Divorce Act*, Contract Law and the 'Religious Thicket

This section analyses 'the plight of the *agunah*' in Canada through the 'official' responses introduced by the State with the aim of comparing them with the 'unofficial' responses of the legal subjects involved. This section aims to outline the challenges faced by practitioners who try to navigate the plurality of legal orders through these State law mechanisms.

In 1968, the Parliament of Canada exercised its jurisdiction over "marriage and divorce"[6] to enact the *Divorce Act*, whose current 1985 version lays out the grounds and procedure for divorce in Canada. Canadian 'official' family law stands as an egalitarian, staunchly contractual and civil regime. For instance, it trumps all other possibly applicable legal systems in a private international law context (Fournier 2011). However, the State reaches out to intervene into the religious domain, specifically addressing the 'plight of the *agunah*' in two distinct instances. The first mechanism, the Supreme Court's ruling in the case of *Bruker v. Marcovitz*, is judicial in nature, and the second, section 21.1 of the *Divorce Act*, is legislative.

The case of *Bruker v. Marcovitz* sheds light on 'the plight of the *agunah*' in particular ways. Mr. Marcovitz had signed a separation agreement, which contained a clause binding him to "appear before the rabbinical authorities in the City and District of Montreal for the purpose of obtaining the traditional religious *get*, immediately upon a Decree Nisi of Divorce being granted" (quoted in *Marcovitz*: para. 39). Mr. Marcovitz then refused to fulfil his contractual obligation despite the granting of the civil divorce and left Ms. Bruker as an *agunah*, unable to remarry within her Orthodox community or to have legitimate children for a period of 15 years, after which he finally granted her a *get*. I note in passing that it may well have been too late for Ms. Bruker to have children when she received her *get*, as she was "almost 47" at the time (*Marcovitz*: para. 29). Ms. Bruker went forward with a petition for damages for breach of contractual obligation, damages that were awarded by the trial judge in the amount of $47,500, at the time equivalent to roughly £21,000 (*S.B.B. v. J.B.M.*). However, the province's Court of Appeal decided to reverse the award because the agreement entered into by the parties, being "religious in nature," was considered unenforceable (*Marcovitz c. Bruker*: para. 76). Hilton J.A. wrote for the

[6] As provided by s. 92(26) the *Constitution Act, 1867.*

unanimous Quebec Court of Appeal that: "if there is any relief available to Ms. Bruker, it is in a religious forum, not a secular one" (*Marcovitz c. Bruker*: para. 90).[7]

Upon appeal to the Supreme Court of Canada, Madame Justice Rosalie Abella, herself a progressive Jewish woman (Abella 2005), writing for the majority, reversed the Court of Appeal's judgement and imposed damages on the recalcitrant husband for his refusal to give the *get* despite contractual commitment to do so. The decision was harshly criticized, particularly in French speaking Quebec, which is closer to French republicanism than other parts of Canada (Gaudreault-Desbiens 2009: 165), on the basis that it runs against a *laïcité*-inspired vision of civil law as a pure body of legal rules that never must enforce any religiously-coloured commitment (Landheer-Cieslak in Langevin et al. 2008; Astengo 2009: 529; DeCoste 2009; Moore 2009: 239). Ironically, refusing to conceive the "religious aspect of the obligation [...] as a barrier to its civil validity" (*Marcovitz*: para. 51) allowed the court to implement wholly secular remedies (damages) to the *agunah* problem. This judgement usefully flies in the face of the secularist conception of the "religious community as an association that members join and quit at will" (Moon 2008b: 62), a view which does not seem to account for the importance of informal religious norms and decentralized community bonds for religious/minority citizens. As put by an observer, the decision intelligently recognizes the existence of "different normative spheres while attempting to reconcile them in the context of particular cases" (Glenn 2008: 439; see also Kleefeld and Kennedy 2008).

While undoubtedly a celebratory decision for many, its power remains uncertain for several Jewish women in Canada. First, the decision only applies in so far as a separation agreement calling for the granting of the *get* is concluded in the course of a civil divorce (*Marcovitz*: para. 23). It does not apply to the *ketubah,* a form of religious prenuptial agreement which includes various provisions such as the husband's duty to provide his wife with adequate food, clothing, shelter and regular intercourse and to pay her a financial compensation upon divorce (Epstein 2005: 163). The Supreme Court was not in a position to reverse the current law on the enforceability of *ketubah* contracts, an issue on which it did not purport to

[7] In an interesting contrast, in France, a country generally considered a secularist hard-liner, the Cour de cassation, the country's highest court, held that awarding damages for *get* refusal does not contravene the separation of Church and State (Cour de cassation, Chambre civile 2, 15 june 1988).

decide (*Marcovitz*: para. 46). The Manitoba Court of Appeal's 1974 ruling in the case of *Morris v. Morris*, which held that the *ketubah* is unenforceable by a civil court, is still applicable. Hence, the Jewish women who could otherwise include in their *ketubah* a so-called 'Lieberman clause', whereby the husband recognizes the jurisdiction of the *Beth Din* and submits in advance to any measures taken to sanction *get* refusal (Finkelman 1995: 156), cannot benefit from this legal strategy.[8] Neither does the current state of the law leave room for a solution based on the idea, adopted by an Illinois court in *In re Marriage of Goldman*, that the generic *ketubah* words on which the argument rested in *Morris* did indeed constitute a contractual obligation to grant the *get*.[9]

The *Morris* Court's decision to declare the Jewish marriage contract unenforceable is based on the idea that Canadian family law is a "civil matter **[that]** cannot be allowed to become uncertain or schismatic by reference to various sects or religions." (*Morris v. Morris*: para. 55) Is religion truly this 'private' matter removed from the power of the State? Conversely, is the State this 'objective' and 'neutral' apparatus? Or should courts and the State be analysed as culturally/ideologically oriented institutions, despite widespread denial of this phenomenon (Caughey 2009: 323; Althusser 1997)? The religious-private/secular-public dichotomy seems built on fragile assumptions, especially in the Jewish context where communities have been installed for centuries in Canada (Tulchinsky 1997; Nigro and Mauro 1999) and 'public' group life bears significant importance. For these communities, a phenomenon of "declining familism" (Hartman and Hartman 2009: 25; Tulchinsky 2008: 490) has partly shifted the prime locus of social regulation from the family, which may have been more important in the immigration context, to important community webs which form a sort of "self-governing quasi-state" (Weinfield 2001: 173) composed of Jewish tribunals, schools, hospitals, old-age centres, sports leagues, cultural centres, newspapers, media, etc. In this context, the unenforceability of the *ketubah* on the grounds adopted in *Morris* seems outdated.

The second limitation of the *Marcovitz* decision is that the Supreme Court was legally unable to extend the civil courts' sanctioning of *get* refusal beyond the post-nuptial contractual realm (Langevin et al. 2008: 684 note 103). Abella J. describes

[8] The civil enforceability of this type of clause in New York family law has been settled by the New York Court of Appeal in *Avitzur v. Avitzur*.

[9] It bears notice that a New Jersey court dismissed a similar claim on the basis of freedom of religion (*Aflalo v. Aflalo*).

the French solution of awarding damages for extra-contractual civil liability as follows: "it is impossible in the circumstances of the case at bar to draw any inspiration from the situation in France." (*Marcovitz*: para. 153) Although "not precluded" (*Marcovitz*: para. 154), this legal response was obviously unnecessary for Ms. Bruker who benefited from a written contract.[10] As for the Israeli solution of allowing "financial compensation" to a wife whose husband refuses to grant her the *get*, the Court affirms that: "the solutions adopted in Israel cannot be imported into Canada without taking account of Canadian legislation and the Canadian context." (*Marcovitz*: para. 153)[11] Thus, in the peculiar situation of *get* refusal, it seems clear that Jewish women in Canada still need to manage for themselves a way to transform their religious commitments into a proper contractual obligation.

Absent a contract, where does the 'plight of the *agunah*' tragically go? What recourse may capture her inability to obtain a religious divorce from her husband? Whom can she reach to pressure a husband acting out of pure bad faith? To answer these questions and further understand the complex, shifting boundaries between the religious and secular spheres, I collected micro-level narratives in the forms of six interviews with Jewish women who had experienced difficulties in obtaining the *get* in Canada. While this work can certainly not be considered quantitatively representative, it is interesting to note that only one out of six participants had included in her separation agreement a clause relating to the *get*. Four others had not been able to include such a clause, for various reasons pertaining to their lack of awareness of the law or incomplete legal counselling. The last participant had not included any clause in her separation agreement for her first divorce, and after having learned the lesson the hard way, negotiated such a clause for her second divorce. For 5 out of 6 participants, the 'official' state law—the *Marcovitz* decision—is of no application (Linderberg 2010). Only section 21.1 of the *Divorce Act* could in theory be of assistance, the second state solution to which I now turn.

---

[10] In the case of Stephanie Bruker, resort to Quebec extra-contractual civil liability (tort) law would have even been precluded by art. 1458 of the *Civil Code of Québec*, which forbids the option between contractual and extra-contractual liability in the presence of a contract. However, there would be a strong case for recognizing *get* refusal as a tort, if not on purely pragmatic grounds, as a matter of principle, to cast a stigma on what is often malevolent, oppressive behaviour, as argued by Cobin (1986: 430).

[11] Interestingly, there is no mention, neither by the majority nor by the dissent, of the *Sanctions Law*, the Israeli statute which allows religious courts to compel the giving of the *get* and sanction the recalcitrant husbands: see *infra* part V.

Section 21.1 of the *Divorce Act* was enacted in 1990, after much lobbying from Jewish women's groups. Four years earlier, the Province of Ontario had amended the *Ontario Family Law Act* to allow for sanctions aimed at recalcitrant husbands regarding the settlement of financial matters related to the divorce (Tager 1999: 447; Freeman 1996: 375). This legislative overlap certainly illustrates the pressing nature of the *agunah* problem in Canada. Given the restricted geographical scope of the Ontario statute, I only discuss the federal pan-Canadian *Divorce Act*, which is more widely known. The federal Minister of Justice of the time, Doug Lewis, thus justified the amendments to the *Divorce Act*:

> I am concerned about protecting the integrity of the *Divorce Act* and preventing persons from avoiding the application of the principles contained in the act. [...] Without a *get*, a Jewish woman cannot remarry in her own faith. Children of a subsequent civil marriage suffer religious disabilities. [...] The government is moving where it can and where it is brought to the government's attention to eliminate sexism and gender bias in the law. (*House of Commons Debates* 1990: 8375-77)

This section of the *Act* was conceived to put pressure on a spouse withholding a religious divorce; it does not allow courts to actually order the granting of a religious divorce, much less pronounce the religious divorce themselves. In this regard, it is in keeping with the fundamental Talmudic rule according to which the granting of the *get* is a "personal act between husband and wife, with the courts (or indeed, the state, as in Israel today) playing or taking no role insofar as the actual effectuation of the divorce in concerned" (Haut 1983: 20).[12] Under the provision, a spouse (most likely the wife) can file an affidavit with the court about any barriers to religious remarriage present in their case. If the barrier has not been removed after the serving of the affidavit, section 21.1(3) allows the court to dismiss applications under the *Divorce Act* filed by the withholding spouse (most likely the husband) and to "strike out any other pleadings and affidavits filled by that spouse under [the] Act." (s.21.1(3)(c) and (d))[13] Subsection 21.1(4) allows the

[12] However, in the case of *E.I. c. A.A.* the Quebec Superior court, in a strange judgement, literally ordered the granting of the *get* (see para. 11).

[13] Subsection 21.1(6) indicates that the provision does not apply to situations where the barrier to religious divorce is in the hands of a religious body or official. I note in passing that this has no bearing on *get* refusal since under Jewish law the husband alone can grant the *get*, and the *Beth Din* in theory can never supersede

recalcitrant husband to circumvent this process if he demonstrates "genuine grounds of a religious or conscientious nature for refusing to remove the barriers [to remarriage]". This subsection has surely been included as a safeguard against a long-expected constitutional challenge to s 21.1 based on freedom of religion (Van Praagh 1993: 245), one of which had been mounted by Mr. Marcovitz and subsequently abandoned at trial, therefore not making it to the Supreme Court: (*Marcovitz*: para. 34). Notably, the 2002 British '*get* bill',[14] the equivalent of s. 21.1, does not contain such a perplexing exception.

Nevertheless, the adoption of s. 21.1 is an extremely positive development in Canadian law, as it allows for a definition of the *agunah* problem that goes beyond strict religious criteria. Since under pure *Halacha* there is no 'right' to divorce, the *agunah* could come to be defined restrictively, encompassing only women who fit within the restrictive (mostly fault-based) grounds for compelling divorce instead of being defined plainly as any woman who is divorced civilly but denied a religious divorce (Broyde 2001: 37). Indeed, the existence of s. 21.1 and the large definition of the *agunah* has thus allowed for an ongoing argument before Quebec courts as to whether "a civil divorce judgment carries with it the implicit obligation to give a *ghet*" (*Abadi v. Emanuel*: para. 7). Moreover, the adoption of s. 21.1 also offers a mechanism of integrative dialogue between the secular and religious, going a long way towards what Ayelet Shachar described as a

> joint-governance framework [which] offers us a vision in which the secular law may be invoked to provide remedies for religious women to protect them from their husbands who might otherwise 'cherry-pick' their religious and secular obligations" (Shachar 2010: 127).

Here, the 'official' state law sees and directly acknowledges how members of minority families navigate among different legal orders to which they are subject. Interestingly, it seems that most of the petitions under s. 21.1 are successful,[15]

---

his will.

[14] The *Divorce (Religious Marriages) Act 2002* (UK), which amends the *Matrimonial Causes Act 1973* (UK) to allow the court to suspend the decree absolute of divorce until each party produces a declaration to the court "that they have taken such steps as are required to dissolve the marriage in accordance with those [religious] usages" (S. 10(2)).

[15] See e.g. *I.L. c. M.A.*; *K.N.H. v. J.S.*; *E.S. c. O.S.*; *D.A. c. J.H.*; *A.D. c. J.P.*;

which indicates that the Canadian State responds to the complex reality of plural family types in an engaged fashion. Moreover, the 'freedom of religion' exception clause of s. 21.1(4) is in practice looked upon with much scepticism by the judiciary. Applications under the exception clause were dismissed in a number of cases, creating a string of interesting precedents (*I.L. c. M.A.*; *K.N.H. v. J.S.*; *E.S. c. O.S.*; *D.A. c. J.H*).

However, despite section 21.1's clear call on Jewish women to seize the civil legal tools, the number of cases in which this legal mechanism was invoked is effectively very small. In addition to the four cases previously mentioned, it was sometimes alluded to but not invoked because the parties had negotiated and worked out the matter through other means (*Darel v. Darel*; *Blumes v. Blumes*; N.K. v. M.K.; *Nathanson, Schachter and Thompson v. Levitt*). Likewise, in the Quebec Superior Court case of *R.M. v. M.S.S.*, proceedings under s. 21.1 were initiated by the wife but the dispute was 'resolved' outside the courtroom (para. 33). Furthermore, although my qualitative fieldwork cannot be considered as necessarily representative, it is again interesting to note that only one of my six interviewees has had recourse to s. 21.1. The other participants were unaware of the existence of the provision, almost twenty years after its enactment. What appears as a powerful legislation drafted to purposely address the 'plight of the *agunah*' seems to sometimes remain a dead letter. The next section investigates some possible reasons for this state of affairs and presents some of the alternatives Jewish women are presented with upon divorce.

'Unofficial' Stories: The Plight of the Canadian *Agunah* in Underground Community-Life

Given the limits of the two 'official' State mechanisms to address 'the plight of the *agunah*', I have sought to explore what lies in the shadow of these legal remedies that might explain their seemingly scant use. The Supreme Court of British Columbia case of *Nathanson, Schachter and Thompson v. Levitt* inspired a working hypothesis. In that case, an application under 21.1 and a consequent challenge to the provision's constitutional validity were abandoned "at the last minute through the intervention of a rabbi." (para. 32) Whether the intervention in that case occurred through the official channel of the *beth din* or through informal

E.F. v. A.K. In some marginal cases such as *Tanny v. Tanny* the provision was used against a refusing wife.

mediation is unknown. Nevertheless, it shows the influential role of the community on religious minority members[16] and clearly invites legal scholars to further explore the impact of non-state forms of power on the behaviour of religious subjects, which I did by engaging in socio-legal fieldwork in Canada and studying the non-State recourses available to Jewish women.

For the *get* to be religiously valid, a rabbinical court or *beth din* (pl. *batei din*) composed of three Jewish judges (*dayanim*)[17] must oversee the divorce process. However, the *beth din* cannot execute the divorce itself, as the "man's consent [is] the *sine qua non* of the entire process" (Berger and Lipstadt 1998: 99). Nevertheless, *batei din* have put in place several non-state mechanisms to pressure recalcitrant husbands. For instance, a *beth din* can decree a *cherem*, an order on the community to marginalize the recalcitrant husband (Fishbayn 2008: 83). A wife can also apply for a *siruv* (sometimes spelled *seruv*), a contempt citation ordered against a person who refuses to appear before a *beth din* to which he or she is summoned (Saris 2006: 375; Guthartz 2004: 48; Fried 2004; Wolf 2009: 1191). Several sanctions can be enacted along with this decree to restrict the husband's position in the synagogue. For instance, the Rabbinical Council of America established a policy to enforce orders of *siruv* in synagogues, against men who are using the *get* as a bargaining tool in their divorce procedures or are refusing to give the *get*. Various forms of excommunication can be applied with the possible consequences that the recalcitrant husband "not be permitted to occupy any elective or appointed position, or position as employee, within the Synagogue" or be downright "excluded from membership in the Synagogue" (Rabbinical Council of America 1993). These sanctions can be very effective given the role of synagogues in maintaining the "religious and cultural cohesion of the community" (Baker 1993: 28). Even though these measures are described as unequally and sometimes reluctantly enforced (Breitowitz 1992: 15; Greenberg-Kobrin 1999: 368), they have the benefit of being efficient in at least *some* religious communities (Wolfe 2006: 441). One of my participants had attempted to yield the power of *siruv* against her husband. She was confident that this

[16] For instance, in Ontario alone, each year about 30 cases of divorce by Jews are overseen in their entirety by the rabbinical *Beth Din*, including issues such as custody and property division (Boyd 2004: 41).

[17] The rabbinate has been closed to women for centuries. However, in recent decades, female rabbis have been admitted in North America, though the importance of this phenomenon varies greatly according to the denomination involved (Joseph 2005: 582).

mechanism would work, as her husband's family would not be able to bear the brunt of public humiliation in the community:

> I have been in contact with many rabbis from the *beth din*, trying to force him to give the *get*. [...] He was called three times to appear before the *beth din* and he did not show up all three times. If he doesn't show up he is put in *siruv*. [...] My ex-husband's family is an established family; they give a lot of money to charity, so they really would not want him to be put in *siruv*, because it would bring public humiliation to the family. (Canadian Participant #10)

This powerful bargaining tool illustrates how community pressure can often be perceived as the most useful option available, more so than 'official' State law. In addition to the formal recourses before the *beth din*, community life presents a plethora of informal alternatives for *agunah* women to explore. This "organizational ecology" (Friedland 2001: 45) endows Jewish women with important resources. For instance, the New York Jewish Press magazine ran a column reporting recalcitrant husbands and *agunah* women, bringing shame on the husbands (Zornberg 1995: 711). Likewise, in January 2011, a New York Orthodox Jewish public figure was publicly shamed by rabbis and campaigners through Jewish media and the internet for his refusal to give the *get* (Oppenheimer 2011). Inherent to many Jewish community dynamics are informal interpersonal bonds, reinforced by "series of interlocking matrices of religious belief and practices" (Unterman 1997: 196), which often work to create informal recourses and opportunities which supersede the civil courts and the 'official' State law.[18] Some of my participants yielded these disciplinary tools through their connections in the Jewish legal and religious *milieus*:

> I retained a great attorney. She's become a very, very close personal friend. My attorney is Jewish, not religious, but she's Jewish. The attorney that he retained is also Jewish, and from what I understand, but I am not 100% sure, I think he was told that his attorney would not represent him, unless he promised to give me the *get*. (Canadian Participant #6)

[18] See Van Praagh's account of some Montreal Chasidic (ultra-orthodox) communities' perception of themselves as self-regulating entities (Van Praagh 1996: 214). Also see Richman (2006).

> In my community, some [people] mentioned to the friend of my ex, who was a president of a synagogue: "Give her the *get*". (Canadian Participant #8)

Other participants used their personal bonds of friendship and family to pressure their recalcitrant husbands, using shame and public reputation as a weapon:

> After thinking about how I could convince him [to give the *get*], I came to the conclusion that it would be impossible to persuade him on my own and enlisted the help of those I thought would be most embarrassed by his behaviour. I called an aunt of his with whom he was quite close and has a great deal of respect for. [...] She said she would absolutely speak to him and encourage him to do the right thing. [...] To this day, I don't know for sure what led to his finally agreeing to a *get*, but I think the pressure and embarrassment of my exposing his behaviour in front of others led to success. (Canadian Participant #4)

State law can no longer ignore this emphasis on community affiliations. For many religious women, the civil sphere is not necessarily the first forum that they will explore upon divorce. Moreover, when they do enter that space, it may not always be reflective of their experience. This is no surprise given that secularism, which is oftentimes paradoxically informed by Protestant emphasis on individual (private) belief as the foundation of religion and the latter's seclusion from the civil domain, does not have the same resonance in non-Christian contexts (Stone 2000: 190; Shah 2006). This should not be taken to suggest that the boundaries between Jewish communities and gentile 'secular' society are not blurry and that multiple community belongings are not overlapping (Cooper 1996; Van Praagh 2008). However, solutions rooted in the civil laws of the State, even when they do reach out to the religious sphere as does section 21.1, may take root less easily in non-Christian communities, for whom the 'unofficial' religious community mechanisms are not seen as divorced from their 'public', 'civil' life and may indeed be seen as preferable to the remedies created by the State. Critical attention to this dynamic may be key for the integrative dialogue to begin between the secular and the religious, and for a meaningful access to justice policy to be implemented among minority religious communities.

'Official' Stories: Sanctions, Jail and the Israeli Rabbinical Courts

I now turn to the case of Israel, which has strong social and religious relevance to most of the Diaspora communities (Ben-Rafael 2006; Stratton 2004: 143). This importance is illustrated by my Canadian participant who had neither used s. 21.1 nor included a *Marcovitz*-type separation agreement, but mentioned the possible use of Israel's 1995 so-called *Sanctions Law*, the *Rabbinical Tribunals (Implementation of Divorce Judgments) Law*, a statute allowing for the punishment of recalcitrant husbands. She was disappointed to learn that the *Sanctions Law* only applies to Israeli residents and citizens, which her husband was not.[19] However, this anecdote underline the large-scale trans-jurisdictional intertwinements that globalization has brought to the realm of family law disputes (Fournier 2010: 2-3; Cossman 2006; Blackett 1998). This section explores the Israeli legislation relating to the *get* from a comparative law perspective, in an attempt to inform the analysis of Canadian law and Western legal systems more generally. The complex forces constraining the Israeli legislation directly affect the ways in which Jewish women worldwide may view the issue of the *agunah*. As Dr. Norma Joseph, a prominent Jewish scholar and public figure (Brown 2005), has argued: "Judaism is at stake over this issue" (quoted in Prentice et al. 1996: 450).

Israel's family law regime, in a large measure dating back to the Ottoman Millet system, confers jurisdiction over divorce and marriage to (religious) rabbinical courts (*The Rabbinical Courts Jurisdictions (Marriage and Divorce) Law*: S. 1; Navot 2007: 21). When the British set out to govern Palestine at the close of the First World War, this system was maintained by article 53 of the Palestine Order-in-Council of 1922 (Shiloh 1970: 481). When the state of Israel was created in 1948, the 'status quo' arrangement, Ben Gurion's compromise with religious parties and authorities, provided that the creation of the state would in no way compromise the "values and way of life of religious Jews". This arrangement confirmed that "Orthodox courts would have jurisdiction in issues of personal law (particularly matters of marriage and divorce)" (Lerner 2009: 447). Moreover, the divorce procedures, which are the focus of this article, are governed by strictly

[19] Even though this is indeed the state of the law, this participant could have tried to petition an Israeli rabbinical court, as it seems that some of them do ascertain jurisdiction over non-resident Jews, who may even have celebrated their marriage outside of Israel, as evidenced by a warning against this extension of Israeli jurisdiction issued by the US Department of State to American citizens travelling to Israel (US Department of State 2012).

religious law, even though certain ancillary areas of divorce law such as custody and matrimonial property are governed by civil law (Shifman 1990: 538). Up to today, there is no civil marriage to speak of for the majority of Israelis.[20] As put by Martin Edelman, even though Israel is not a formally theocratic State, "Judaism functions in the Israeli polity as if it were the official state religion" (Edelman 1994: 3-4).

The problem of the Israeli *agunah* has gotten significant international media coverage. A 1995 source estimated that between 8,000 and 10,000 Israeli women were being denied a *get* (Fisher 1995). By comparison, a study found that 462 Jewish women across Canada and the United States had declared being *agunah*, even though authors of the study indicate that the actual number of *agunahs* in both countries could be from 20 to 50 per cent higher (Jewish Tribune 2011). That being said, the Israeli figures are highly contested. For instance, in 2007 the Rabbinical Courts Administration published statistics which indicate that there is a mere total of 69 *agunah* women in Israel, taking into consideration only the cases registered at the rabbinical and pending for more than two years. There are obviously huge political stakes behind this debate, including the very definition and control over the scale of the *agunah* problem. Going beyond cases where downright refusal drags on for years, it is interesting to note that Israeli men often use the *get* as a bargaining tool to extract concessions in alimony custody of property matters, before granting the *get*. It is estimated that almost 100,000 divorced women have been victims of such '*get* extortion' in Israel (Yefet 2009: 447).

In order to combat the '*agunah* problem', the Knesset enacted the *Sanctions Law*, which allows women to use sanctions against their recalcitrant husband to pressure them into giving the *get*. The rabbinical court can only order the parties to divorce on very specific halachic grounds but may not enact the divorce itself. If there are no grounds for divorce, there is nothing short of an agreement of the spouses that can dissolve the marriage. While the grounds for ordering divorces vary tremendously across jurisdictions and religious authorities, generally, if the wife is subject to physical or verbal abuse by her husband, if the husband is impotent or sterile or if he fails to provide maintenance, an order to grant divorce may be issued (Lieber et al. 2007: 712-713). Although the Israeli rabbinical court judges,

[20] A bill was passed in May 2010 to allow civil marriage for partners who are both considered as "lacking a religion", a group which may not be very important numerically in Israel (Lerner 2011: 213 footnote 12).

like their Canadian *beth din* counterparts, do not often issue orders of *get* compulsion, when they do, the *Sanctions Law* allows them to issue sanctions and to withhold certain benefits from the husband to ensure compliance with the order. The *Sanctions Law*, unlike Canada's s. 21.1, is thus conditioned upon the existence of these grounds for compelling divorce (Einhorn 2000: 152). Nevertheless, the *Sanctions Law* is intended to be binding on religious authorities. The power of the community to use indirect pressure to influence a husband to issue a bill of divorce, which in the past was done through ostracism and excommunication, is now said to be translated into legislation by allowing the courts to withhold certain benefits from the husband. For instance, the law allows for the imposition of restrictions on the right to leave the country, obtain an Israeli passport, maintain a driver's license, work in a profession regulated by law or operate a business requiring a license or legal permit, open or maintain a bank account (Kaplan 2004: 123). Section 3 of the *Law* even allows for imprisonment to ensure compliance with a divorce order. The period of imprisonment that a rabbinical court may impose is limited to five years, a term that may be extended by the court as long as the total term does not exceed ten years (*Sanctions Law*: s. 3(b)). A further section of the *Law* goes as far as to allow the rabbinical court to impose sanctions upon a husband who may already be serving a jail sentence (*Sanctions Law*: s. 2(7)). So we see that the 'official' law ostensibly provides a solution for *agunah* women. Let us now see how this plays out in the realm of 'unofficial' law.

'Unofficial' Stories: Unenforced Laws, Indeterminacy and Informal Strategizing

This section aims to go beyond the official legal discourse to examine how the *Sanctions Law* is applied and how various actors shape it on a day-to-day basis.[21] Despite the enactment of the *Sanctions Law*, which is a clear indication that the 'plight of the *agunah*' must be addressed, very few sanctions have actually been enacted. Statistics show that between 1995 and 1998, only 163 restraining orders were issued against recalcitrant husbands, of which 76 came from the same rabbinical court in a single district (Halperin-Kaddari 2004: 239). The *Sanctions*

[21] This article does not study the all-important phenomenon of the growth of parallel non-state Haredim courts in Israel. It focuses on the State rabbinical courts, which most observant sectors of Israeli society still abide by and support (Hofri-Winogradow 2010-2011: 65).

Law was used only 73 times in 2008; only 20 arrest warrants were issued, and private investigators were hired by the courts only 36 times to locate men who had disappeared in Israel or abroad to avoid giving their wives a *get* (Administration of the Rabbinical Courts 2008). In 2009, only six of the verdicts imposing sanctions included arrests warrants (Ettinger 2010). These numbers are quite low for a nation of more than 7 million people. The *Sanctions Law* was thus often unenforced. Through my fieldwork, I sought to analyse the variables that affect and complicate the *Sanctions Law*'s disciplinary power. For my participants, the ineffectiveness of the sanctions stemmed from judicial actors and the police in charge of executing the ordinances rendered under the *Sanctions Law*:

> The rabbinical court put out a warrant to arrest him and the police didn't do anything with it. For more than a year the police did nothing, they didn't arrest him and then the rabbinical court decided to close the case. (Israeli Participant #3)

> The police went and looked for him, but he wasn't there. I told them to look at his sister's house, I told them to look at his brother's house, everywhere they went to look, he wasn't there. He ended up showing up anyways. What did I learn from that? I can't count on the police that they're going to find him. Court order, shmourt order! [...] I can sit at home and hold this nice piece of paper and have it framed on the wall, and he's going to still do whatever he wants. (Israeli Participant #6)

Almost all of my participants shared this criticism of police and judicial actors. Furthermore, the ineffectiveness of the sanctions was also said to stem from the rabbis themselves. In fact, the participants indicated that hearings at the rabbinical courts were delayed because the rabbis were reticent and unsympathetic to the women's plight:

> I don't think that the rabbis do their job the way they should. We go into a hearing and we're invited for 10:30, and we go in at like 12:30 and at one o'clock, when they have to go home, they put on their coat and their hat and they say "Ok, we've heard enough and we'll send you a decision in the mail." [...] The rabbis wait a long time until they actually go ahead and give you an arrest warrant. (Israeli Participant #5)

> We started all of [the sanctions] but [the rabbis] actually didn't

> want to do [the sanctions]. You see I learned the rabbinical court's ways [...] They start something but they don't follow it all the way through to the end. It's like they feel... it's not comfortable for them to hurt people. [...] It was a waste of time! (Israeli Participant #4)

Many scholars have noted, echoing the testimonies of my participants, that the rabbinical courts are reluctant to issue orders compelling the granting of the *get* out of fear that applying sanctions upon the recalcitrant husband will render the eventual giving of the *get* invalid due to force or undue pressure (Blecher-Prigat and Shmueli 2009: 283; Einhorn 2000: 151; Shifman 1999: 245). Indeed, a *get* that is given forcibly, or because a man *felt* pressured to do so, is halachically invalid (a "*get* meuseh") (Yefet 2009: 446; Bitton, 2009: 117-118; Kaplan 2004: 61). This may explain why in 2006, for instance, only 41 compulsion decrees were issued in Israel (Ratzlav-Katz 2007). Furthermore, as revealed in the statistics quoted above, "[e]ven when men are commanded to divorce, the court seldom applies the coercive measures that it was legislatively authorized to use in 1995" (Yefet 2009: 448). Robyn Shames[22] also explained to me that rabbis sometimes encourage women to settle by saying "pay him what he wants, you see what type of person he is, just pay him what he wants". She also described the conception of rabbis she encountered: for them, women will only hurt themselves by refusing the conditions men put forth in order to grant them a *get,* sometimes becoming 'get refusers' in the eyes of the court.

A rabbi's ideological and personal inclinations may thus influence the adjudicative process. Accordingly, the religious composition of Israeli courts was always the object of much academic interest. Scholars have described the "monopoly" (Raday 1996: 214) orthodox groups enjoy over family law in Israel. Orthodox rabbis are considered to form the majority of rabbinical court judges in the country (Woods 2008: xvi; Halperin-Kaddari 2000-2001: 348). The most orthodox rabbis are often said to be overly sympathetic to the husband (Halperin-Kaddari 2004: 233; Clinton 2000: 306) and to be very reticent to order the granting of the *get*, except in extreme cases "like those involving a violent, ill or sterile husband" (Ettinger 2010). Thus, the 'official' law here again needs to account for decentralized normative belongings and religious ideology that affect and circumvent the 'official' law.

---

[22] Director, International Coalition for Agunah Rights (online: http://www.icar.org.il/en), sent by email on March 8, 2011.

However, the 'unofficial' does not only hamper the *Sanctions Law*. It can also allow *some* legal subjects to find their way around the insufficiencies of 'official' law. Participants mentioned that in addition to being often unenforced, the *Sanctions Law* is indeterminate in its application, in the sense of being permeable to ideological manipulation. Some participants have indicated that the rulings issued by the rabbinical courts depend on the backgrounds, personalities and religious ideologies of the judges and are inconsistent:

> [The rabbis] only care about what the man wants not what the woman wants. They treated me like I wasn't even there. Then I said: "I came to ask to be free, not for money or anything, just to be free..." [...] When the rabbis saw that I have a rabbinical advocate and that I am determined, that I want [a divorce] and that I am doing everything to get it, then they were easier. (Israeli Participant #2)

> Once in a while we will get a rabbinical court that has guts, that will put the pressure on the guy. But it is unpredictable, there's nothing uniform in the decision-making. It's all based on whim and which three judges are sitting and half the time there aren't even three judges there so they can't make a decision. They show up late for work, they leave early from work... There is nothing uniform about the rabbinical courts, one rabbi is rigid, one is not rigid. (Social Worker, *Mavoi Satum*[23])

Lawyers and rabbinical advocates, as a result of the indeterminacy of religious adjudication, will strategize to bring their clients in front of judges who they deem more lenient. Participants had often wanted a particular rabbi to adjudicate their divorce petition because of these perceived ideological, religious or personal inclinations:

> I knew that I needed to be in [rabbi] Rav Feldman's[24] group, the panel with the three of them. [...] Now in the *beit hadin hagadol* (high rabbinical court), there was only one *dayan*, one of those

[23] Organization which supports *agunah* women (online: http://www.mavoisatum.org).

[24] All personal names have been changed to protect the anonymity of the individuals concerned.

> rabbis who would understand. [....] So we knew that we needed to get to Rav Shmuel Feldman. (Israeli Participant #6)

Accordingly, notwithstanding widespread complaints that rabbis are overly sympathetic to men, some participants were able to play out their image against that of their husband's to successfully influence the rabbis. According to Halperin-Kaddari, the religious courts, when rendering decisions, will put more emphasis on 'moral' and religious questions than do the Israeli civil courts. Their application of the law and appreciation of the facts may be tainted by their religious perspective (Halperin-Kaddari 2004: 250). For instance, Ariel Rosen-Zvi indicates that the rabbinical court will likely favour the 'more religious' parent for custody purposes (Rosen-Zvi 1989: 352). As some of my participants demonstrated, exploiting the perception that the rabbis had of their personal ethics could constitute a fertile strategic avenue for many religious women:

> Watching him in action yelling at the judges, [...] that was what convinced them that I needed a *get*. [...] I'm this together lady, and when they saw him ranting and raving they didn't like him. [...] So then, at one point, towards the end, we finally got a *chiyuv* [order that the *get* be given]. (Israeli Participant #6)

> Three rabbis were sitting at the *beit din*, and I said "When you go to sleep think that I am your daughter. Would you relate to your daughter like you are acting to me?" I don't know if it did anything to them but the next time, they changed, they decided they had to give me a *get*. They treated me like a human. (Israeli Participant #2)

In addition to this ideological breach in some rabbi's misogynistic attitudes, the community-based nature of the rabbinical courts allowed some women to personally put pressure on the rabbis, using personal connections and networks:

> We needed to go to the high rabbinical court. And only there was I saved, because we had there rabbi Lazare who worked with my boss, and he came to a lot of the hearings. I called him many times and asked him to help. (Israeli Participant #1)

Thus, we see that while the *Sanctions Law* cannot be considered a success in terms of women empowerment, some women do exploit informal avenues in the shadow of the law. 'Unofficial' Israeli law not only helps explain why the *Sanctions Law* fails, it also gives us examples of how the limitations of the law can be overcome by women who take on the rabbis, using a variety of techniques and tricks which I have only begun to discover in my fieldwork. If the stories of my participants cannot be considered as numerically representative of all women in Israel, they echo the findings of many socio-legal studies and thus complement the latter with a qualitative account. My study aligns with that of Sezgin, who brilliantly demonstrates (2010a) that there are many other "coping strategies" being used by Israeli women and men like marrying abroad, common law partnerships or claiming damages for *get* refusal (Eglash 2011), which are redrawing the boundaries of the (religious) legal system from within. Perhaps these coping strategies can serve as inspiration to women around the world struggling to obtain a *get*. Revealing as I have done the indeterminacy of the *Sanctions Law* and its permeability to ideological manipulation[25] can thus be a political gesture in itself and hopefully contribute to alleviating the plight of the *agunah* in unexpected ways.

Conclusion

In this article, I have developed an approach that navigates and analyses the intersection between the religious and the secular and its impacts on Jewish women divorcing in Canada and Israel. Drawing from my fieldwork and the literature, I have emphasized the necessity to explore the sites of regulation that lie beyond the locus of the State but nevertheless highly influence the shape and the impacts of the law. For instance, Canadian public policy values contract law as a solution to the *agunah* problem, but is limited if women do not use this form of legal regulation. Moreover, remedies enshrined in the Canadian civil *Divorce Act* can only assist those women who have penetrated the civil sphere upon divorce *and* have been correctly informed of the existence of section 21.1. Whereas the Canadian approach to the *agunah* problem brings positive results when used by Jewish women, the Israeli response seems attractive on its face but is rarely applied in the manner in which it was intended (albeit with notable exceptions where women were able to play out the indeterminacy of religious law to their advantage). In fact, the law enforcement mechanisms will be given all sorts of fair and unfair directions depending on the rabbi appointment process and the parties'

[25] This is not to suggest, of course, that secular law is determinate and free of ideological influences. For the application of the indeterminacy thesis in Western secular systems, see Kennedy (1997) and Tushnet (1996).

strategies.

The lessons Canada and Israel have to learn from each other are wholly methodological. Both cases underline that one cannot only understand law through the ontological tools of "legal evangelicalism", which "breeds a reliance on the rituals, catechism and creed of official institutions that focus on the word (especially on the definitive pronouncements of the *curia* that sits at the top of an institutional hierarchy)" (Macdonald 2011: 306). As *critical* legal pluralism teaches us, legal subjects shape and produce law as much as Parliament does, through their constructive creativity and normative interpersonal interactions. In the Canadian context, this has entailed going beyond the civil law recourses to wander into the private sphere of community affiliations to understand why state law sometimes fails, and why community interactions can sometimes be more efficient than state law. Recent research done in the plight of the *agunah* in the United Kingdom has also taken the promising approach of investigating the reasons of the insufficiencies of State responses to the *agunah* problem (Jackson et al. 2009: 10-11) and the reactions of non-State actors to these policies (Douglas et al. 2011: 48). In the Israeli context, the *critical* legal pluralist outlook has led me to assess the role of religious ideology and informal bonds of religious community to explain at once why the *Sanctions Law* fails for so many women yet is used by *some* women to successfully put an end to their plight. While at first the socio-legal landscapes of both polities seemed to be polar opposites, we have seen that many conclusions from both studies can be connected. In both polities, we have seen that legal agents navigate through "different legal spaces superimposed, interpenetrated, and mixed in [their] mind as much as in [their] actions" (Santos 1987: 297-298). Moreover, my fieldwork in both countries illustrates how legal pluralist inquiry can at once be attentive to State law and be committed to non-State normativities. In this regard, my invocation of *critical* legal pluralism may be unorthodox, informed as it is by a vision of the State as an important source of bargaining endowments, which intersect with non-state power relations (Fournier 2012). My findings illustrate how legal subjects' socio-economic bargaining may straddle the fence between State and non-State law, two phenomena which have been pitted against one another by some strands of legal pluralism, but which "dynamically interact with one another" (Sezgin 2004: 102-103) and are in fact mutually constitutive (Corrin 2009). I have begun to chronicle these interactions through the eyes of *agunah* women that confront State and non-State recourses and intertwine them as they bargain with religious law.

These findings could be shown to have significant repercussions on our conception of access to justice. As put by Canadian Participant #4, who had not been able to get adequate counselling on religious divorce matters:

> One of the questions when you're first going through a consult should be, you know, "Are there any religious issues?" And that did not come up. [...] I really do think that, you know, family law attorneys should be aware that sometimes there are really strange religious issues that come up in divorce, and it should be addressed.

Understanding the unofficial norms that shape the 'law in action' can thus be seen as a fundamental professional duty, analogous to those encountered in multicultural contexts (Bryant 2001; Jacobs 1997; Hartley and Petrucci 2004). This is also key to ensuring professional services that incorporate basic commitments to equality and access to justice (Way 2002: 214). As put by Roderick A. Macdonald, meaningful "empirical research [on access to justice] must target the everyday law of social interaction where inaccessible justice is first perceived" (Macdonald 2010: 517). This does not imply that lawyers should assume any systematic hierarchy between a legal subject's normative commitments, which are unevenly distributed and perpetually re-designed (Macdonald 2011: 325). Rather, legal practitioners must adapt their consultations on a case-by-case basis by finding the appropriate way to combine State and non-State law to further the interests of Jewish women. Any access to justice policy must acknowledge and embrace the messiness of the "multiple networks, constant transitions and mixing of legal spaces" (Van Praagh 1996: 214) that are characteristic of legal systems as seemingly different as Canada and Israel. In these two polities, the relationship between the civil state and religious law is one of "tension and opposition" (Leckey 2006: 18), leading to many unexpected outcomes as this tension is played out by judges, rabbis, wives and husbands. Jukier and Van Praagh emphasize that:

> Deference to religion by the state, and a corresponding refusal to interfere, may seem to be one option; authority over religion by the state, with an accompanying eagerness to fix the perceived failures of traditional faiths, may seem to be another. A careful reading of *Bruker* should suggest that neither is feasible or desirable, and that a sometimes seemingly chaotic coexistence of normative commitments, of religion 'at' law, is closer to reality (Jukier and Van Praagh 2008: 338).

Moreover, the twelve Jewish women I interviewed have shown that the interaction and intertwinement of State and non-State regulation orders, when it is duly acknowledged by legal practitioners, has "generated interesting and creative solutions to problems of marriage and divorce in a number of communities" (Estin 2009: 471), as evidenced by the recourse to members of the religious community by some of my participants to pressure their husbands. As Sezgin notes, these internal pluralist solutions may be more productive than "top-down secular solutions" (Sezgin 2010b: 30). Thus, engaging in inter-normative empirical work that chronicles those solutions may be the way to better understand the 'plight of the *agunah*'. As a result of this work, could Israeli *agunah* women, following my Canadian participant who strategized across borders in considering the Israeli legislation, be inspired by Western Jewish women's navigation of Jewish community institutions? Moreover, could Canadian *beth dins* develop their own *Sanctions Law*, taking cues from what Israeli rabbinical courts and Canadian civil courts have been trying to achieve? The 'plight of the *agunah*', which travels from the (Canadian) civil State to the (Israeli) religious State to the (Canadian) private religious sphere of the *beth din*, can perhaps only be addressed by borrowing solutions across countries, communities, normative orders and boundaries.

References

Statutes: Canada

Civil Code of Québec, S.Q. 1991, c. 64.
Constitution Act, 1867 (U.K.), 30 & 31 Victoria, c. 3.
Divorce Act, R.S.C. 1970 c. D-8.
Divorce Act, R.S.C. 1985, c. 3 (2nd Supp).
Ontario Family Law Act, R.S.O. 1990, c. M.3.

Statutes: Israel

Rabbinical Tribunals (Implementation of Divorce Judgments) Law, 5755-1995, Law Book of the State of Israel [Sanctions Law].
The Rabbinical Courts Jurisdictions (Marriage and Divorce) Law, 5713-1953, Law Book of the State of Israel.

Statutes: UK

Divorce (Religious Marriages) Act 2002 (U.K.).
Matrimonial Causes Act 1973 (U.K.).

Cases

Abadi v. Emanuel, 2011 QCCS 147 (Quebec Superior Court).
A.D. c. J.P., [2004] J.Q. no 1078 (Quebec Superior Court).
Aflalo v. Aflalo, 295 N.J. Super 527 (1996) (Superior Court of New Jersey).
Avitzur v. Avitzur, 449 NYS2d 83, 86 AD2d 133 (App. Div., 1982) (New York Court of Appeal).
Blumes v. Blumes, [1995] A.J. No. 452, 175 A.R. 253 (Alberta Court of Queen's Bench).
Bruker v. Marcovitz, [2007] 3 S.C.R. 607, 2007 SCC 54 (Supreme Court of Canada).
Cour de cassation, Chambre civile 2, 15 June 1988, No. 86-15476, Bulletin civil 1988 II p. 78, No. 146.
D.A. c. J.H., 2008 QCCS 838 (Quebec Superior Court).
Darel v. Darel, 1999 ABQB 881 (Alberta Court of Queen's Bench).
E.F. v. A.K., [2001] Q.J. No. 2067 (Quebec Superior Court).
E.I. c. A.A. [1995] J.Q. no 990 (Quebec Superior Court).
E.S. c. O.S., [1995] R.D.F. 728 (Quebec Superior Court).
I.L. c. M.A., 2009 QCCS 538 (Quebec Superior Court).
In re Marriage of Goldman, 554 N.E. 2d 1016 (1990) (Appellate Court of Illinois).
K.N.H. v. J.S., [2000] Q.J. No. 2147, [2000] R.D.F. 268 (Quebec Superior Court).
Marcovitz c. Bruker, 2005 QCCA 835, [2005] R.J.Q. 2482 (Quebec Court of Appeal).
Morris v. Morris (1974) 42 D.L.R. (3d) 550 (Manitoba Court of Appeal).
Nathanson, Schachter and Thompson v. Levitt, 2006 BCSC 730 (Supreme Court of British Columbia).
N.K. v. M.K., [2000] Q.J. No. 1461(Quebec Superior Court).
R.M. v. M.S.S. [1995] Q.J. No. 1569 (Quebec Superior Court).
S.B.B. v. J.B.M., [2003] R.J.Q. 1189, [2003] R.D.F. 342 (Quebec Superior Court).
Tanny v. Tanny, [2000] O.J. No. 2472, 8 R.F.L. (5th) 427 (Ontario Superior Court).

Parliamentary Documents

House of Commons Debates, vol. VI, 2nd Sess., 34th Parl., February 15, 1990.

Literature

ABELLA, Irving
2005 'Rosalie Silberman Abella.' available at http://jwa.org/encyclopedia/article/abella-rosalie-silberman (accessed August 14 2012).
ADMINISTRATION OF THE RABBINICAL COURTS
2008 'Yearly Summary 2008.' (Hebrew) available at http://www.rbc.gov.il/statistics/2008/2008.pdf (accessed August 14 2012).
ALTHUSSER, Louis
1997 'Ideology and Ideological State Apparatuses.' Pp.85-126 in Louis Althusser, *Lenin and Philosophy and Other Essays*, translated by Ben Brewster, New York: Monthly Review Press.
ASTENGO, Francesca
2009 'Liberté de religion ou égalité entre les sexes? La Cour suprême du Canada se prononce sur un cas de divorce.' *Revue de droit de l'Université de Sherbrooke* 39(2): 507-529.
BAKER, Adrienne
1993 *The Jewish Woman in Contemporary Society: Transitions*. New York: New York University Press.
BARON, Jane B.
1994 'Resistance to Stories.' *Southern California Law Review* 67(2): 255-285.
BARTLETT, Katharine T.
1990 'Feminist Legal Methods.' *Harvard Law Review* 103: 829-888.
BENDA-BECKMANN, Franz von, and Keebet von BENDA-BECKMANN
2006 'The Dynamics of Change and Continuity in Plural Legal Orders.' *Journal of Legal Pluralism* 53(1): 17-32.
BEN-RAFAEL, Eliezer
2006 'Contemporary Dilemmas of Identity: Israel and the Diaspora.' Pp. 279-288 in Eliezer Ben Rafael, Thomas Gergely and Yosef Gorny (eds.), *Jewry Between Tradition and Secularism: Europe and Israel Compared*, Leiden: Koninklijke Brill NV.
BERGER, Michael S. and Deborah E. LIPSTADT
1998 'Women in Judaism from the Perspective of Human Rights.' Pp.77-111 in

Michael J. Broyde and John Witte Jr. (eds.), *Human Rights in Judaism: Cultural, Religious and Political Perspectives*, Jerusalem: Jason Aronson.

BIALE, Rachel

1984 *Women and the Jewish Law: The Essential Texts, Their History and Their Relevance for Today*. New York: Schocken Books.

BITTON, Yifat

2009 'Public Hierarchy and Private Harm: Tort Law as a Remedy for Gender Inequality in Israeli Family Law.' Pp. 115-132 in Lisa Dresdner and Laurel S. Peterson (eds.), *(Re)Interpretations: The Shapes of Justice in Women's Experience*, Newcastle: Cambridge Scholars Publishing.

BLACKETT, Adelle

1998 'Globalization and its Ambiguities: Implications for Law School Curricular Reform.' *Columbia Journal of Transnational Law* 37: 57-79.

BLECHER-PRIGAT, Ayelet, and SHMUELI, Benjamin

2009 'The Interplay between Tort Law and Religious Family Law: The Israeli Case.' *Arizona Journal of International and Comparative Law* 26: 279-301.

BOYD, Marion

2004 'Dispute Resolution in Family law: Protecting Choice, Promoting Inclusion.' Available at http://www.attorneygeneral.jus.gov.on.ca/english/about/pubs/boyd/fullreport.pdf (accessed August 14 2012).

BREITOWITZ, Irving

1992 'The 'Plight of the Agunah:' A Study in 'Halacha,' Contract, and the First Amendment.' *Maryland Law Review* 51(2): 312-421.

1993 *Between Civil and Religious Law: The Plight of the Agunah in American Society*. Westport Connecticut: Greenwood Press.

BROWN, Michael

2005 'Norma Bauel Joseph.' Available at http://jwa.org/encyclopedia/article/joseph-norma-baumel (accessed August 14 2012).

BROYDE, Michael

2001 *Marriage, Divorce, and the Abandoned Wife in Jewish Law: a Conceptual Understanding of the Agunah Problems in America*. Hoboken New Jersey: KTAV Publication House.

BRYANT, Susan

2001 'The Five Habits: Building Cross-Cultural Competence in Lawyers.' *Clinical Law Review* 8(1): 33-107.

CAMPBELL, Angela

2008 'Wives' Tales: Reflecting on Research in Bountiful.' *Canadian Journal of Law and Society* 23: 121-141.

2009 'Bountiful Voices.' *Osgoode Hall Law Journal* 47: 183-234.

CAUGHEY, John L.

2009 'The Anthropologist as Expert Witness: The Case of a Murder in Maine.' Pp.321-334 in Marie-Claire Foblets and Alison Dundes Renteln (eds.), *Multicultural Jurisprudence: Comparative Perspectives on the Cultural Defence,* Oxford: Hart Publishing.

CLINTON, Erica

2000 'Chains of Marriage: Israeli Women's Fight for Freedom.' *Journal of Gender Race and Justice* 3: 283-288.

COBIN, David M.

1986 'Jewish Divorce and the Recalcitrant Husband - Refusal to Give a Get as Intentional Infliction of Emotional Distress.' *Journal of Law and Religion* 4(2): 405-430.

COHN, Margit

2004 'Women, Religious Law and Religious Courts in Israel – The Jewish Case.' *Retfaerd, Scandinavian Journal of Social Sciences* 27: 57-76.

COOPER, Davina

1996 'Talmudic Territory? Space, Law and Modernist Discourse.' *The Journal of Law and Society* 23(4): 529-548.

CORRIN, Jennifer

2009 'Moving Beyond the Hierarchical Approach to Legal Pluralism in the South Pacific.' *Journal of Legal Pluralism* 59: 29-48.

COSSMAN, Brenda

2006 'Migrating Marriages and Comparative Constitutionalism.' Pp. 209-229 in Sujit Choudhry (ed.), *The Migration of Constitutional Ideas*, Cambridge: Cambridge University Press.

DECOSTE, Frederick C.

2009 'Caesar's Faith: Limited Government and Freedom of Religion in Bruker v. Marcovitz.' *Dalhousie Law Journal* 32(1): 153-176.

DELGADO, Richard

1993 'Rodrigo's Second Chronicle: The Economics and Politics of Race.' *Michigan Law Review* 91: 1193-98.

DOUGLAS, Gillian, Norman DOE, Sophie GILLIAT-RAY, Russell SANDBERG and Asma KHAN

2011 'Social Cohesion and Civil Law: Marriage, Divorce and Religious Courts.' Available at http://www.law.cf.ac.uk/clr/Social%20Cohesion%20and%20Civil%20La

w%20Full%20Report.pdf (accessed August 14 2012).

EDELMAN, Martin
1994 *Courts, Politics, and Culture in Israel*. Charlottesville, VA: University of Virginia Press.

EGLASH, Ruth
2011 'District Court sets precedent by upholding right of "aguna".' *Jerusalem Post*, dated 2 March 2011, available at http://www.jpost.com/NationalNews/Article.aspx?id=206488 (accessed August 14 2012).

EINHORN, Talia
2000 'Jewish Divorce in the International Arena.' Pp.135-153 in Jürgen Basedow et al. (eds.), *Private International Law in the International Arena*, The Hague: T.M.C. Asser Press.

EPSTEIN, Louis M.
2005 *The Jewish Marriage Contract: A study of the Status of the Woman in Jewish Law*. New Jersey: Lawbook Exchange.

ESTIN, Ann L.
2009 'Unofficial Family Law.' *Iowa Law Review* 94(2): 449-480.

ETTINGER, Yair
2010 'Rabbinical Courts Softened Stance on Husbands Refusing Their Wives Divorce.' *Haaretz*, dated 27 January 2010, available at http://www.haaretz.com/hasen/spages/1145446.html (accessed August 14 2012).

EWICK, Patricia, and Susan S. SILBEY
1998 *The Common Place of Law: Stories from Everyday Life*. Chicago: University of Chicago Press.

FAJET, Marc A.
1994 'Authority, Credibility, and Pre-Understanding: A Defence of Outsider Narratives in Legal Scholarship.' *Georgetown Law Journal* 82: 1845-1867.

FINKELMAN, Paul
1995 'Bad Marriage: Jewish Divorce and the First Amendment.' *Cardozo Women's Law Journal* 2: 131-172.

FISHBAYN, Lisa
2008 'Gender, Multiculturalism and Dialogue: The Case of Jewish Divorce.' *Canadian Journal of Law and Jurisprudence* 21(1): 71-96.

FISHER, Allyn
1995 'Feminists Challenge Divorce Laws in Israel: Cards Are Stacked in Favor of Men.' *San Francisco Chronicle*, dated 10 January 1995, available at http://www.sfgate.com/news/article/Feminists-Challenge-Divorce-Laws-

in-Israel-3049001.php (accessed August 14 2012).

FOBLETS, Marie-Claire, Jean-François GAUDREAULT-DESBIENS and Alison Dundas RENTELN

2010 *Cultural Diversity and the Law: State Responses from Around the World.* Brussels: Bruylant.

FOURNIER, Pascale

2010 *Muslim Marriage in Western Courts: Lost in Transplantation.* Farnham: Ashgate Publishing.

2011 'Borders and Crossroads: Comparative Perspectives on Minorities and Conflicts of Laws.' *Emory International Law Review* 25(2): 987-1006.

2012 'Calculating Claims: Jewish and Muslim Women Navigating Religion, Economics and Law in Canada.' *International Journal of Law in Context* 8(3): 47-72.

FREEMAN, Michael

1996 'Law, Religion and The State: The *Get* Revisited.' Pp.361-384 in Nigel Lowe and Gillian Douglas (eds.), *Families Across Frontiers*, The Hague: Kluwer Law International.

FRIED, Ginnie

2004 'The Collision of Church and State: A Primer to Beth Din Arbitration and the New York Secular Courts.' *Fordham Urban Law Journal* 31(2): 633-656.

FRIEDLAND, Lewis A.

2001 'Reform Judaism and Modern American Community.' Pp.39-48 in Dana Evan Kaplan (ed.), *Contemporary Debates in American Reform Judaism: Conflicting Visions*, New York: Routledge.

GAUDREAULT-DESBIENS, Jean-François

2009 'Religious Challenges to the Secularized Identity of an Insecure Polity: A Tentative Sociology of Québec's 'Reasonable Accommodation' Debate.' Pp.151-176 in Ralph Grillo et al. (eds.), *Legal Practice and Cultural Diversity*, Farnham: Ashgate.

GLENN, Patrick H.

2008 'A Concept of Legal Tradition.' *Queen's Law Journal* 34(1): 427-445.

GREENBERG-KOBRIN, Michell

1999 'Civil Enforceability of Religious Prenuptial Agreements.' *Columbia Journal of Law and Social Problems* 32(4): 359-400.

GRIFFITHS, John

1986 'What is Legal Pluralism?' *Journal of Legal Pluralism* 24: 1-55.

GRILLO, Ralph, Roger BALLARD, Alessandro FERRARI, André HOEKEMA, Marcel MAUSSEN and Prakash SHAH (eds.)

2009 *Legal Practice and Cultural Diversity*, Farnham: Ashgate.

GUTHARTZ, Stacey A.
2004 'Domestic Violence and the Jewish Community.' *Michigan Journal of Gender and Law* 11: 27-62.
HACOHEN, Aviad and Blu GREENBERG
2004 *Tears of the Oppressed: An Examination of the Agunah Problem: Background and Halakhic Sources.* Jersey City: KTAV Publishing House.
HALPERIN-KADDARI, Ruth
2000-2001 'Women, Religion and Multiculturalism in Israel.' *UCLA Journal of International Law and Foreign Affairs* 5(2): 339-366.
2004 *Women in Israel: A State of Their Own.* Philadelphia: University of Pennsylvania Press.
HARTLEY, Carolyn Copps, and Carrie J. PETRUCCI
2004 'Practicing Culturally Competent Therapeutic Jurisprudence: A Collaboration between Social Work and Law.' *Washington University Journal of Law and Policy* 14: 133-181.
HARTMAN, Harriet and Moshe HARTMAN
2009 *Gender and American Jews: Patterns in Work, Education and Family in Contemporary Family Life.* Lebanon, NH: Brandeis University Press.
HAUT, Irwin H.
1983 *Divorce in Jewish Law and Life,* Vol. 5. New York: Sepher-Hermon Press.
HOFRI-WINOGRADOW, Adam
2010-2011 'Plurality of Discontent: Legal Pluralism, Religious Adjudication and the State.' *Journal of Law and Religion* 26(1): 57-90.
JACKSON, Bernard, Yehudah ABEL, Avishalom WESTREICH, Shoshana BOROCIN-KNOL and Nechama HADARI
2009 'Agunah: The Manchester Analysis.' Available at www.mucjs.org/ARUDraftFinal.pdf (accessed August 14 2012).
JACOBS, Michelle S.
1997 'People From The Footnotes: The Missing Element in Client-Centered Counseling.' *Golden Gate University Law Review* 27(3): 345-422.
JEWISH TRIBUNE
2011 'Agunot study turns up unexpected results.' dated 8 November 2011, available at http://www.jewishtribune.ca/uncategorized/2011/11/08/agunot-study-turns-up-unexpected-results (accessed August 14 2012).
JOSEPH, Norma B.
2005 'Jewish Law and Gender.' Pp. 576-588 in Rosemary Keller and Rosemary Radford Reuther, (eds.), *Encyclopedia of Women and Religion*, Indiana:

Indiana University Press.

JUKIER, Rosalie, and Shauna VAN PRAAGH

2008 'Civil Law and Religion in the Supreme Court of Canada: What Should We *Get* out of *Bruker v. Marcovitz.*' *Supreme Court Law Review* 43(2): 381-413.

KAPLAN, Yehiel S.

2004 'Enforcement of Divorce Judgements by Imprisonment: Principles of Jewish Law.' *Jewish Law Annual* 15: 57-145.

KENNEDY, Duncan

1997 *A Critique of Adjudication: fin de siècle.* Cambridge MA: Harvard University Press.

KLEEFELD, John C. and Amanda KENNEDY

2008 '"A Delicate Necessity": Bruker v. Marcovitz and the Problem of Jewish Divorce.' *Canadian Journal of Family Law* 24(2): 205-282.

KLEINHANS Martha-Marie and Roderick A. MACDONALD

1997 'What is Critical Legal Pluralism?' *Canadian Journal of Law and Society* 12: 25-46.

KORTEWEG, Anna C.

2008 'The Sharia Debate in Ontario: Gender, Islam, and Representations of Muslim Women's Agency.' *Gender and Society* 22(4): 434-454.

LANGEVIN, Louise, Louis-Philippe LAMPRON, Christelle LANDHEER-CIESLAK, Alain PRUJINER andPatrick TAILLON

2008 'L'affaire *Bruker c. Marcovitz*: variations sur un thème.' *Cahiers de Droit* 49(4): 655-708.

LECKEY, Robert

2006 'Profane Matrimony.' *Canadian Journal of Law and Society* 21(2): 1-23.

LERNER, Hanna

2009 'Entrenching the Status-Quo: Religion and State in Israel's Constitutional Principles.' *Constellations* 16: 445-461.

2011 *Making Constitutions in Deeply Divided Societies.* New York: Cambridge University Press.

LIEBER, David, Ben-Zion SCHERESCHEWSKY and Moshe DRORI

2007 'Divorce.' Pp.710-721 in Michael Berenbaum and Fred Skolnik (eds.), *Encyclopaedia Judaica*, 2nd ed. Detroit: Macmillan Reference USA.

LINDERBERG, Joanna

2010 '(Un)Chained Wives: Understanding the Bruker v. Markovitz Decision and Possible Alternative Legal Claims for Jewish Women Who are Denied a Get.' Available at http://works.bepress.com/infraread/3 (accessed August 14 2012).

MACDONALD, Roderick A.
2002 *Lessons of Everyday Law*. Montreal: McGill University Press.
2010 'Access to Civil Justice.' Pp. 492-521 in P. Cane and H. Kritzer (eds.), *Oxford Handbook of Empirical Legal Research*, Oxford: Oxford University Press.
2011 'Custom made: for a non-chirographic critical legal pluralism.' *Canadian Journal of Law and Society* 26(1): 301-327.
MACLEAN, Mavis and John EEKELAAR
n.d. *Managing Family Justice in Diverse Societies*. Oxford: Hart Publishing (forthcoming).
MANDERSON, Desmond
2005 'Interstices: New Work on Legal Spaces.' *Law Text Culture* 9: 1-10.
MELISSARIS, Emmanuel
2004 'The More the Merrier? A New Take on Legal Pluralism.' *Social and Legal Studies* 13(1): 57-79.
2009 *Ubiquitous Law: Legal Theory and the Space for Legal Pluralism.* Farnham: Ashgate Publishing.
MERRY, Sally E.
1986 'Everyday Understandings of the Law in Working-Class America.' *American Ethnologist* 13(2): 253-270.
1988 'Legal Pluralism: A Literature Review.' *Law and Society Review* 22(5): 869-896.
MOON, Richard J.
2008a *Law and Religious Pluralism in Canada.* Vancouver: UBC Press.
2008b 'Bruker v. Marcovitz: Divorce and the Marriage of Law and Religion.' *Supreme Court Law Review* 42: 37-62.
MOORE, Benoît
2009 'Contrat et religion – À la volonté de Dieu ou des contractants? Commentaire sur l'affaire Marcovitz c. Bruker.' *Revue Juridique Thémis* (43)1: 219-241.
NAVOT, Suzi
2007 *Constitutional Law of Israel.* Alphen aan den Rijn Netherlands: Kluwer Law International.
NICHOLS, Joel A.
2007 'Multi-Tiered Marriage: Ideas and Influences from New York and Louisiana to the International Community.' *Vanderbilt Journal of Transnational Law* 40(1): 135-196.
2011 *Marriage and Divorce in a Multicultural Context, Multi-Tiered Marriage and the Boundaries of Civil Law and Religion*. Cambridge: Cambridge University Press.

NIGRO, Mario and MAURO, Clare
1999 'Jewish Immigrant Experience and the Practice of Law in Montreal, 1830-1990.' *McGill Law Journal* 44(4): 999-1046.
OPPENHEIMER, Mark
2011 Religious Divorce Dispute Leads to Secular Protest.' *New York Times*, dated 3 January 2011, available at http://www.nytimes.com/2011/01/04/us/04divorce.html (accessed August 14 2012).
PRENTICE, Alison L., Paula BOURNE, Gail Cuthbert BRANDT, Beth LIGHT, Wendy MITCHINSON and Naomi BLACK
1996 *Canadian Women: A History*. Toronto: Harcourt Brace Jovanovich.
RABBINICAL COUNCIL OF AMERICA
1993 'Resolution: Matter of Pre-Nuptial Agreements and Recalcitrant Spouses.' Available at http://www.rabbis.org/news/article.cfm?id=101025 (accessed August 14 2012).
RADAY, Frances
1996 'Religion, Multiculturalism and Equality: The Israeli Case.' *Israel Yearbook on Human Rights* 25: 193-280.
RATZLAV-KATZ, Nissan
2007 'Statistics Dispel Claims of Thousands of Israeli Agunot.' *Israel National News*, dated 27 June 2007, available at http://www.israelnationalnews.com/News/News.aspx/122884# (accessed August 14 2012).
RAYNER, John D.
2001 'The Gender Issue in Jewish Divorce.' Pp.33-57 in Walter Jacob and Moshe Zemer (eds.), *Gender Issues in Jewish Law*, Oxford: Bergahn Books.
RICHMAN, Barak D.
2006 'How Community Institutions Create Economic Advantage: Jewish Diamond Merchants in New York.' *Law and Social Inquiry* 31(2) 383-420.
ROSEN-ZVI, Ariel
1989 'Forum Shopping Between Religious and Secular Courts (And its Impact on the Legal System).' *Tel Aviv University Studies in Law* 9: 347-396.
SANTOS, Boaventura de Sousa
1987 'Law: A Map of Misreading. Toward a Postmodern Conception of Law.' *Journal of Law and Society* 14(3): 279-302.
SARAT, Austin
1990 'The Law is all Over: Power, Resistance and the Legal Consciousness of the Welfare Poor.' *Yale Journal of Law and Humanities* 2: 343-379.

SARAT, Austin and Thomas R. KEARNS
1993 'Beyond the Great Divide: Forms of Legal Scholarship and Everyday Life.' Pp.21-62 in Austin Sarat and Thomas R. Kearns (eds.), *Law in Everyday Life*, Ann Arbor: University of Michigan Press.
SARIS, Anne
2006 'Les tribunaux religieux dans les contextes canadien et québécois.' *Revue Juridique Thémis* 40(2): 353-428.
SEZGIN, Yüksel
2004 'Theorizing Formal Pluralism: Quantification of Legal Pluralism for Spatio-Temporal Analysis.' *Journal of Legal Pluralism* 50: 101-118.
2010a 'The Israeli Millet System: Examining Legal Pluralism through Lenses of Nation-Building and Human Rights.' *Israel Law Review* 43(3): 631-653
2010b 'How to Integrate Universal Human Rights into Customary and Religious Legal Systems?' *Journal of Legal Pluralism* 60: 5-40.
SHACHAR, Ayelet
2008 'Privatizing Diversity: A cautionary Tale from Religious Arbitration in Family Law.' *Theoretical Inquiries in Law* 9(2): 573-607.
2010 'State, Religion and the Family: The New Dilemmas of Multicultural Accommodation.' Pp.115-133 in Rex Ahdar and Nicholas Aroney (eds.), *Shari'a in the West*, Oxford: Oxford University Press.
SHAH, Prakash
2006 'Thinking Beyond Religion: Legal Pluralism in Britain's South Asian Diaspora.' *The Australian Journal of Asian Law* 8(3): 237-260.
SHALEV, Carmel
1995 '*Women in Israel: Fighting Tradition.*' Pp.89-95 in Julie Peters and Andrea Wolper (eds.), *Women's Rights, Human Rights: International Feminist Perspectives*. New York: Routledge.
SHIFMAN, Pinhas
1990 'Family Law in Israel: The Struggle Between Religious and Secular Law.' *Israel Law Review* 24: 537-552.
1999 'The Status of Women in Israeli Family Law – the Case for Reform.' pp.245-248 in Herbert Hausmaninger et al. (eds.), *Developments in Austrian and Israeli Private Law*. New York: Springer-Verlag Wien.
SHILOH, Isaac S.
1970 'Marriage and Divorce in Israel.' *Israel Law Review* 5(4): 479-498.
STONE, Suzanne L.
2000 'The Intervention of American Law in Jewish Divorce: A Pluralist Analysis.' *Israel Law Review* 34(2): 170-210.
STOPLER, Gila
2004 'The Free Exercise of Discrimination: Religious Liberty, Civic

Community and Women's Equality.' *William and Mary Journal of Women and Law* 10(3): 459-532.

STRATTON, Jon

2004 *Coming Out Jewish: Constructing Ambivalent Identities*. New York: Routledge.

TAGER, Esther

1999 'The Chained Wife.' *Netherlands Quarterly of Human Rights* 17(4): 425-457.

TULCHINSKY, Gerald

1997 *Taking Root: The Origins of the Canadian Jewish Community*. Toronto: Stoddart.

2008 *Canada's Jews: A People's Journey*. London: University of Toronto Press.

TUSHNET, Mark

1996 'Defending the Indeterminacy Thesis.' *Quinnipac Law Review* 16(3): 339-356.

UNTERMAN, Alan

1997 *The Jews: Their Religious Beliefs and Practices*. East Sussex: Sussex Academic Press.

US DEPARTMENT OF STATE

2012 'Israel, the West Bank and Gaza Country Specific Information,' dated 9 August 2012, available at http://travel.state.gov/travel/cis_pa_tw/cis/cis_1064.html#special_circumstance (accessed August 14 2012).

VAN PRAAGH, Shauna

1993 Book Review of *Religion and Culture in Canadian Family Law* by John Tibor Syrtash.' *McGill Law Journal* 38: 233-262.

1996 'The Chutzpah of Chasidism.' *Canadian Journal of Law and Society* 11(2): 193-215.

1999 'Faith, Belonging, and the Protection of 'Our' Children.' *Windsor Yearbook of Access to Justice* 17: 154-203.

2008 'View From the *Succah*: Religion and Neighbourly Relations.' Pp.21-40 in Richard Moon (ed.), *Law and Religious Pluralism in Canada*, Vancouver: UBC Press.

WAY, Rosemary C.

2002 'Reconceptualizing Professional Responsibility: Incorporating Equality.' *Dalhousie Law Journal* 25(1): 27-46.

WEINFIELD, Morton

2001 *Like Everyone Else... But Different: The Paradoxical Success of Canadian Jews*. Toronto: McClelland and Stewart.

WOLF, Benjamin C.
2009 'Resolving the Conflict Between Jewish and Secular State Law.' *Hofstra Law Review* 37(4): 1171-1201.

WOLFE, Caryn L.
2006 'Faith-Based Arbitration: Friend Or Foe? An Evaluation of Religious Arbitration Systems and their Interaction with Secular Courts.' *Fordham Law Review* 75(1): 427-470.

WOODS, Patricia J.
2008 *Judicial Power and National Politics: Courts and Gender in the Religious-Secular Conflict in Israel.* Albany NY: State University of New York Press.

YEFET, Karin C.
2009 'Unchaining the *Agunot*: Enlisting the Israeli Constitution in the Service of Women's Marital Freedom.' *Yale Journal of Law and Feminism* 20(2): 441-504.

ZORNBERG, Lisa
1995 'Beyond the Constitution: Is the New York Get Legislation Good Law.' *Pace Law Review* 15(3): 703-786.